Mastering TypeScript and Zod: A Guide to Type-Safe Programming and Validation for Next-Level Application Design

Jayden Reed

2

Preface

TypeScript has revolutionized the way developers write JavaScript by adding a layer of type safety that reduces bugs, enhances developer productivity, and makes codebases more maintainable. Yet, despite TypeScript's power, one challenge remains: ensuring runtime validation of data. That's where Zod steps in. Combining TypeScript with Zod creates a seamless synergy between compile-time type safety and runtime data validation, enabling developers to build robust, error-resilient applications with confidence.

This book, **"Mastering TypeScript and Zod: A Guide to Type-Safe Programming and Validation for Next-Level Application Design,"** is the culmination of years of hands-on experience with these tools. Whether you're new to Zod, exploring TypeScript in-depth, or seeking best practices for combining the two, this book is designed for you.

Why Write This Book?

The journey of mastering TypeScript is often filled with "aha!" moments as you discover its capabilities. But as many developers (myself included) have learned, type safety at compile time doesn't necessarily guarantee safety at runtime. Real-world applications need to deal with untrusted data—user inputs, API responses, or even database records—and validating this data is critical. Enter Zod: a library that bridges this gap elegantly by offering a developer-friendly way to validate data and ensure it aligns with your TypeScript types.

When I first started using Zod, I was struck by how naturally it complemented TypeScript. The clean, intuitive API and the ability to define schemas that double as TypeScript types felt like a missing puzzle piece. But like any powerful tool, mastering Zod requires understanding not just its features but also how to use it effectively in real-world scenarios. That's what I aim to deliver with this book: practical knowledge that helps you become not just a user but a confident master of TypeScript and Zod.

Who Is This Book For?

This book is for developers at all levels who are looking to:

- Deepen their understanding of TypeScript's type system and its advanced features.

- Leverage Zod to validate and transform data seamlessly.

- Build scalable, type-safe applications that minimize runtime errors.

- Solve real-world problems with practical examples and best practices.

Whether you're a frontend developer working with React, a backend developer building APIs, or a full-stack developer looking for end-to-end type safety, this book has something for you.

What Can You Expect?

In this book, we'll cover:

1. **Core TypeScript Concepts:** From types and interfaces to generics and utility types, we'll ensure you have a solid foundation.

2. **Mastering Zod:** Learn how to define schemas, validate data, handle errors, and extend Zod for custom use cases.

3. **Real-World Applications:** See how TypeScript and Zod can be integrated into frontend, backend, and full-stack projects, with detailed examples and case studies.

4. **Best Practices:** Explore strategies for testing, debugging, scaling, and maintaining type-safe applications.

A Personal Note

As developers, we're always seeking tools that make our lives easier and our code more reliable. TypeScript and Zod are two such tools that have transformed the way I approach development. Writing this book has been both a challenge and a joy—a chance to distill years of learning into a guide that I hope will empower you on your journey.

My goal is to make this book as engaging and practical as possible. You'll find examples, insights, and tips that reflect the realities of software development—because theory alone isn't enough. By the end of this book, you'll not only understand how to use TypeScript and Zod but also how to think about designing applications with type safety and validation as core principles.

Let's embark on this journey together and unlock the full potential of TypeScript and Zod.

Table of Contents

Chapter 1: Introduction

Welcome to **"Mastering TypeScript and Zod"**! In this chapter, we'll lay the foundation for what this book is about and why it matters. You'll learn about TypeScript and Zod, why they're a powerful combination, and how this book can help you level up your development skills. Let's dive in!

1.1 What is TypeScript?

TypeScript is a **superset of JavaScript** that brings static typing and additional language features to JavaScript's already rich ecosystem. In simple terms, it extends JavaScript by adding a type system and other powerful tools, making it easier to write robust, error-free code. The end result is a language that retains the flexibility of JavaScript but with a safety net.

A Better JavaScript

At its core, TypeScript builds on JavaScript, meaning any valid JavaScript code is also valid TypeScript. However, TypeScript introduces types—such as `string`, `number`, and `boolean`—to describe the data your code works with.

Here's a simple example of JavaScript:

```javascript
---
function greet(name) {
   return "Hello, " + name + "!";
}

greet(42); // This will produce "Hello, 42!", which may not
be what we wanted.
```

This JavaScript code works but allows unintended input, leading to unpredictable results. Now, let's look at how this would work in TypeScript:

```typescript
```

```
---
function greet(name: string): string {
  return `Hello, ${name}!`;
}

// greet(42); // ✗ Error: Argument of type 'number' is not
assignable to parameter of type 'string'.
```

By explicitly stating that `name` must be a `string`, TypeScript catches the error before the code even runs, saving you from potential runtime bugs.

Why TypeScript Matters

JavaScript's lack of strict typing often results in subtle bugs that are difficult to track down, especially in larger codebases. TypeScript addresses these issues by enabling developers to:

1. **Catch Errors Early:** With TypeScript, many errors are caught at compile time, long before your code runs.
2. **Understand Your Codebase:** Type annotations act as documentation, making it easier to understand what a function or variable is supposed to do.
3. **Refactor with Confidence:** TypeScript's type system ensures that changes you make in one part of the codebase don't inadvertently break another.

Key Features of TypeScript

1. **Static Typing:**
   TypeScript lets you define the shape of your data upfront. This is especially useful when working on teams, as it ensures everyone adheres to the same data contracts.

```
typescript
---
let age: number = 25;
age = "twenty-five"; // ✗ Error: Type 'string' is not
assignable to type 'number'.
```

2. **Interfaces and Types:**

   TypeScript allows you to define complex data structures using interfaces or type aliases. This is particularly helpful when working with objects.

```typescript
---
interface User {
  name: string;
  age: number;
}

const user: User = { name: "Alice", age: 30 };
```

3. **Generics:**

   Generics allow you to write reusable and type-safe code. For instance, you can create a function that works with any data type:

```typescript
---
function identity<T>(value: T): T {
  return value;
}

const result = identity<string>("Hello"); // Result is
inferred as string.
```

4. **Type Inference:**

   TypeScript often infers types for you, reducing the need for explicit annotations. For example:

```typescript
---
let count = 10; // TypeScript infers this as a number.
```

5. **Tooling and IDE Support:**

   One of the most tangible benefits of TypeScript is its integration with modern development tools. Editors like Visual Studio Code provide real-time feedback, auto-completion, and refactoring tools that make coding more efficient and enjoyable.

Why Developers Love TypeScript

One of the most common sentiments I hear about TypeScript is that it "makes you a better developer." While that may sound like an exaggeration, it reflects how TypeScript encourages discipline and best practices. For instance, by enforcing type definitions, you're naturally inclined to think about your data structures more carefully.

In my own experience, adopting TypeScript wasn't just about preventing bugs—it was about regaining control over my codebase. In one project, a sprawling JavaScript application turned into a TypeScript-powered system where everything felt predictable and intentional. I no longer had to guess what a function was expecting or returning—it was all there in the types.

When to Use TypeScript

TypeScript is most valuable when:

- You're working on **large-scale applications** that require long-term maintenance.
- Your team needs clear **data contracts** and reduced risk of miscommunication.
- You want to **catch bugs early** and ensure code quality during development.
- You're integrating with **complex APIs** or third-party libraries.

However, TypeScript might not be the right choice for every project. For quick prototypes or projects with minimal complexity, plain JavaScript could be sufficient.

The TypeScript Ecosystem

TypeScript's popularity has resulted in a vibrant ecosystem, with strong support from libraries and frameworks. Tools like Next.js, Angular, and React integrate seamlessly with TypeScript, and its type definitions are maintained for thousands of third-party libraries via **DefinitelyTyped**.

Conclusion

TypeScript is more than just a tool—it's a mindset shift. By introducing static typing to JavaScript, it helps you write code that's safer, more maintainable, and easier to understand. Whether you're working solo or on a team, TypeScript empowers you to build applications that you can trust to work as intended. As we move through this book, you'll see how TypeScript serves as the foundation for building type-safe systems and how Zod enhances this further by tackling runtime validation. Let's continue exploring!

1.2 What is Zod?

Zod is a powerful **TypeScript-first schema declaration and validation library** that allows you to define, parse, and validate the shape of your data. If TypeScript ensures your code is type-safe at compile time, Zod ensures your data is safe and conforms to expected shapes at runtime. This combination creates a robust development experience, reducing errors and improving overall code reliability.

In this section, we'll explore what Zod is, why it's essential for modern development, and how it integrates seamlessly with TypeScript.

The Role of Schema Validation

In any application, data comes from various sources—user input, API responses, databases, or third-party services. While TypeScript provides a type-safe development environment, it doesn't validate the actual data your application receives or processes. For example, an API might promise a response structure but send something unexpected. This is where runtime validation becomes critical.

Zod bridges this gap by:

1. Defining schemas for your data structures.
2. Validating incoming data against these schemas.
3. Ensuring your application works with data that conforms to expected formats.

How Zod Works

Zod revolves around schemas, which are blueprints for your data. These schemas define the shape, type, and constraints of your data. You can think of Zod as a rules engine for your data: if the data fits the rules, it's valid; if not, Zod throws meaningful errors.

Here's a simple example:

```typescript
---
import { z } from "zod";

const userSchema = z.object({
  name: z.string(),
  age: z.number().min(18), // User must be at least 18 years old.
});

const userData = {
  name: "Alice",
  age: 25,
};

// Validate the data
const result = userSchema.safeParse(userData);

if (result.success) {
  console.log("Valid data:", result.data);
} else {
  console.error("Validation errors:", result.error.errors);
}
```

In this example:

- `z.object()` defines a schema for an object with two fields: `name` (a string) and `age` (a number with a minimum value of 18).
- `safeParse()` checks if `userData` matches the schema and returns either the valid data or detailed errors.

Why Zod Stands Out

There are several libraries for runtime validation, like Joi and Yup, but Zod offers some unique advantages:

1. **TypeScript-First Design:**

   Zod is built specifically for TypeScript, making it incredibly intuitive for TypeScript developers. When you define a schema in Zod, it automatically infers the TypeScript type for you.

```typescript
---
const userSchema = z.object({
  name: z.string(),
  age: z.number(),
});

type User = z.infer<typeof userSchema>;
```

In this example, `User` is automatically inferred as:

```typescript
---
{
  name: string;
  age: number;
}
```

2. **Composability:**

   Zod allows you to combine and reuse schemas, making it ideal for large, complex projects.

```typescript
---
const addressSchema = z.object({
  street: z.string(),
  city: z.string(),
  zipCode: z.string().length(5),
});

const userSchema = z.object({
  name: z.string(),
  age: z.number(),
  address: addressSchema,
});
```

3. **Validation and Transformation:**

   Zod can transform data while validating it. For example, you can trim whitespace from a string or parse a string as a number during validation.

```typescript
---
const trimmedStringSchema = z.string().transform((val) =>
val.trim());
```

```
const result = trimmedStringSchema.parse("  hello ");
console.log(result); // Outputs: "hello"
```

4. **Rich Error Messages:**
   Zod provides detailed and human-readable error messages, making debugging much easier.
5. **Lightweight and Flexible:**
   Despite its powerful features, Zod is lightweight and easy to integrate with various frameworks and libraries, including React, Next.js, and Express.

Use Cases for Zod

Zod is incredibly versatile and can be used in a wide range of scenarios:

- **Form Validation in Frontend Applications:**
  Validate user inputs directly in the browser.
- **API Payload Validation:**
  Ensure that incoming requests to your backend match the expected structure.
- **API Response Validation:**
  Verify that responses from external APIs conform to your application's requirements.
- **Data Transformation:**
  Clean and standardize data during validation.
- **Config File Validation:**
  Validate configuration files to ensure they contain valid values.

Why I Chose Zod

While working on a large project involving user-generated content, I frequently encountered data inconsistencies—API responses with missing fields, user inputs that didn't match the expected format, and so on. TypeScript helped during development, but runtime issues were still slipping through.

After trying several validation libraries, I found Zod. Its TypeScript integration and clean API design were a revelation. Unlike other libraries,

Zod didn't require separate type definitions, which meant fewer opportunities for errors. Using Zod, I could confidently validate data at runtime while ensuring type safety across the codebase. The result was fewer bugs and much cleaner code.

A Quick Comparison: TypeScript vs. Zod

Feature	TypeScript	Zod
Type Checking	Compile-time only	Runtime
Validation	No	Yes
Error Messages	Compiler errors	Human-readable runtime errors
Schema Definition	Static typing	Explicit runtime schemas
Data Transformation	No	Yes

Conclusion

Zod is more than just a validation library—it's a tool that enhances your TypeScript workflow, ensuring your applications handle data reliably and predictably. By combining the static guarantees of TypeScript with Zod's runtime validation, you create a powerful safety net that catches issues early and minimizes surprises.

In the next sections, you'll learn how to use Zod in tandem with TypeScript to build robust, type-safe applications. Whether you're working on the frontend, backend, or both, Zod has your back. Let's continue!

1.3 Why TypeScript and Zod Together?

Combining TypeScript and Zod is like pairing two master craftspeople to tackle a single challenge. TypeScript ensures that your code is type-safe during development, catching errors at compile time, while Zod validates that your data behaves as expected at runtime. Together, they create a robust safety net that covers both the code you write and the data you process.

Let's dive into why this combination is so powerful, and how it can transform the way you build applications.

---

1. Static vs. Runtime: Covering Both Bases

TypeScript is a static type checker, which means it ensures type correctness during the development process. It catches errors like mismatched types, missing properties, or incorrect function arguments *before* your code is executed. But there's a limit to what TypeScript can do—it can't guarantee that the data your application interacts with at runtime (like API responses, user inputs, or database records) matches its expected type.

Here's an example to illustrate this limitation:

```typescript
---
type User = {
  name: string;
  age: number;
};

// TypeScript sees no issue with this data during
development.
const user: User = JSON.parse('{"name": "Alice", "age":
"25"}');
```

While the code compiles, it will throw a runtime error because `age` is a string, not a number. This is where Zod steps in.

Zod validates data *at runtime* by parsing it against schemas you define. Let's rewrite the example with Zod:

```typescript
---
import { z } from "zod";

const userSchema = z.object({
  name: z.string(),
  age: z.number(),
});

const user = userSchema.parse(JSON.parse('{"name": "Alice",
"age": "25"}'));
// Throws a clear error: "Expected number, received string."
```

By pairing TypeScript and Zod, you ensure:

1. **Static Safety:** Your code is well-typed and consistent.
2. **Runtime Assurance:** Your application only works with valid, trusted data.

2. Seamless Integration

One of the best things about Zod is its TypeScript-first design. When you define a Zod schema, you're also defining a TypeScript type—there's no need to duplicate your efforts. This reduces friction and keeps your codebase DRY (Don't Repeat Yourself).

```typescript
---
const userSchema = z.object({
  name: z.string(),
  age: z.number(),
});

// Infer TypeScript type directly from the Zod schema
type User = z.infer<typeof userSchema>;

const user: User = userSchema.parse({ name: "Alice", age: 30 });
```

This seamless integration allows you to focus on building your application without worrying about mismatches between type definitions and validation logic.

3. Enhanced Developer Productivity

By combining TypeScript and Zod, you eliminate entire classes of bugs:

- **Compile-Time Errors:** Caught by TypeScript (e.g., typos in property names, mismatched types).
- **Runtime Errors:** Caught by Zod (e.g., unexpected API responses, invalid user inputs).

This leads to:

- **Fewer Debugging Sessions:** Errors are caught early, often before they make it to production.
- **Clearer Error Messages:** Zod provides detailed runtime error feedback, making issues easier to identify and fix.
- **Faster Refactoring:** TypeScript and Zod's type inference ensure that changes to your code are propagated consistently.

---

4. Real-World Scenarios

Let's look at some scenarios where TypeScript and Zod together provide unmatched value:

1. **API Integration:**
   When consuming third-party APIs, you often have to deal with incomplete or incorrect documentation. While TypeScript can help you define the expected response structure, it can't validate the actual response. Zod lets you parse and validate API responses, ensuring your application doesn't break when the API sends unexpected data.

```typescript
---
const apiResponseSchema = z.object({
  id: z.string(),
  name: z.string(),
  email: z.string().email(),
});

async function fetchUserData(userId: string) {
  const response = await fetch(`/api/user/${userId}`);
  const data = await response.json();
  return apiResponseSchema.parse(data);
}
```

2. **Form Validation:**
   Forms are notorious for unpredictable user inputs. With Zod, you can validate form submissions on the client-side, ensuring the data sent to your backend is clean and well-structured.

```typescript
---
const formSchema = z.object({
  username: z.string().min(3),
  password: z.string().min(6),
```

```
});

const formData = { username: "ab", password: "123456" };
const result = formSchema.safeParse(formData);

if (!result.success) {
  console.error(result.error.errors); // Detailed feedback
for invalid fields
}
```

3. **Database Interactions:**
    When working with databases, you may receive data that doesn't match your application's expectations due to schema changes or data corruption. Zod helps validate this data before your application processes it.

5. Simplifying Complex Applications

In large applications, managing data consistency across multiple layers—frontend, backend, and APIs—can be challenging. TypeScript and Zod help streamline this by enforcing type and schema consistency throughout your stack. For example, you can:

- Define a shared Zod schema for an API payload.
- Use TypeScript's `z.infer` to ensure type safety in both the API handler and the client consuming the API.
- Validate the payload with Zod at runtime on both ends.

This approach reduces duplication and ensures that any schema updates are automatically reflected across the application.

6. A Balanced Approach to Safety

One of the best things about TypeScript and Zod is how they balance strictness with flexibility:

- **TypeScript:** Catches obvious mistakes during development without imposing unnecessary constraints.

- **Zod:** Validates data only when needed, avoiding performance overhead in parts of your application that don't require runtime validation.

Together, they let you enforce safety where it matters most without slowing you down.

Conclusion

TypeScript and Zod complement each other beautifully, addressing each other's weaknesses and amplifying their strengths. While TypeScript ensures that your code is type-safe at compile time, Zod ensures that your application handles data safely at runtime. This combination empowers you to write robust, maintainable, and scalable applications.

As we move through this book, you'll see how these tools work together in real-world scenarios, from form validation to API integrations. By the end, you'll not only understand why TypeScript and Zod are a perfect match— you'll know how to wield them to build better applications. Let's keep going!

1.4 Who is This Book For?

Every book has an audience, and this one is no different. Whether you're a seasoned developer or someone just starting their programming journey, this book offers something valuable. But let's break it down further to understand exactly who will benefit the most from mastering TypeScript and Zod.

---

1. Frontend Developers

As a frontend developer, you're constantly working with forms, user inputs, and APIs—all potential sources of unpredictable data. You know the pain of debugging issues caused by invalid input or unexpected API responses. TypeScript helps you catch these issues during development, while Zod ensures they don't slip through at runtime.

This book is for frontend developers who want:

- To eliminate common bugs related to input validation.
- To build type-safe forms without relying on cumbersome validation libraries.
- To create applications that are predictable and maintainable, especially when working with modern frameworks like React, Next.js, or Angular.

2. Backend Developers

For backend developers, handling incoming requests and ensuring the integrity of your data pipeline is paramount. When working with APIs, database operations, or complex business logic, invalid or inconsistent data can quickly become a nightmare. TypeScript and Zod together allow you to enforce data contracts, validate payloads, and confidently process data without fear of introducing subtle bugs.

This book is for backend developers who:

- Build REST or GraphQL APIs and need reliable request/response validation.
- Want to integrate runtime validation without duplicating schema definitions.
- Handle sensitive data and want to enforce strict constraints to ensure security and correctness.

3. Full-Stack Developers

Full-stack developers have the unique challenge of juggling responsibilities across the frontend and backend. You need a consistent way to handle data validation and type safety throughout the entire stack. With TypeScript and Zod, you can define schemas once and use them everywhere, ensuring seamless integration between client and server.

This book is for full-stack developers who:

- Want end-to-end type safety to reduce the friction of context switching.
- Need reusable schemas that work across layers of their applications.
- Aim to streamline development processes while maintaining reliability.

4. Teams Working on Large Applications

If you're part of a team building a complex application, maintaining code consistency and avoiding regressions can feel like an uphill battle. TypeScript enforces shared standards during development, while Zod ensures the data flowing through your system adheres to agreed-upon contracts.

This book is for teams who:

- Struggle with inconsistencies in data handling across their codebase.
- Want a single source of truth for data validation that's easy to maintain.
- Need tools that scale well with growing projects and teams.

5. Developers Integrating with External APIs

When working with third-party APIs, the promise of a well-documented response structure doesn't always match reality. Missing fields, unexpected data types, and incomplete responses are all too common. TypeScript helps you define the expected structure, and Zod validates the actual response at runtime, preventing unpleasant surprises.

This book is for developers who:

- Frequently integrate with external APIs and need to handle inconsistencies.
- Want to avoid assumptions about data correctness and handle edge cases gracefully.
- Seek tools to make API integrations more reliable and predictable.

6. New Developers Exploring TypeScript

If you're new to TypeScript, this book offers a structured introduction to its core concepts while showing you how to pair it with Zod for even greater benefits. By combining these tools, you'll not only learn TypeScript but also gain a practical understanding of how to build reliable applications.

This book is for new developers who:

- Are transitioning from JavaScript and want to adopt TypeScript effectively.
- Want to understand how to manage real-world data challenges.
- Need a hands-on guide to mastering modern development practices.

7. Developers Focused on Code Quality

For developers who prioritize clean, maintainable, and bug-free code, TypeScript and Zod are invaluable. They force you to think critically about your data structures, write code that adheres to strict contracts, and catch potential issues before they escalate.

This book is for developers who:

- Believe in the power of tooling to improve productivity and code quality.
- Want to adopt best practices for data validation and type safety.
- Are tired of runtime errors caused by unvalidated or mismatched data.

8. Developers Building for Scale

When building applications designed to scale, having reliable tools to enforce type safety and validate data is essential. As your application grows, TypeScript and Zod ensure that your codebase remains predictable and easy to manage.

This book is for developers who:

- Need tools that scale well with the complexity of their applications.
- Work in distributed teams where clear data contracts are essential.
- Want to future-proof their projects by adopting modern development paradigms.

Why You Should Read This Book

If you've ever struggled with debugging an issue caused by bad data, felt overwhelmed managing types and validation logic separately, or wanted to bring more rigor and predictability to your development process, this book is for you.

By mastering TypeScript and Zod, you'll gain the tools to write cleaner, safer, and more maintainable code. Whether you're working solo, as part of a small team, or on a massive enterprise project, these skills will transform how you approach application development.

Let's continue this journey together and dive deeper into how TypeScript and Zod can reshape the way you build software.

1.5 How to Use This Book

This book is designed to be a practical, hands-on guide for mastering TypeScript and Zod. Whether you prefer to follow a structured path or dive into specific topics as needed, this book provides the flexibility to suit your learning style. By the time you finish, you'll have the confidence and knowledge to build robust, type-safe applications with ease.

Here's how you can get the most out of this book.

---

1. Start at the Beginning (or Jump Ahead)

If you're new to TypeScript or Zod, it's best to start at the beginning. The chapters are designed to build on each other, gradually introducing key concepts and techniques. Early chapters focus on the fundamentals, such as setting up TypeScript and understanding Zod's schema validation. These foundational topics are essential if you're just starting out.

However, if you're already familiar with one or both tools, feel free to skip to the sections that interest you most. For example:

- Experienced with TypeScript? Jump ahead to the chapters on Zod and its advanced features.
- Familiar with Zod but new to TypeScript? Start with the basics of TypeScript before diving into their integration.

2. Follow Along with Hands-On Examples

This book isn't just a theoretical guide—it's packed with practical examples you can apply immediately. To get the most out of these examples:

- Set up a local development environment with TypeScript and Zod installed.
- Write the code as you read through the examples. Experiment with modifying the examples to see how changes affect the behavior.
- Pay close attention to error messages and how TypeScript and Zod help you catch and fix issues.

The process of writing and experimenting with the code will help solidify your understanding.

3. Focus on Problem-Solving

This book is organized around solving real-world problems. Each chapter addresses common challenges faced by developers, such as:

- Validating user input in forms.
- Ensuring API responses match expected data structures.
- Safely handling dynamic or untrusted data.

By learning to solve these problems, you'll gain practical skills that are directly applicable to your projects. Don't just read the solutions—think about how you could adapt them to similar challenges in your own work.

4. Learn by Building

Throughout the book, you'll encounter progressively larger examples and case studies. These sections are designed to help you see how TypeScript and Zod fit into the bigger picture of application development. Treat these as mini-projects:

- Build the examples as described, testing and debugging along the way.
- Extend the examples by adding new features or incorporating tools you already know.
- Use the techniques you learn to create your own applications.

By the end of the book, you'll have a strong portfolio of examples and a solid understanding of how to use TypeScript and Zod in real-world scenarios.

5. Engage with the Broader Ecosystem

While this book focuses on TypeScript and Zod, these tools don't exist in isolation. They integrate seamlessly with many popular frameworks and libraries, such as React, Next.js, Express, and Prisma. As you progress, you'll see how to use TypeScript and Zod effectively in these contexts. This will prepare you to tackle larger projects and work within modern tech stacks.

If you're already working with a specific framework or library, think about how the concepts in this book can enhance your workflow.

6. Embrace Iterative Learning

Programming is an iterative process, and so is learning. Don't worry if you don't understand everything immediately. Some concepts, especially advanced ones, may take time to sink in. Here's how you can approach this book for maximum benefit:

- **First Pass:** Focus on understanding the main ideas and following along with the examples.
- **Second Pass:** Revisit challenging sections, testing your knowledge by solving problems or extending examples.
- **On-the-Job Learning:** As you work on your own projects, refer back to relevant sections of the book to reinforce your understanding.

7. Use This Book as a Reference

This book is structured to serve not only as a learning guide but also as a reference you can return to. Each chapter is self-contained, with clear explanations and examples that can stand alone. Whether you need to brush up on a concept or look for a specific solution, this book is here to support you long after you've finished reading it.

8. Experiment Freely

The beauty of TypeScript and Zod lies in their flexibility and depth. Experimentation is one of the best ways to learn:

- Try using Zod in ways the examples don't explicitly cover.
- Challenge yourself by re-creating schemas or types from scratch without looking back at the examples.
- Push the boundaries of what you think TypeScript and Zod can do—you might discover new patterns or techniques.

9. Balance Learning with Practice

It's tempting to try and absorb everything in one go, but the real learning happens when you apply the concepts. As you read this book, pair your learning with small projects or exercises:

- Create a simple application to practice type safety and validation.
- Refactor an existing project to use TypeScript and Zod.
- Share your experiences with peers or in developer communities to solidify your understanding.

10. Adapt the Book to Your Goals

Every developer has different goals. Whether you're learning TypeScript and Zod to improve your existing projects, impress potential employers, or simply for personal growth, tailor your approach to your objectives:

- Focus on the chapters and examples that align most closely with your work or interests.
- Use the additional resources and suggested tools at the end of the book to dive deeper into areas that excite you.

Final Thoughts

This book is more than just a tutorial—it's a roadmap for mastering TypeScript and Zod. By following the guidance here and applying it to your own work, you'll not only gain technical skills but also develop the confidence to build type-safe, robust applications.

Remember, learning is a journey. Take your time, embrace challenges, and celebrate your progress. I'm excited to be part of your journey, and I hope this book becomes a trusted companion as you grow as a developer. Let's continue and start building together!

Chapter 2: Getting Started with TypeScript

TypeScript has become an essential tool for modern development, offering a layer of safety and predictability that makes coding less stressful and more enjoyable. In this chapter, we'll guide you through the basics of TypeScript, exploring how to set up your environment, understand its core concepts, dive into advanced features, and adopt best practices for writing clean, type-safe code.

2.1 Setting Up Your TypeScript Environment

Setting up a proper environment for TypeScript is the first step in leveraging its power for robust, type-safe application development. Whether you're adding TypeScript to an existing project or starting a new one from scratch, this guide will walk you through the process step by step.

By the end of this section, you'll have a fully functional TypeScript environment ready for development.

Step 1: Install Node.js

Before diving into TypeScript, you need to have Node.js installed on your system. TypeScript is distributed as an npm package, and Node.js provides the runtime and package manager (npm) needed for installation.

1. Visit the official Node.js website.
2. Download and install the **LTS (Long-Term Support)** version, which is recommended for most users.
3. Verify the installation by running the following commands in your terminal:

```bash
---
node -v
npm -v
```

Step 2: Install TypeScript

Once Node.js is installed, you can install TypeScript globally using npm. This makes the `tsc` (TypeScript Compiler) command available globally on your system.

Run the following command in your terminal:

```bash
---
npm install -g typescript
```

To verify that TypeScript was installed correctly, check the version:

```bash
---
tsc -v
```

Step 3: Set Up a New Project

Now that TypeScript is installed, let's set up a new project to get started.

1. **Create a Project Directory:** Open your terminal and create a new directory for your project:

```bash
---
mkdir my-typescript-project
cd my-typescript-project
```

2. **Initialize the Project:** Initialize a new Node.js project using npm. This creates a `package.json` file to manage your project's dependencies.

```bash
---
npm init -y
```

3. **Install TypeScript Locally (Optional):** While TypeScript is installed globally, it's a good practice to install it locally in your project to ensure version consistency:

```bash
---
```

```
npm install --save-dev typescript
```

Step 4: Create a tsconfig.json File

The `tsconfig.json` file is the heart of any TypeScript project. It defines the configuration options for the TypeScript compiler, specifying how TypeScript should transpile your code into JavaScript.

To create a default `tsconfig.json`, run:

```bash
---
tsc --init
```

This generates a configuration file with commented options. Here's a minimal configuration:

```json
---
{
  "compilerOptions": {
    "target": "ES6", // Transpile TypeScript to ES6
JavaScript
    "module": "CommonJS", // Use CommonJS for module
resolution
    "outDir": "./dist", // Output directory for transpiled
files
    "strict": true, // Enable strict type-checking
    "esModuleInterop": true // Enable compatibility with
CommonJS modules
  },
  "include": ["src/**/*"], // Include all TypeScript files in
the src directory
  "exclude": ["node_modules"] // Exclude node_modules from
compilation
}
```

Step 5: Organize Your Project Structure

A well-organized project structure improves maintainability and readability. Here's a simple structure for a TypeScript project:

```graphql
---
```

```
my-typescript-project/
│
├── src/                   # Source files
│   └── index.ts           # Entry file
├── dist/                  # Transpiled JavaScript files
(generated by TypeScript)
├── node_modules/          # Installed dependencies
├── package.json           # Project metadata and dependencies
└── tsconfig.json          # TypeScript configuration
```

1. Create the `src` directory:

```bash
---
mkdir src
```

2. Create an `index.ts` file inside the `src` directory.

Step 6: Write Your First TypeScript Code

Let's write a simple TypeScript program in the `src/index.ts` file to test your setup. Add the following code:

```typescript
---
const greet = (name: string): string => {
  return `Hello, ${name}!`;
};

console.log(greet("TypeScript"));
```

Step 7: Compile and Run Your TypeScript Code

1. **Compile the Code:** Use the `tsc` command to compile the TypeScript file into JavaScript. The output will be placed in the `dist` directory as specified in the `tsconfig.json`.

```bash
---
tsc
```

32

2. **Run the JavaScript Output:** Run the compiled JavaScript file using Node.js:

```bash
---
node dist/index.js
```

You should see the following output:

```
Hello, TypeScript!
```

Step 8: Use a Development Workflow

To streamline development, consider using tools like **ts-node** or **nodemon**:

- **ts-node:** Allows you to run TypeScript files directly without compiling them manually.

    ```bash
    ---
    npm install --save-dev ts-node
    npx ts-node src/index.ts
    ```

- **nodemon:** Automatically restarts your application when changes are detected, speeding up development.

    ```bash
    ---
    npm install --save-dev nodemon
    ```

Update the `package.json` file to include a script for starting the project:

```json
---
"scripts": {
  "start": "nodemon --watch src --exec ts-node src/index.ts"
}
```

Run your project with:

```bash
---
npm start
```

Personal Insight: Why Setup Matters

When I first started with TypeScript, I underestimated the importance of a good setup. My initial projects were chaotic—files scattered, configurations mismatched, and debugging a nightmare. Taking the time to set up a proper structure and configuration changed everything. It made my codebase cleaner, debugging easier, and collaboration smoother. A good foundation saves time and frustration down the road.

Conclusion

Congratulations! You've successfully set up a TypeScript environment and written your first TypeScript program. This foundational setup will serve as the backbone of your projects, allowing you to explore TypeScript's features with confidence. In the next section, we'll dive into TypeScript's core concepts—types, interfaces, and generics—to build a solid understanding of its type system. Let's continue!

2.2 Core Concepts: Types, Interfaces, and Generics

TypeScript's core strength lies in its ability to describe the shape and behavior of your data through types, interfaces, and generics. These tools provide structure, improve readability, and catch errors before they reach production. In this section, we'll explore these concepts in detail, with practical examples and clear explanations.

---

1. Types: Building Blocks of TypeScript

A **type** in TypeScript describes the shape and behavior of a value. It acts as a contract, ensuring that your variables, functions, and objects adhere to expected structures.

Basic Types

TypeScript provides a rich set of built-in types, such as:

- **Primitive Types:** string, number, boolean, null, undefined
- **Composite Types:** object, array, tuple
- **Special Types:** any, unknown, void, never

Here's a quick example of using types:

```typescript
---
let userName: string = "Alice";
let userAge: number = 25;
let isActive: boolean = true;
```

Union and Intersection Types

- **Union Types** allow a variable to hold multiple possible types:

  ```typescript
  ---
  let id: string | number;
  id = 42; // Valid
  id = "abc123"; // Also valid
  ```

- **Intersection Types** combine multiple types into one:

  ```typescript
  ---
  type Address = { street: string; city: string };
  type Contact = { phone: string; email: string };
  type User = Address & Contact;
  ```

Custom Types

Custom types allow you to create aliases for complex structures. They're especially useful for readability and reusability.

```typescript
---
type User = {
  name: string;
  age: number;
  isActive: boolean;
};
```

---

2. Interfaces: Structuring Your Data

Interfaces are similar to types but are specifically designed to define the structure of objects. They are particularly useful when working with APIs, classes, or large data models.

Defining an Interface

An interface defines the expected properties and their types.

```typescript
---
interface User {
  name: string;
  age: number;
  email?: string; // Optional property
}
```

Extending Interfaces

Interfaces can be extended to create new structures without duplicating code:

```typescript
---
interface Address {
  street: string;
  city: string;
}

interface ExtendedUser extends Address {
  name: string;
  age: number;
}
```

Key Differences Between Types and Interfaces

While types and interfaces often overlap in functionality, they have subtle differences:

1. **Extensibility:** Interfaces are designed for extension; types require unions or intersections.
2. **Use Cases:** Interfaces are often preferred for object modeling, while types are more versatile.

---

3. Generics: Writing Flexible and Reusable Code

Generics allow you to write code that works with multiple types while maintaining type safety. They're particularly useful for creating reusable components like data structures, utility functions, or APIs.

Generic Functions

A generic function operates on any data type, specified by a placeholder like `<T>`.

```typescript
---
function identity<T>(value: T): T {
  return value;
}
```

Here, `T` acts as a placeholder for the type that the function will handle. When the function is called, the actual type is determined automatically.

Generic Interfaces

You can also use generics in interfaces to define reusable structures:

```typescript
---
interface ApiResponse<T> {
  data: T;
  error?: string;
}
```

This flexibility allows you to define APIs that work with various data types.

Generic Constraints

To ensure that a generic type meets specific requirements, you can apply constraints:

```typescript
---
function getLength<T extends { length: number }>(item: T):
number {
  return item.length;
}
```

Here, the generic type `T` is constrained to types that have a `length` property.

4. Practical Examples: Bringing It All Together

Let's combine types, interfaces, and generics in a real-world scenario.

Example 1: Modeling a User Profile

Define a user profile structure using an interface:

```typescript
---
interface UserProfile {
  name: string;
  age: number;
  address: Address;
}

interface Address {
  street: string;
  city: string;
}
```

Create a function that processes a user profile:

```typescript
---
function printUserProfile(user: UserProfile): void {
  console.log(`${user.name}, ${user.age}, lives at
${user.address.street}, ${user.address.city}`);
}
```

Example 2: API Response Handling with Generics

Define a generic API response:

```typescript
---
interface ApiResponse<T> {
  success: boolean;
  data: T;
}

function fetchData<T>(endpoint: string):
Promise<ApiResponse<T>> {
  return fetch(endpoint)
    .then((response) => response.json())
```

```
    .then((data) => ({ success: true, data }))
    .catch(() => ({ success: false, data: null as unknown as
T })));
}
```

This approach ensures type safety for any API response.

---

5. Why These Concepts Matter

When I started using TypeScript, the ability to define types and interfaces brought immediate clarity to my projects. Generics, on the other hand, required more practice to fully grasp their power. Over time, I realized that combining these tools not only made my code more robust but also reduced the time spent debugging edge cases.

These concepts are foundational for writing clean, scalable TypeScript code. Types ensure correctness, interfaces provide structure, and generics enable flexibility. Together, they form the building blocks of TypeScript's type system.

Conclusion

Understanding types, interfaces, and generics is crucial for mastering TypeScript. They allow you to describe, structure, and generalize your data, making your code more predictable, maintainable, and reusable. In the next section, we'll explore TypeScript's advanced features, such as utility types and conditional types, to enhance your skills further. Let's continue!

2.3 Advanced Features: Utility Types and Conditional Types

As you progress with TypeScript, you'll encounter situations where defining types manually becomes cumbersome or repetitive. This is where **utility types** and **conditional types** come in. These advanced features enhance your ability to create flexible, reusable, and efficient type definitions, making your code more concise and maintainable.

In this section, we'll explore these features in depth, understand their use cases, and see how they can simplify your development workflow.

1. Utility Types

Utility types are built-in tools in TypeScript that allow you to manipulate and transform existing types. They're designed to save time and reduce boilerplate by handling common tasks like making properties optional, extracting subsets of types, or creating new types from existing ones.

Key Utility Types

Here are some of the most commonly used utility types:

1. **Partial<T>** Converts all properties of a type T into optional properties.

   ```typescript
   ---
   interface User {
     name: string;
     age: number;
     email: string;
   }

   type PartialUser = Partial<User>;
   // Result: { name?: string; age?: number; email?:
   string }
   ```

   Use Case: Use Partial<T> when updating objects, as not all fields may be modified.

2. **Required<T>** Converts all properties of a type T into required properties.

   ```typescript
   ---
   type RequiredUser = Required<PartialUser>;
   // Result: { name: string; age: number; email: string }
   ```

   Use Case: Use Required<T> to enforce the presence of optional fields.

3. **Pick<T, K>** Extracts a subset of properties K from a type T.

```typescript
---
type UserContactInfo = Pick<User, "name" | "email">;
// Result: { name: string; email: string }
```

Use Case: Use Pick<T, K> when you need a lighter version of a type.

4. **Omit<T, K>** Removes specific properties K from a type T.

```typescript
---
type UserWithoutEmail = Omit<User, "email">;
// Result: { name: string; age: number }
```

Use Case: Use Omit<T, K> to exclude unnecessary fields from an object.

5. **Readonly<T>** Converts all properties of a type T into read-only properties, preventing modification.

```typescript
---
type ReadonlyUser = Readonly<User>;
```

Use Case: Use Readonly<T> for immutable data structures.

6. **Record<K, T>** Constructs an object type where keys K are associated with values of type T.

```typescript
---
type UserRoles = Record<"admin" | "editor" | "viewer",
boolean>;
// Result: { admin: boolean; editor: boolean; viewer:
boolean }
```

Use Case: Use Record<K, T> to define a map-like structure.

2. Conditional Types

Conditional types are a way to create types dynamically based on conditions. They allow you to perform type-level logic, similar to conditional statements in regular programming.

The syntax for a conditional type is:

```typescript
---
T extends U ? X : Y
```

This means: "If T is assignable to U, then the type is X; otherwise, it's Y."

Examples of Conditional Types

1. **Basic Example**

```typescript
---
type IsString<T> = T extends string ? true : false;

type Test1 = IsString<string>; // Result: true
type Test2 = IsString<number>; // Result: false
```

2. **Extracting a Subtype** The Extract<T, U> utility type (built into TypeScript) uses conditional logic to extract types that are assignable to U.

```typescript
---
type StringsOnly = Extract<"a" | "b" | 1 | 2, string>;
// Result: "a" | "b"
```

3. **Excluding a Subtype** The Exclude<T, U> utility type excludes types that are assignable to U.

```typescript
---
type NonStrings = Exclude<"a" | "b" | 1 | 2, string>;
// Result: 1 | 2
```

4. **Infer Keyword** Conditional types can use infer to extract types dynamically.

```typescript
---
```

```typescript
type ReturnType<T> = T extends (...args: any[]) =>
infer R ? R : never;

type ExampleFunction = () => string;
type ExampleReturn = ReturnType<ExampleFunction>;
// Result: string
```

3. Practical Implementations

Let's see how utility and conditional types work together in real-world scenarios.

Example 1: API Response Transformation

Imagine you're working with an API that returns a response containing various properties, but your application only needs a subset.

```typescript
---
interface ApiResponse {
  id: string;
  name: string;
  email: string;
  createdAt: string;
  updatedAt: string;
}

type ClientResponse = Pick<ApiResponse, "id" | "name" |
"email">;
// Result: { id: string; name: string; email: string }
```

This reduces the size of the object being passed around, improving performance and readability.

Example 2: Dynamic Form Validation

Suppose you're building a dynamic form where only specific fields are required based on user input. You can use `Partial` and conditional types to define these rules:

```typescript
---
```

```
interface FormFields {
  username: string;
  password: string;
  confirmPassword?: string;
}

type OptionalConfirmPassword<T extends { confirmPassword?:
any }> = T extends {
  confirmPassword: string;
}
  ? Required<T>
  : T;

type BasicUser = OptionalConfirmPassword<{ username: string;
password: string }>;
type FullUser = OptionalConfirmPassword<{
  username: string;
  password: string;
  confirmPassword: string;
}>;
// BasicUser: { username: string; password: string }
// FullUser: { username: string; password: string;
confirmPassword: string }
```

4. Why These Features Matter

When I first encountered utility and conditional types, they seemed intimidating. However, as my projects grew, I realized they were essential for managing complex type logic. For example, utility types drastically reduced repetitive code, while conditional types allowed me to create dynamic solutions tailored to my applications. These tools not only improved code quality but also helped me write more expressive, maintainable type definitions.

Conclusion

Utility types and conditional types are powerful tools that simplify type definitions and enhance code reusability in TypeScript. They allow you to handle complex scenarios with ease, ensuring your applications remain scalable and maintainable.

In the next section, we'll focus on writing clean, type-safe code using the principles and tools we've covered so far. Let's continue building your TypeScript expertise!

2.4 Writing Clean, Type-Safe Code

Writing clean, type-safe code is one of the main benefits of using TypeScript. It's not just about ensuring your code compiles without errors; it's about creating a codebase that is **readable**, **maintainable**, and **predictable**. This section will guide you through the principles of clean TypeScript code, demonstrating best practices and practical examples to help you maximize the benefits of type safety.

---

1. Principles of Clean, Type-Safe Code

1.1 Be Explicit About Types

While TypeScript's type inference is powerful, being explicit about types in key areas improves readability and reduces ambiguity, especially in collaborative projects.

When to Be Explicit:

- Function parameters and return types.
- Public APIs or library exports.
- Complex objects that could confuse developers.

When to Rely on Inference:

- Local variables or straightforward assignments.

1.2 Use Interfaces and Types Consistently

Decide whether to use `interface` or `type` and stick to it consistently across your project. While they overlap in functionality, `interface` is better for object shapes and `type` is more versatile for unions and primitives.

Best Practice:

- Use `interface` for modeling objects or class shapes.
- Use `type` for unions, aliases, or more advanced constructs.

1.3 Avoid the `any` Type

Using `any` effectively disables type checking, defeating the purpose of TypeScript. Instead, use alternatives like:

- **unknown:** Safer than `any`, as it requires type checking before use.
- **Narrowing:** Use TypeScript's type narrowing to determine the exact type dynamically.

1.4 Leverage Utility and Conditional Types

When dealing with repetitive or complex type definitions, utility types (`Partial`, `Pick`, etc.) and conditional types simplify the code, reducing redundancy and improving maintainability.

1.5 Validate at the Edges

TypeScript provides compile-time type safety, but it doesn't validate runtime data. Combine it with runtime validation libraries like **Zod** to ensure your application handles external data (e.g., API responses, user input) safely.

---

2. Best Practices in Action

Let's put these principles into practice with real-world examples.

2.1 Explicit Types for Functions

Always define types for function parameters and return values to ensure clarity.

```typescript
---
// Function to calculate the area of a rectangle
function calculateArea(width: number, height: number): number
{
  return width * height;
}

// Enforces correct usage:
const area = calculateArea(5, 10); // Valid
// const invalid = calculateArea("5", "10"); // Compile-time
error
```

By explicitly defining types, you avoid misunderstandings and potential runtime errors.

2.2 Using Interfaces for Structured Objects

Interfaces improve clarity when working with structured data like API responses.

```typescript
---
interface User {
  id: string;
  name: string;
  email: string;
}

const user: User = {
  id: "123",
  name: "Alice",
  email: "alice@example.com",
};

// Compile-time checks ensure all properties are present and
correctly typed.
```

2.3 Avoiding the any Type

Instead of `any`, use `unknown` and narrow the type with checks.

```typescript
---
function processInput(input: unknown): string {
  if (typeof input === "string") {
    return input.toUpperCase();
  } else if (typeof input === "number") {
    return input.toFixed(2);
  }
  throw new Error("Unsupported input type");
}

// This ensures TypeScript enforces checks before using the
value.
```

2.4 Leveraging Utility Types

Utility types help you create clear and concise definitions.

```typescript
---
interface User {
  id: string;
  name: string;
  email: string;
  isActive: boolean;
}

// Create a type with only selected properties
type BasicUser = Pick<User, "id" | "name">;

// Create a type with optional properties
type UpdateUser = Partial<User>;
```

Using utility types reduces boilerplate and improves type reuse.

2.5 Validating External Data

Combine TypeScript with runtime validation to ensure type safety when
working with untrusted data.

```typescript
---
```

```typescript
import { z } from "zod";

// Define a runtime validation schema
const userSchema = z.object({
  id: z.string(),
  name: z.string(),
  email: z.string().email(),
});

// Validate data from an API
function fetchUserData(data: unknown): User {
  const parsedData = userSchema.parse(data); // Throws an
error if invalid
  return parsedData;
}

// By validating at runtime, you ensure the data conforms to
the User interface.
```

3. Writing Maintainable TypeScript Code

3.1 Modularize Types

Break your types into smaller, reusable modules to avoid duplication.

```typescript
---
// address.ts
export interface Address {
  street: string;
  city: string;
  zipCode: string;
}

// user.ts
import { Address } from "./address";

export interface User {
  id: string;
  name: string;
  address: Address;
}
```

This makes your code more maintainable, especially in large projects.

3.2 Use Readable Naming Conventions

Choose descriptive names for your types and interfaces. Avoid abbreviations or overly generic terms like `Data` or `Info`.

3.3 Enable Strict Mode

Always enable `strict` mode in your `tsconfig.json`. This enforces best practices like null checks and strict type assignment, reducing potential bugs.

```json
---
{
  "compilerOptions": {
    "strict": true
  }
}
```

3.4 Comment Complex Types

If a type or interface is complex, add comments to clarify its purpose.

```typescript
---
// Represents a product in the shopping cart
interface CartItem {
  productId: string;
  quantity: number;
  price: number;
}
```

---

4. Common Pitfalls to Avoid

1. **Overusing `any`:** This weakens TypeScript's benefits.
2. **Ignoring Type Errors:** Address errors immediately; they often reveal hidden issues.
3. **Skipping Type Inference:** Trust TypeScript to infer types for simple cases, but don't rely on it entirely.
4. **Mixing Types and Interfaces:** Use them consistently to avoid confusion.

Conclusion

Writing clean, type-safe TypeScript code isn't just about following rules—it's about developing habits that make your code easier to understand, maintain, and extend. By using explicit types, leveraging utility types, validating runtime data, and adopting a modular approach, you'll create a codebase that scales gracefully and minimizes bugs.

In the next chapter, we'll explore how TypeScript pairs with Zod to bring runtime validation and type safety together, creating even more powerful applications. Let's keep building!

Chapter 3: Understanding Zod

Zod is a powerful library designed to simplify schema declaration and runtime validation. It complements TypeScript by adding the missing layer of runtime data validation, ensuring that your application not only compiles correctly but also handles real-world data safely. In this chapter, we'll explore what Zod is, how to set it up, its core features, and why it stands out among alternatives.

3.1 Introduction to Schema Validation

In software development, data is at the heart of nearly every application. Whether it's user input, API responses, or database records, your application's functionality depends on data being in the correct format. This is where **schema validation** becomes crucial. It acts as a gatekeeper, ensuring that the data entering your application is structured, consistent, and reliable.

In this section, we'll explore what schema validation is, why it's essential, and how it integrates with modern development practices.

What is Schema Validation?

Schema validation is the process of checking whether data conforms to a predefined structure or set of rules, called a schema. A schema acts as a blueprint, describing the expected format of the data, including:

- **Types:** Is the data a string, number, boolean, or object?
- **Constraints:** Are there specific ranges, lengths, or patterns the data must meet?
- **Structure:** Does the data include the required fields, and are they in the right format?

Think of schema validation as quality control for your data pipeline. It ensures that only valid data passes through, reducing the risk of bugs, crashes, and other issues caused by invalid or unexpected data.

Why is Schema Validation Important?

1. Handling Untrusted Data

Modern applications often interact with external systems, such as APIs, third-party services, or user inputs. This external data can be unpredictable, incomplete, or outright malicious. Schema validation safeguards your application by verifying that data meets the expected criteria before it's processed.

2. Preventing Errors Early

Invalid data can lead to subtle bugs that are hard to detect and debug. Schema validation catches these issues early, ensuring that errors are flagged and resolved before they propagate through your application.

3. Enforcing Consistency

Applications often rely on data flowing through various layers, such as the frontend, backend, and database. Schema validation enforces a consistent structure, making it easier to maintain and scale your application.

4. Enhancing Security

Schema validation helps mitigate security risks by ensuring that incoming data is sanitized and conforms to expected formats. This reduces vulnerabilities to injection attacks and other exploits.

5. Improving Developer Experience

For developers, schema validation provides clear feedback on data issues, making it easier to debug and maintain the application. It also serves as a form of documentation, outlining the exact structure and requirements of your data.

How Does Schema Validation Work?

Schema validation typically involves three steps:

1. Define the Schema

The first step is to create a schema that describes the structure and rules for the data. This includes defining types, required fields, and constraints.

Example: A user schema might require a `name` (string), `email` (string matching a specific pattern), and `age` (number greater than 18).

2. Apply the Schema

Once the schema is defined, it is applied to incoming data. This process involves checking whether the data conforms to the schema's rules.

3. Handle Validation Results

If the data passes validation, it's processed by the application. If it fails, an error is returned, often with details about what went wrong. These error messages can be used to provide meaningful feedback to users or to debug issues in the data pipeline.

Schema Validation in Modern Development

Schema validation is particularly important in today's development landscape, where applications are more interconnected than ever. Here are a few scenarios where schema validation plays a critical role:

1. Validating API Requests and Responses

When building APIs, schema validation ensures that incoming requests include the required fields and that responses sent to clients are well-formed. This is especially important when working with external consumers who rely on consistent API contracts.

2. User Input Validation

From form submissions to interactive components, user input is one of the most common sources of data. Schema validation ensures that user inputs are complete, valid, and safe to process.

3. Database Interactions

Data retrieved from a database might not always match your application's expectations, especially if schema changes occur over time. Validating database records before use prevents unexpected errors.

4. Integration with Third-Party Services

When consuming external APIs, schema validation ensures that data returned by these services is correctly formatted and safe to process, even if the service documentation is inaccurate or outdated.

5. Frontend-Backend Consistency

Schema validation ensures that data passed between the frontend and backend is consistent, reducing the likelihood of runtime errors caused by mismatched expectations.

Schema Validation vs. TypeScript

You might wonder: "If I'm using TypeScript, why do I need schema validation?" While TypeScript ensures that your code is type-safe during development, it doesn't validate data at runtime. Schema validation fills this gap by verifying that real-world data conforms to the expected structure, complementing TypeScript's static type checking.

My Insight

Early in my career, I encountered a bug in an application caused by a single missing field in an API response. The application crashed, and debugging the issue took hours. This experience taught me the importance of validating external data. Once I started incorporating schema validation into my projects, these kinds of issues became a thing of the past. It's one of those practices that pays off immediately and continuously as your application evolves.

Conclusion

Schema validation is a foundational practice for building reliable, secure, and maintainable applications. It ensures that your application processes only well-formed data, reducing errors, improving security, and enhancing the overall development experience. As we continue in this chapter, we'll dive into Zod—a powerful library that makes schema validation intuitive and efficient, particularly in TypeScript projects. Let's move on to installing and configuring Zod.

3.2 Installing and Configuring Zod

Zod is a powerful, TypeScript-first library designed for runtime schema validation. Installing and configuring Zod is a straightforward process, making it accessible for projects of any size. This section will guide you through setting up Zod in your development environment, with practical steps and explanations to help you get started seamlessly.

1. Installing Zod

To begin using Zod, you'll need to install it in your project. It's distributed as an npm package and can be added with a single command.

Step 1: Install Zod

In your terminal, navigate to your project directory and run:

```bash
---
npm install zod
```

Alternatively, if you're using Yarn:

```bash
bash
---
yarn add zod
```

This command adds Zod as a dependency in your project.

Step 2: Install TypeScript (if not already installed)

Zod works best in a TypeScript environment. If you haven't already set up TypeScript, install it as a development dependency:

```bash
bash
---
npm install --save-dev typescript
```

Once TypeScript is installed, ensure you have a `tsconfig.json` file to configure TypeScript compilation.

---

2. Configuring Zod

Zod doesn't require complex configuration to get started, but understanding its integration points will help you make the most of it.

Step 1: Import Zod

Once installed, you can start using Zod by importing it into your TypeScript files:

```typescript
typescript
---
import { z } from "zod";
```

Step 2: Define a Schema

The first step in using Zod is to define a schema that describes the structure and rules of your data. Here's an example schema for user data:

```typescript
typescript
---
const userSchema = z.object({
  name: z.string(),
  age: z.number().min(18),
```

```
  email: z.string().email(),
});
```

Step 3: Validate Data

Once you've defined a schema, use it to validate data at runtime. If the data passes validation, Zod returns the validated object; if not, it throws a detailed error:

```typescript
---
const validData = userSchema.parse({
  name: "Alice",
  age: 25,
  email: "alice@example.com",
});
```

3. Working with TypeScript

One of Zod's standout features is its ability to infer TypeScript types directly from schemas. This eliminates the need to write separate type definitions, ensuring consistency between your types and validation logic.

Step 1: Infer Types

To infer a TypeScript type from a Zod schema, use the `z.infer` utility:

```typescript
---
type User = z.infer<typeof userSchema>;
```

This automatically generates the following type:

```typescript
---
type User = {
  name: string;
  age: number;
  email: string;
};
```

Step 2: Use in Functions

You can use the inferred type in functions or other parts of your code to ensure type safety:

```typescript
---
function greetUser(user: User): string {
  return `Hello, ${user.name}!`;
}
```

4. Integrating Zod into Your Workflow

Zod is highly versatile and can be integrated into various parts of your application. Here are some common use cases:

Frontend Validation

Use Zod to validate form inputs or user interactions before sending data to a backend. This ensures that only well-structured data reaches your APIs.

Backend Validation

Validate incoming API requests in a Node.js application. Zod ensures that all required fields are present and correctly formatted.

API Response Validation

When consuming external APIs, Zod can validate the responses to ensure they conform to the expected schema, even if the API documentation is outdated or incomplete.

5. Debugging and Error Handling

When validation fails, Zod provides detailed error messages, making it easy to debug issues.

Accessing Error Details

If you want to handle errors gracefully instead of throwing them, use the `safeParse` method:

```typescript
---
const result = userSchema.safeParse({
  name: "Alice",
  age: "not-a-number", // Invalid
  email: "alice@example.com",
});

if (!result.success) {
  console.error(result.error.errors);
}
```

This approach is particularly useful for user-facing applications where you need to display meaningful feedback.

6. My Insight

When I first started using Zod, its simplicity stood out to me. Unlike other libraries, I didn't have to spend hours configuring it or learning complex APIs. Within minutes, I was able to define schemas, validate data, and integrate it into my existing TypeScript projects. Its ability to infer types directly from schemas saved me time and eliminated errors caused by mismatched type definitions. For anyone working with TypeScript, Zod feels like a natural extension of the language.

7. Conclusion

Installing and configuring Zod is a quick and painless process that sets the stage for powerful runtime validation and type safety. With just a few commands and basic setup, you can start using Zod to validate data, enforce schema rules, and ensure consistency across your application. In the next section, we'll explore Zod's core features—schemas, parsing, and validation—in greater depth, unlocking its full potential for your projects. Let's continue!

3.3 Core Features: Schemas, Parsing, and Validation

Zod is built around three core functionalities: defining **schemas**, parsing data through those schemas, and performing **validation** to ensure data integrity. Together, these features provide a powerful toolkit for handling real-world data in your TypeScript applications.

In this section, we'll dive into each feature with practical examples and detailed explanations to help you master Zod.

---

1. Schemas: Defining the Blueprint of Your Data

A **schema** in Zod is a declarative description of what your data should look like. It acts as a blueprint, specifying the structure, types, and constraints of the data you want to validate.

Step 1: Defining a Basic Schema

The most common use case is defining an object schema with properties of different types.

```typescript
---
import { z } from "zod";

const userSchema = z.object({
  name: z.string(),
  age: z.number(),
  email: z.string().email(),
});
```

- `z.string()` ensures that name is a string.
- `z.number()` ensures that age is a number.
- `z.string().email()` validates that email is a properly formatted email address.

Step 2: Nested and Complex Schemas

Zod allows you to define schemas for nested objects or arrays.

```typescript
```

61

```
---
const userWithAddressSchema = z.object({
  name: z.string(),
  age: z.number().min(18), // Minimum age is 18
  email: z.string().email(),
  address: z.object({
    street: z.string(),
    city: z.string(),
    zipCode: z.string().length(5), // Exactly 5 characters
  }),
});
```

- **Nested Objects:** Use `z.object()` for substructures like `address`.
- **Constraints:** Add rules like `min()`, `max()`, or `length()` to refine validation.

---

2. Parsing: Applying the Schema to Data

Once you've defined a schema, the next step is to apply it to your data. This process is called **parsing**. Zod checks if the data matches the schema and either returns the parsed data or throws an error.

Step 1: Valid Data

When data matches the schema, `parse()` returns the validated object.

```typescript
---
const userData = {
  name: "Alice",
  age: 25,
  email: "alice@example.com",
  address: {
    street: "123 Main St",
    city: "Wonderland",
    zipCode: "12345",
  },
};

const validatedUser = userWithAddressSchema.parse(userData);
console.log(validatedUser);
// Output: Validated user object
```

Step 2: Invalid Data

When data doesn't match the schema, `parse()` throws an error with detailed feedback.

```typescript
---
const invalidData = {
  name: "Alice",
  age: 15, // Invalid: less than 18
  email: "alice@example.com",
  address: {
    street: "123 Main St",
    city: "Wonderland",
    zipCode: "123", // Invalid: not 5 characters
  },
};

try {
  userWithAddressSchema.parse(invalidData);
} catch (e) {
  console.error(e.errors);
}
// Output: Detailed errors indicating what failed
```

3. Validation: Fine-Tuning Data Rules

Zod goes beyond basic type checking by allowing you to define constraints and rules for your data. This feature ensures that your application adheres to business logic and domain requirements.

Step 1: Adding Constraints

Constraints are additional rules applied to fields. Zod provides built-in methods for numbers, strings, arrays, and more.

```typescript
---
const productSchema = z.object({
  name: z.string(),
  price: z.number().positive(), // Must be greater than 0
  tags: z.array(z.string()).min(1), // At least one tag
required
});

const validProduct = productSchema.parse({
  name: "Laptop",
  price: 999.99,
```

```
  tags: ["electronics", "gadgets"],
});
```

Step 2: Custom Validation

If built-in constraints aren't enough, Zod allows you to define custom validation rules.

```typescript
---
const customSchema = z.string().refine((value) =>
value.startsWith("T"), {
  message: "String must start with 'T'",
});

customSchema.parse("TypeScript"); // Passes
customSchema.parse("JavaScript"); // Throws an error with a
custom message
```

4. Error Handling: Managing Validation Failures

Zod provides detailed error messages when validation fails, helping you debug issues or provide meaningful feedback to users.

Step 1: Handling Errors Gracefully

Instead of throwing an error, use `safeParse()` to return the validation result as an object with `success` and `error` properties.

```typescript
---
const result = userWithAddressSchema.safeParse(invalidData);

if (!result.success) {
  console.log(result.error.errors);
} else {
  console.log(result.data); // Validated data
}
```

Step 2: Error Format

Zod errors include:

- **Path:** The property that failed validation.

- **Message:** A human-readable explanation of the failure.
- **Code:** The type of validation error (e.g., "invalid_type").

---

5. Transforming Data

In addition to validation, Zod can transform data during parsing. This is useful for standardizing or cleaning inputs.

Example: Trimming Strings

```typescript
---
const trimmedStringSchema = z.string().transform((val) =>
val.trim());

const userInput = "  Hello World  ";
const transformedData = trimmedStringSchema.parse(userInput);
console.log(transformedData); // "Hello World"
```

---

6. Practical Use Cases

Use Case 1: API Request Validation

Zod ensures incoming API requests are well-structured, reducing errors caused by unexpected inputs.

Use Case 2: User Input Validation

Validate form submissions or query parameters to prevent invalid data from reaching your application logic.

Use Case 3: API Response Validation

When consuming external APIs, Zod validates responses to ensure they match the expected schema, even when documentation is incomplete.

---

7. Why This Matters

As a developer, I've often struggled with bugs caused by invalid or unexpected data, especially in projects where data flows between multiple layers. Zod has been a game-changer, allowing me to catch these issues early and confidently handle external inputs. The detailed error reporting has saved me hours of debugging, and its seamless integration with TypeScript keeps my codebase clean and consistent.

Conclusion

The core features of Zod—schemas, parsing, and validation—offer a robust framework for handling data in your applications. By defining schemas, applying them through parsing, and enforcing validation rules, you can ensure that your data is reliable and predictable. In the next section, we'll explore why Zod stands out among validation libraries and how it compares to alternatives like Joi and Yup. Let's continue building!

3.4 Why Choose Zod Over Alternatives?

In the world of schema validation libraries, several options stand out, including **Zod**, **Yup**, and **Joi**. While all these libraries serve the same purpose—validating and shaping data—Zod distinguishes itself with its **TypeScript-first design**, clean API, and flexibility. This section explores why Zod is a compelling choice for modern application development, particularly when working with TypeScript.

1. TypeScript-First Design

One of Zod's defining features is its seamless integration with TypeScript. It's designed from the ground up to complement TypeScript's static type-checking capabilities. Here's why this matters:

Type Inference

When you define a schema in Zod, it automatically infers the corresponding TypeScript type. This eliminates the need to write duplicate type definitions, saving time and reducing the risk of mismatches.

Example:

```typescript
---
import { z } from "zod";

const userSchema = z.object({
  name: z.string(),
  age: z.number(),
});

type User = z.infer<typeof userSchema>;
// User is automatically inferred as { name: string; age:
number }
```

This tight integration ensures that your validation logic and type definitions stay in sync, reducing errors and improving maintainability.

No Extra Configuration

Unlike alternatives like Joi, which require additional tools or configurations to work effectively with TypeScript, Zod's TypeScript support is built-in and effortless to use.

---

2. Intuitive and Clean API

Zod's API is designed to be simple, expressive, and easy to understand. Whether you're a beginner or an experienced developer, Zod's syntax is straightforward, reducing the learning curve.

Example: Defining a Schema

Here's how Zod compares to other libraries for a basic schema:

Zod:

```typescript
---
```

```
const schema = z.object({
  name: z.string(),
  age: z.number(),
});
```

Yup:

```javascript
---
import * as yup from "yup";

const schema = yup.object({
  name: yup.string().required(),
  age: yup.number().required(),
});
```

Joi:

```javascript
---
import Joi from "joi";

const schema = Joi.object({
  name: Joi.string().required(),
  age: Joi.number().required(),
});
```

Zod's syntax is concise, requires fewer method calls, and focuses on clarity. This simplicity makes Zod a pleasure to work with, especially in large projects.

---

3. Runtime Validation and Data Transformation

Zod combines validation and data transformation in a single, cohesive package. While libraries like Joi also offer transformations, Zod simplifies the process and tightly integrates it with schema definitions.

Example: Trimming Strings

```typescript
---
const trimmedStringSchema = z.string().transform((val) =>
val.trim());
```

```
const userInput = "  Hello World  ";
const validatedInput = trimmedStringSchema.parse(userInput);
console.log(validatedInput); // "Hello World"
```

This ability to transform data while validating it is especially useful for cleaning inputs, applying defaults, or standardizing data formats.

4. Detailed and Customizable Error Reporting

Zod provides rich, human-readable error messages out of the box. This is particularly useful for debugging or providing meaningful feedback to users.

Example: Error Handling

When validation fails, Zod errors include:

- **Path:** The specific property that failed validation.
- **Message:** A clear explanation of the failure.
- **Code:** The type of error (e.g., "invalid_type").

```typescript
---
const schema = z.object({
  name: z.string(),
  age: z.number().min(18),
});

try {
  schema.parse({ name: "Alice", age: 15 });
} catch (e) {
  console.error(e.errors);
}
// Output: [{ path: ['age'], message: 'Number must be greater
than or equal to 18', ... }]
```

Zod's error handling is more structured and easier to interpret compared to alternatives like Joi or Yup, which often return more generic error messages.

5. Composability and Modularity

Zod excels at composability, allowing you to build complex schemas by combining smaller, reusable ones. This is ideal for large applications with interrelated data models.

Example: Composing Schemas

```typescript
---
const addressSchema = z.object({
  street: z.string(),
  city: z.string(),
  zipCode: z.string().length(5),
});

const userSchema = z.object({
  name: z.string(),
  age: z.number(),
  address: addressSchema,
});
```

This modular approach ensures that your code remains DRY (Don't Repeat Yourself) and easy to maintain.

---

6. Performance and Lightweight Design

Zod is lightweight and optimized for performance, making it suitable for use in both frontend and backend environments. Its efficient validation engine ensures fast execution even with large or deeply nested schemas.

In contrast, Joi is known to be heavier and may introduce performance bottlenecks in resource-constrained environments, such as serverless functions.

---

7. Versatility Across Use Cases

Zod's flexibility makes it applicable to a wide range of scenarios:

- **API Validation:** Validate request payloads and responses in backend services.
- **Form Validation:** Validate user inputs in frontend forms.

- **Type-Safe Configuration Files:** Ensure that application configurations meet expected standards.
- **Third-Party API Integration:** Validate data from external APIs to ensure reliability.

Unlike Yup, which is more focused on form validation, Zod's versatility makes it suitable for both frontend and backend use cases.

---

8. Active Community and Ecosystem

Zod is backed by an active community and regular updates. Its growing popularity ensures strong support, comprehensive documentation, and integrations with popular frameworks like React, Next.js, and Express.

While Joi and Yup are mature libraries with their own communities, Zod's momentum in the TypeScript ecosystem has made it the go-to choice for modern developers.

Comparison with Alternatives

Feature	Zod	Yup	Joi
TypeScript Support	Built-in, seamless	Requires manual typing	Requires manual typing
API Simplicity	Clean and intuitive	Verbose	Verbose
Error Reporting	Rich and structured	Basic	Basic
Composability	Excellent	Good	Limited
Performance	Lightweight and fast	Lightweight	Heavy
Transformation	Integrated	Limited	Supported
Use Cases	Frontend and backend	Mostly frontend	Mostly backend

My Insight

As someone who has worked extensively with both frontend and backend systems, I've found Zod to be a breath of fresh air compared to its alternatives. Its intuitive syntax and seamless TypeScript integration have saved me hours of work, especially in projects with complex data models. The composability of schemas and detailed error messages have made debugging a breeze, even in high-pressure situations.

Conclusion

Zod stands out as the ideal choice for TypeScript developers, offering a TypeScript-first approach, a clean API, and unparalleled flexibility. Whether you're building a small application or scaling a large system, Zod's core features ensure that your data validation is efficient, maintainable, and robust.

In the next chapter, we'll delve deeper into real-world applications of Zod, showcasing its power in frontend and backend scenarios. Let's continue!

Chapter 4: Integrating TypeScript and Zod

Integrating TypeScript and Zod brings together the strengths of compile-time type safety and runtime data validation, creating a robust foundation for building reliable applications. This chapter explores how these two powerful tools complement each other, ensuring that your code is both type-safe and resilient against unexpected data. We will delve into the synergy between TypeScript's static typing and Zod's runtime validation, guide you through creating and utilizing Zod schemas, discuss handling optional and nullable values effectively, and provide strategies for managing validation errors seamlessly.

4.1 Runtime Validation Meets Compile-Time Safety

In the realm of software development, ensuring that your application handles data correctly is paramount. TypeScript and Zod each provide unique strengths in this endeavor: TypeScript offers **compile-time type safety**, while Zod delivers **runtime validation**. When combined, they create a comprehensive safety net that enhances both development efficiency and application reliability. This section explores how these two tools complement each other, providing a seamless development experience that guards against a wide array of potential issues.

Understanding the Two Layers of Safety

Compile-Time Safety with TypeScript: TypeScript's primary role is to catch type-related errors during the development phase. By enforcing type annotations and leveraging TypeScript's type system, developers can identify and rectify issues before the code runs. This static analysis helps prevent common bugs, such as passing incorrect types to functions or accessing nonexistent properties on objects.

Runtime Validation with Zod: While TypeScript ensures type safety during development, it doesn't offer protection once the application is running. Data can originate from various sources—user inputs, API responses, databases, or third-party services—that TypeScript cannot validate at runtime. Zod fills this gap by providing robust schema validation, ensuring that incoming data adheres to expected structures and constraints.

Together, TypeScript and Zod Provide:

- **Comprehensive Error Detection:** TypeScript catches errors early in the development process, while Zod handles unexpected data at runtime.
- **Enhanced Code Quality:** Combining static and dynamic validation leads to more reliable and maintainable codebases.
- **Seamless Integration:** Zod's TypeScript-first design ensures that type definitions and validation schemas remain synchronized.

Practical Implementation: Bridging TypeScript and Zod

Let's walk through a practical example to illustrate how TypeScript and Zod work together to provide both compile-time and runtime safety.

Step 1: Setting Up the Project

1. **Initialize a New Project:** Create a new directory and initialize it with npm.

```bash
---
mkdir ts-zod-integration
cd ts-zod-integration
npm init -y
```

2. **Install Dependencies:** Install TypeScript and Zod as development dependencies.

```bash
---
npm install --save-dev typescript zod
```

3. **Initialize TypeScript Configuration:** Generate a `tsconfig.json` file with default settings.

```bash
---
npx tsc --init
```

Step 2: Defining Types and Schemas

1. **Create a TypeScript File:** Create a `src` directory and an `index.ts` file.

```bash
bash
---
mkdir src
touch src/index.ts
```

2. **Define a TypeScript Interface:** Define the shape of the data using a TypeScript interface.

```typescript
typescript
---
// src/index.ts
interface User {
   name: string;
   age: number;
   email: string;
}
```

3. **Create a Zod Schema:** Define a Zod schema that mirrors the TypeScript interface.

```typescript
typescript
---
import { z } from "zod";

const userSchema = z.object({
   name: z.string(),
   age: z.number().int().min(18, "Age must be at least
18"),
   email: z.string().email("Invalid email address"),
});

type User = z.infer<typeof userSchema>;
```

Explanation:

- `z.object` defines the structure of the `User` object.
- `.int()` ensures that `age` is an integer.
- `.min(18)` sets a minimum age requirement.
- `.email()` validates the email format.

- z.infer<typeof userSchema> automatically infers the User type from the schema, ensuring consistency between TypeScript types and Zod schemas.

Step 3: Parsing and Validating Data

1. **Function to Handle User Data:** Create a function that accepts user data, validates it using Zod, and processes it.

```typescript
---
// src/index.ts
import { z } from "zod";

const userSchema = z.object({
  name: z.string(),
  age: z.number().int().min(18, "Age must be at least 18"),
  email: z.string().email("Invalid email address"),
});

type User = z.infer<typeof userSchema>;

function processUserData(data: unknown): User {
  const parsedData = userSchema.parse(data);
  // Proceed with processing the validated data
  console.log(`Processing user: ${parsedData.name}`);
  return parsedData;
}
```

Explanation:

- The function processUserData takes data of type unknown, emphasizing that the input could be anything.
- userSchema.parse(data) validates the data against the schema. If validation fails, Zod throws an error with detailed messages.
- Upon successful validation, the data is treated as a User type, ensuring type safety within the function.

Step 4: Handling Errors Gracefully

1. **Using safeParse for Error Handling:** Modify the function to handle validation errors without throwing exceptions.

```typescript
---
// src/index.ts
```

```typescript
function safeProcessUserData(data: unknown): void {
  const result = userSchema.safeParse(data);

  if (result.success) {
    const user = result.data;
    console.log(`Processing user: ${user.name}`);
    // Further processing
  } else {
    console.error("Validation failed:", result.error.errors);
    // Handle errors appropriately
  }
}
```

Explanation:

- o safeParse returns an object with a success flag and either data or error.
- o This approach allows for graceful error handling, enabling the application to respond to invalid data without crashing.

Step 5: Testing the Integration

1. **Valid Data Example:**

```typescript
---
const validUserData = {
  name: "Alice",
  age: 30,
  email: "alice@example.com",
};

processUserData(validUserData);
// Output: Processing user: Alice
```

2. **Invalid Data Example:**

```typescript
---
const invalidUserData = {
  name: "Bob",
  age: 16,
  email: "bob-at-example.com",
};

try {
  processUserData(invalidUserData);
```

```
} catch (e) {
  console.error(e.errors);
  // Output: Detailed validation errors
}

safeProcessUserData(invalidUserData);
// Output: Validation failed: [ { path: ['age'], message:
'Age must be at least 18', ... }, { path: ['email'], message:
'Invalid email address', ... } ]
```

Explanation:

- o The first example with `validUserData` passes both TypeScript's compile-time checks and Zod's runtime validation.
- o The second example with `invalidUserData` fails validation:
  - `processUserData` throws an error that can be caught and handled.
  - `safeProcessUserData` logs detailed error messages without throwing exceptions, allowing the application to continue running.

Benefits of Combining TypeScript and Zod

1. **Enhanced Reliability:**
   - o **TypeScript** ensures that your code adheres to defined types during development.
   - o **Zod** validates that incoming and outgoing data matches expected structures at runtime.
2. **Reduced Redundancy:**
   - o Zod's ability to infer TypeScript types from schemas eliminates the need to maintain separate type definitions, reducing duplication and potential inconsistencies.
3. **Improved Developer Experience:**
   - o TypeScript's editor integrations provide real-time feedback and autocompletion, while Zod's detailed error messages aid in debugging and provide clear guidance on data issues.
4. **Scalability:**
   - o This combination is particularly effective in large codebases or teams, where maintaining consistency and reliability across different parts of the application is crucial.
5. **Security:**

- Validating data at runtime helps prevent security vulnerabilities related to unexpected or malformed data inputs.

Conclusion

Integrating TypeScript and Zod leverages the strengths of both compile-time type safety and runtime data validation, resulting in a robust and maintainable codebase. TypeScript catches type-related errors during development, while Zod ensures that your application handles real-world data correctly and safely. By combining these tools, developers can build applications that are not only error-resistant but also easier to understand and maintain.

In the upcoming sections, we'll explore how to create and use Zod schemas effectively, handle optional and nullable values, and manage validation errors to further enhance your TypeScript and Zod integration. Let's continue building a solid foundation for type-safe, reliable application development!

4.2 Creating and Using Zod Schemas

Creating and utilizing Zod schemas is fundamental to harnessing the full power of runtime validation in your TypeScript applications. Zod's intuitive API allows developers to define clear, concise, and reusable schemas that ensure data integrity across various parts of an application. In this section, we'll explore the process of creating Zod schemas, using them for validation, and integrating them seamlessly into your TypeScript workflow through practical, step-by-step examples.

---

1. Defining Basic Schemas

At the core of Zod's functionality is the ability to define schemas that describe the shape and constraints of your data. Let's start with the basics.

Step 1: Importing Zod

Before you can create schemas, you need to import Zod into your TypeScript file.

```typescript
---
import { z } from "zod";
```

Step 2: Creating a Simple Object Schema

Suppose you want to define a schema for a user object that includes a name, age, and email. Here's how you can do it:

```typescript
---
const userSchema = z.object({
  name: z.string(),
  age: z.number(),
  email: z.string().email(),
});
```

Explanation:

- `z.object({...})` creates a schema for an object.
- Each property within the object defines the expected type and any additional constraints.
- `z.string().email()` ensures that the email field contains a valid email address.

Step 3: Inferring TypeScript Types from Schemas

Zod can automatically infer TypeScript types from your schemas, ensuring consistency between your validation logic and type definitions.

```typescript
---
type User = z.infer<typeof userSchema>;
```

Explanation:

- `z.infer<typeof userSchema>` extracts the TypeScript type from the Zod schema.
- This eliminates the need to manually define TypeScript interfaces or types, reducing redundancy.

Step 4: Using the Schema to Validate Data

Once your schema is defined, you can use it to validate data.

```typescript
---
const validUserData = {
  name: "Alice",
  age: 30,
  email: "alice@example.com",
};

const validatedUser = userSchema.parse(validUserData);
console.log(validatedUser);
// Output: { name: "Alice", age: 30, email:
"alice@example.com" }
```

Explanation:

- `userSchema.parse(data)` validates the data against the schema.
- If the data is valid, it returns the parsed object.
- If invalid, it throws a detailed error.

---

2. Enhancing Schemas with Constraints

Zod allows you to add constraints to your schemas, ensuring that data not only matches the expected types but also adheres to specific rules.

Step 1: Adding Minimum and Maximum Constraints

Let's enhance the `age` property to ensure that users are at least 18 years old.

```typescript
---
const userSchema = z.object({
  name: z.string(),
  age: z.number().min(18, { message: "Age must be at least
18" }),
  email: z.string().email(),
});
```

Explanation:

- `.min(18)` ensures that the `age` is at least 18.

- The second argument provides a custom error message for clarity.

Step 2: Making Properties Optional or Nullable

Sometimes, certain properties may not always be present or can be `null`. Zod provides methods to handle these scenarios.

- **Optional Properties:**

```typescript
---
const userSchema = z.object({
  name: z.string(),
  age: z.number().min(18),
  email: z.string().email(),
  phone?: z.string(), // Optional property
});
```

Explanation:

- Adding a `?` after the property name makes it optional.
- Users can omit the `phone` field without causing validation to fail.

- **Nullable Properties:**

```typescript
---
const userSchema = z.object({
  name: z.string(),
  age: z.number().min(18),
  email: z.string().email(),
  phone: z.string().nullable(), // Property can be a
string or null
});
```

Explanation:

- `.nullable()` allows the property to be `null` in addition to its defined type.

Step 3: Setting Default Values

Zod can assign default values to properties if they are missing from the data.

```typescript
```

```
---
const userSchema = z.object({
  name: z.string(),
  age: z.number().min(18),
  email: z.string().email(),
  isActive: z.boolean().default(true), // Default value
});
```

Explanation:

- `.default(true)` sets `isActive` to `true` if it's not provided in the data.

---

3. Composing and Reusing Schemas

Zod promotes reusability and modularity by allowing schemas to be composed from smaller, reusable pieces.

Step 1: Creating Reusable Subschemas

Suppose you have an address that multiple objects might share. Define an address schema separately.

```typescript
---
const addressSchema = z.object({
  street: z.string(),
  city: z.string(),
  zipCode: z.string().length(5, { message: "Zip Code must be
5 characters long" }),
});
```

Step 2: Integrating Subschemas into Larger Schemas

Use the `addressSchema` within the `userSchema` to validate nested objects.

```typescript
---
const userSchema = z.object({
  name: z.string(),
  age: z.number().min(18),
  email: z.string().email(),
  address: addressSchema, // Nested schema
});
```

Explanation:

- Nesting schemas ensures that complex data structures are validated comprehensively.
- Reusing `addressSchema` avoids duplication and enhances maintainability.

---

4. Parsing and Handling Data

Zod provides robust methods for parsing and handling data, ensuring that your application can respond appropriately to both valid and invalid inputs.

Step 1: Parsing Data with `parse`

The `parse` method validates the data and returns the parsed object if valid or throws an error if invalid.

```typescript
---
try {
  const user = userSchema.parse(invalidUserData);
  // Proceed with using the validated user data
} catch (e) {
  console.error(e.errors);
  // Handle validation errors
}
```

Explanation:

- Wrapping `parse` in a `try-catch` block allows you to handle validation errors gracefully.
- `e.errors` contains detailed information about each validation failure.

Step 2: Safe Parsing with `safeParse`

For scenarios where you prefer not to throw errors, `safeParse` returns an object indicating success or failure.

```typescript
---
const result = userSchema.safeParse(userData);
```

```
if (result.success) {
  const user = result.data;
  console.log("Valid user:", user);
} else {
  console.error("Validation errors:", result.error.errors);
}
```

Explanation:

- `safeParse` avoids throwing exceptions, making it easier to handle
  validation results within conditional logic.
- This approach is particularly useful in applications where validation
  errors need to be displayed to users without disrupting the flow.

---

5. Integrating Zod Schemas into Your Workflow

Incorporating Zod schemas into your development workflow enhances both
frontend and backend processes, ensuring data consistency and reliability
across your application.

Step 1: Frontend Integration

Use Zod schemas to validate user inputs in forms, ensuring that data
submitted to the backend meets the expected criteria.

```typescript
---
// Example: Validating form data before submission
const formData = {
  name: "Bob",
  age: 20,
  email: "bob@example.com",
};

const validationResult = userSchema.safeParse(formData);

if (validationResult.success) {
  // Submit the validated data
} else {
  // Display validation errors to the user
}
```

Step 2: Backend Integration

Validate incoming API requests to ensure that the data received from clients is well-structured and adheres to the expected schema.

```typescript
---
// Example: Validating API request body in an Express route
app.post("/api/user", (req, res) => {
  const validationResult = userSchema.safeParse(req.body);

  if (validationResult.success) {
    const user = validationResult.data;
    // Proceed with processing the valid user data
    res.status(200).send("User created successfully");
  } else {
    res.status(400).json({ errors:
validationResult.error.errors });
  }
});
```

Step 3: Consistency Across Layers

By defining Zod schemas that mirror your TypeScript types, you ensure consistency across different layers of your application, from the frontend to the backend and beyond.

Example: Shared Schema Definitions

```typescript
---
// schemas/userSchema.ts
import { z } from "zod";

export const userSchema = z.object({
  name: z.string(),
  age: z.number().min(18),
  email: z.string().email(),
});

// types/user.ts
import { z } from "zod";
import { userSchema } from "../schemas/userSchema";

export type User = z.infer<typeof userSchema>;
```

Explanation:

- Sharing schema definitions across your application ensures that all parts of your codebase adhere to the same data contracts.
- This reduces the risk of inconsistencies and makes maintaining large codebases more manageable.

---

6. My Insight: The Power of Combined Validation

Integrating TypeScript and Zod has transformed the way I approach data handling in my projects. Initially, relying solely on TypeScript for type safety was sufficient during development, but runtime data inconsistencies often led to frustrating bugs. Introducing Zod provided the necessary layer of runtime validation, ensuring that data entering my application met all necessary criteria. This combination not only reduced bugs but also made the codebase more maintainable and understandable for the entire team. By defining clear schemas and leveraging TypeScript's type inference, we achieved a seamless and efficient development workflow.

Conclusion

Creating and using Zod schemas is a critical step in building type-safe and reliable TypeScript applications. By defining clear schemas, leveraging Zod's powerful parsing and validation capabilities, and integrating schemas seamlessly into your workflow, you ensure that your application handles data consistently and securely. The synergy between TypeScript's compile-time safety and Zod's runtime validation provides a robust foundation for developing scalable and maintainable software. In the next section, we'll explore how to handle optional, nullable, and default values effectively, further enhancing your data validation strategy. Let's continue!

4.3 Handling Optional, Nullable, and Default Values

In real-world applications, not all data fields are mandatory. Some fields might be optional, nullable, or require default values. Effectively managing these scenarios is crucial for building flexible and resilient applications. TypeScript and Zod provide robust mechanisms to handle optional, nullable, and default values seamlessly. This section delves into these concepts, illustrating how to implement them using TypeScript and Zod with practical, step-by-step examples.

---

1. Understanding Optional, Nullable, and Default Values

Before diving into the implementation, it's essential to understand what optional, nullable, and default values mean:

- **Optional Values:** Fields that may or may not be present in the data. In TypeScript, this is denoted using the ? symbol.
- **Nullable Values:** Fields that can hold a value of a specified type or null. This is represented using union types (e.g., string | null).
- **Default Values:** Fields that automatically receive a predefined value if they are missing from the data.

---

2. Handling Optional Values

TypeScript Perspective:

In TypeScript, optional properties are defined using the ? syntax. This indicates that the property may or may not be present.

```typescript
---
interface User {
  name: string;
  age: number;
  email?: string; // Optional property
}
```

Zod Perspective:

Zod mirrors this functionality by providing the .optional() method, allowing properties to be optional within schemas.

Step-by-Step Implementation:

1. **Define the TypeScript Interface:**

```typescript
---
interface User {
  name: string;
  age: number;
  email?: string;
}
```

2. Create the Zod Schema with Optional Property:

```typescript
---
import { z } from "zod";

const userSchema = z.object({
  name: z.string(),
  age: z.number(),
  email: z.string().optional(), // Optional property
});

type User = z.infer<typeof userSchema>;
```

3. Validate Data with and without the Optional Property:

```typescript
---
const userWithEmail = {
  name: "Alice",
  age: 30,
  email: "alice@example.com",
};

const userWithoutEmail = {
  name: "Bob",
  age: 25,
};

// Parsing user with email
const validatedUserWithEmail =
userSchema.parse(userWithEmail);
console.log(validatedUserWithEmail);
// Output: { name: "Alice", age: 30, email:
"alice@example.com" }

// Parsing user without email
const validatedUserWithoutEmail =
userSchema.parse(userWithoutEmail);
console.log(validatedUserWithoutEmail);
// Output: { name: "Bob", age: 25 }
```

Explanation:

- The `email` property is marked as optional using `.optional()`.
- When validating `userWithoutEmail`, Zod accepts the data even though the `email` field is missing.

---

3. Handling Nullable Values

TypeScript Perspective:

Nullable properties can hold a value of a specified type or `null`. This is represented using union types.

```typescript
---
interface User {
  name: string;
  age: number;
  email: string | null; // Nullable property
}
```

Zod Perspective:

Zod provides the `.nullable()` method to allow properties to be `null`.

Step-by-Step Implementation:

1. **Define the TypeScript Interface:**

```typescript
---
interface User {
  name: string;
  age: number;
  email: string | null;
}
```

2. **Create the Zod Schema with Nullable Property:**

```typescript
---
import { z } from "zod";
```

```typescript
const userSchema = z.object({
  name: z.string(),
  age: z.number(),
  email: z.string().nullable(), // Nullable property
});

type User = z.infer<typeof userSchema>;
```

3. **Validate Data with and without `null` in the Nullable Property:**

```typescript
---
const userWithEmail = {
  name: "Alice",
  age: 30,
  email: "alice@example.com",
};

const userWithNullEmail = {
  name: "Bob",
  age: 25,
  email: null, // Explicitly set to null
};

// Parsing user with email
const validatedUserWithEmail =
userSchema.parse(userWithEmail);
console.log(validatedUserWithEmail);
// Output: { name: "Alice", age: 30, email:
"alice@example.com" }

// Parsing user with null email
const validatedUserWithNullEmail =
userSchema.parse(userWithNullEmail);
console.log(validatedUserWithNullEmail);
// Output: { name: "Bob", age: 25, email: null }
```

Explanation:

- The `email` property is marked as nullable using `.nullable()`.
- Zod accepts the `email` field when it is either a string or `null`.

---

4. Handling Default Values

TypeScript Perspective:

TypeScript allows setting default values in function parameters or class properties, but it doesn't inherently support default values within interfaces.

Zod Perspective:

Zod provides the .default() method to assign default values to properties if they are missing from the data.

Step-by-Step Implementation:

1. **Define the TypeScript Interface with Optional Property:**

```typescript
---
interface User {
  name: string;
  age: number;
  isActive?: boolean; // Optional property with a default value
}
```

2. **Create the Zod Schema with a Default Value:**

```typescript
---
import { z } from "zod";

const userSchema = z.object({
  name: z.string(),
  age: z.number(),
  isActive: z.boolean().default(true), // Default value
});

type User = z.infer<typeof userSchema>;
```

3. **Validate Data with and without the Property to Observe Default Behavior:**

```typescript
---
const userWithIsActive = {
  name: "Alice",
  age: 30,
  isActive: false,
};

const userWithoutIsActive = {
```

```
  name: "Bob",
  age: 25,
};

// Parsing user with isActive
const validatedUserWithIsActive =
userSchema.parse(userWithIsActive);
console.log(validatedUserWithIsActive);
// Output: { name: "Alice", age: 30, isActive: false }

// Parsing user without isActive
const validatedUserWithoutIsActive =
userSchema.parse(userWithoutIsActive);
console.log(validatedUserWithoutIsActive);
// Output: { name: "Bob", age: 25, isActive: true }
```

Explanation:

- The `isActive` property is assigned a default value of `true` using `.default(true)`.
- When `isActive` is missing from the input data, Zod automatically assigns the default value.

---

5. Combining Optional, Nullable, and Default Values

TypeScript and Zod allow you to combine these features to handle complex data scenarios.

Example Scenario:

Consider a user profile where `middleName` is optional, `nickname` can be `null`, and `isActive` should default to `true` if not provided.

Step-by-Step Implementation:

1. **Define the TypeScript Interface:**

```typescript
---
interface User {
  firstName: string;
  middleName?: string; // Optional
  lastName: string;
  nickname: string | null; // Nullable
```

```typescript
  isActive?: boolean; // Optional with default
}
```

2. Create the Zod Schema with Combined Features:

```typescript
---
import { z } from "zod";

const userSchema = z.object({
  firstName: z.string(),
  middleName: z.string().optional(), // Optional
  lastName: z.string(),
  nickname: z.string().nullable(), // Nullable
  isActive: z.boolean().default(true), // Default value
});

type User = z.infer<typeof userSchema>;
```

3. Validate Data Examples:

```typescript
---
const userFullData = {
  firstName: "Alice",
  middleName: "Marie",
  lastName: "Smith",
  nickname: "Ally",
  isActive: false,
};

const userPartialData = {
  firstName: "Bob",
  lastName: "Brown",
  nickname: null, // Explicitly set to null
};

// Parsing user with full data
const validatedUserFull = userSchema.parse(userFullData);
console.log(validatedUserFull);
// Output: { firstName: "Alice", middleName: "Marie",
lastName: "Smith", nickname: "Ally", isActive: false }

// Parsing user with partial data
const validatedUserPartial =
userSchema.parse(userPartialData);
console.log(validatedUserPartial);
// Output: { firstName: "Bob", lastName: "Brown", nickname:
null, isActive: true }
```

Explanation:

- `middleName` is optional and can be omitted.
- `nickname` can be a string or `null`.
- `isActive` defaults to `true` if not provided.

---

6. Best Practices for Handling Optional, Nullable, and Default Values

To maximize the benefits of TypeScript and Zod in handling optional, nullable, and default values, consider the following best practices:

1. **Consistency Between TypeScript and Zod:**
   - Ensure that your TypeScript interfaces and Zod schemas consistently handle optional and nullable properties.
   - Use `z.infer` to derive TypeScript types directly from Zod schemas to maintain synchronization.
2. **Clear Schema Definitions:**
   - Clearly define which properties are optional, nullable, or have default values within your schemas.
   - Avoid overcomplicating schemas with unnecessary optional or nullable properties unless required by your application logic.
3. **Leverage Zod's Methods:**
   - Utilize `.optional()`, `.nullable()`, and `.default()` methods to handle different scenarios effectively.
   - Combine these methods to cater to complex data requirements.
4. **Document Your Schemas:**
   - Add comments to your schema definitions to explain the rationale behind optional, nullable, or default properties.
   - This enhances readability and aids team members in understanding data structures.
5. **Use Utility Types When Appropriate:**
   - For repetitive patterns, consider using utility types or helper functions to streamline schema definitions.

---

7. My Insight: Streamlining Data Handling

Incorporating optional, nullable, and default values into your TypeScript and Zod workflows significantly enhances the flexibility and robustness of your applications. Early in my experience, managing these scenarios felt cumbersome due to the need for repetitive type definitions and validation logic. However, leveraging Zod's intuitive methods alongside TypeScript's type system streamlined this process, reducing boilerplate and minimizing errors. By clearly defining data contracts, I was able to focus more on building features rather than wrestling with data inconsistencies.

Conclusion

Handling optional, nullable, and default values is a fundamental aspect of robust application development. TypeScript provides the tools to define these scenarios at compile time, while Zod ensures that data adheres to these definitions at runtime. By effectively integrating these features, you create applications that are both flexible and resilient, capable of gracefully handling a wide range of data inputs. In the next section, we'll explore strategies for managing validation errors effectively, ensuring that your applications can respond to data issues in a user-friendly and maintainable manner. Let's continue building a solid foundation for type-safe and reliable application development!

4.4 Managing Validation Errors Effectively

Effective error management is crucial for building resilient and user-friendly applications. When working with data validation using Zod and TypeScript, handling validation errors gracefully ensures that your application can respond appropriately to invalid or unexpected data inputs. This section explores strategies for managing validation errors effectively, leveraging Zod's robust error handling capabilities alongside TypeScript's type safety. We'll walk through practical implementations to help you provide meaningful feedback to users and maintain application stability.

1. The Importance of Managing Validation Errors

Validation errors occur when data does not conform to the expected schema. Properly handling these errors is essential for several reasons:

- **User Experience:** Providing clear and actionable error messages helps users correct their input, enhancing their interaction with your application.
- **Application Stability:** Gracefully handling errors prevents unexpected crashes and ensures that your application remains robust under various data conditions.
- **Security:** Validating and managing errors effectively can mitigate security vulnerabilities related to malformed or malicious data inputs.

By implementing effective error management, you create a safer and more reliable application environment.

---

2. Zod's Error Handling Mechanisms

Zod offers comprehensive error handling features that make it easier to manage validation failures. Understanding these mechanisms allows you to implement robust error management strategies.

a. The `parse` Method

The `parse` method validates data against a schema. If the data is valid, it returns the parsed object. If invalid, it throws a `ZodError` containing detailed information about the validation failures.

Example:

```typescript
---
import { z } from "zod";

const userSchema = z.object({
  name: z.string(),
  age: z.number().min(18, { message: "Age must be at least
18" }),
  email: z.string().email({ message: "Invalid email address"
}),
});

const invalidUserData = {
```

```
  name: "Bob",
  age: 16,
  email: "bob-at-example.com",
};

try {
  const user = userSchema.parse(invalidUserData);
} catch (e) {
  if (e instanceof z.ZodError) {
    console.error(e.errors);
    // Output: Detailed validation errors
  }
}
```

Explanation:

- When `parse` is called with `invalidUserData`, it throws a `ZodError` because `age` is below 18 and `email` is improperly formatted.
- The `catch` block checks if the error is an instance of `ZodError` and then logs the detailed error messages.

b. The `safeParse` Method

Unlike `parse`, the `safeParse` method does not throw an error. Instead, it returns an object indicating whether the validation was successful, along with either the parsed data or the error details.

Example:

```typescript
---
const result = userSchema.safeParse(invalidUserData);

if (result.success) {
  console.log("Valid user:", result.data);
} else {
  console.error("Validation errors:", result.error.errors);
  // Output: Detailed validation errors
}
```

Explanation:

- `safeParse` returns an object with a `success` property.
- If `success` is `true`, `result.data` contains the validated data.
- If `success` is `false`, `result.error.errors` contains detailed error information.

3. Strategies for Handling Validation Errors

Implementing effective error handling involves more than just catching errors. It requires thoughtful strategies to ensure that errors are managed in a way that enhances the overall application experience.

a. Using Try-Catch Blocks with `parse`

When you prefer to handle errors using exception handling, wrapping the `parse` method in a `try-catch` block is a straightforward approach.

Step-by-Step Implementation:

1. **Define the Schema:**

```typescript
---
const userSchema = z.object({
  name: z.string(),
  age: z.number().min(18, { message: "Age must be at least
18" }),
  email: z.string().email({ message: "Invalid email address"
}),
});
```

2. **Parse Data with Error Handling:**

```typescript
---
const userData = {
  name: "Charlie",
  age: 17,
  email: "charlie@example.com",
};

try {
  const user = userSchema.parse(userData);
  console.log("Valid user:", user);
} catch (e) {
  if (e instanceof z.ZodError) {
    console.error("Validation failed:", e.errors);
    // Handle errors, e.g., inform the user
  }
}
```

Explanation:

- The `parse` method validates `userData`.
- If validation fails, the `catch` block captures the `ZodError`.
- Detailed error information can be logged or used to inform the user.

b. Using `safeParse` for Conditional Handling

For scenarios where throwing exceptions is not desirable, `safeParse` provides a clean alternative by returning a structured result.

Step-by-Step Implementation:

1. **Define the Schema:**

```typescript
---
const userSchema = z.object({
  name: z.string(),
  age: z.number().min(18, { message: "Age must be at least 18" }),
  email: z.string().email({ message: "Invalid email address" }),
});
```

2. **Parse Data and Handle Results:**

```typescript
---
const userData = {
  name: "Diana",
  age: 20,
  email: "diana@example.com",
};

const result = userSchema.safeParse(userData);

if (result.success) {
  console.log("Valid user:", result.data);
  // Proceed with processing the valid data
} else {
  console.error("Validation errors:", result.error.errors);
  // Inform the user or take corrective action
}
```

Explanation:

- `safeParse` validates `userData` without throwing an error.
- The result object indicates whether validation succeeded.
- Based on the `success` flag, you can handle the data accordingly.

---

4. Formatting and Presenting Error Messages

Clear and user-friendly error messages are essential for both developers and end-users. Zod provides detailed error information, which can be formatted and presented in various ways to suit different needs.

a. Understanding ZodError Structure

A `ZodError` contains an array of error objects, each detailing a specific validation failure.

Error Object Properties:

- **path:** An array indicating the location of the error within the data structure.
- **message:** A descriptive message explaining the validation failure.
- **code:** A string identifier for the type of validation error.

Example Error Output:

```json
---
[
  {
    "path": ["age"],
    "message": "Age must be at least 18",
    "code": "too_small"
  },
  {
    "path": ["email"],
    "message": "Invalid email address",
    "code": "invalid_string"
  }
]
```

b. Formatting Errors for User Display

To enhance user experience, format these errors into a more readable and actionable form.

Step-by-Step Implementation:

1. **Define a Function to Format Errors:**

```typescript
---
function formatZodErrors(errors: z.ZodIssue[]): string[] {
  return errors.map((error) => {
    const path = error.path.join(".");
    return `${path}: ${error.message}`;
  });
}
```

2. **Use the Function to Present Errors:**

```typescript
---
const result = userSchema.safeParse(invalidUserData);

if (!result.success) {
  const formattedErrors =
formatZodErrors(result.error.errors);
  formattedErrors.forEach((err) => console.error(err));
  // Output:
  // age: Age must be at least 18
  // email: Invalid email address
}
```

Explanation:

- The `formatZodErrors` function transforms each error object into a readable string.
- Errors are displayed in a clear format, indicating the exact field and the issue.

c. Integrating with Frontend Frameworks

When building user interfaces, integrate error formatting with form handling libraries or UI components to provide immediate feedback.

Example with React:

1. Define the Schema and Validation Function:

```typescript
---
const userSchema = z.object({
  name: z.string(),
  age: z.number().min(18, { message: "Age must be at least
18" }),
  email: z.string().email({ message: "Invalid email address"
}),
});

type User = z.infer<typeof userSchema>;
```

2. Handle Form Submission:

```typescript
---
import React, { useState } from "react";

const UserForm: React.FC = () => {
  const [formData, setFormData] =
useState<Partial<User>>({});
  const [errors, setErrors] = useState<string[]>([]);

  const handleSubmit = (e: React.FormEvent) => {
    e.preventDefault();
    const result = userSchema.safeParse(formData);

    if (result.success) {
      console.log("Valid user:", result.data);
      setErrors([]);
      // Proceed with form submission
    } else {
      const formattedErrors =
formatZodErrors(result.error.errors);
      setErrors(formattedErrors);
    }
  };

  return (
    <form onSubmit={handleSubmit}>
      {/* Form fields for name, age, email */}
      <button type="submit">Submit</button>
      {errors.length > 0 && (
        <div className="error-messages">
          {errors.map((err, index) => (
            <p key={index}>{err}</p>
          ))}
        </div>
```

```
    )}
    </form>
  );
};
```

Explanation:

- Upon form submission, `safeParse` validates the data.
- If validation fails, formatted errors are displayed to the user within the UI.

---

5. Best Practices for Managing Validation Errors

Adopting best practices ensures that your error management strategy is both effective and maintainable.

a. Centralize Error Handling Logic

Centralizing error handling logic promotes consistency and reduces duplication across your application.

Step-by-Step Implementation:

1. **Create an Error Handling Utility:**

```typescript
---
// utils/errorHandler.ts
import { z } from "zod";

export function handleZodErrors(errors: z.ZodIssue[]):
string[] {
  return errors.map((error) => {
    const path = error.path.join(".");
    return `${path}: ${error.message}`;
  });
}
```

2. **Use the Utility in Multiple Places:**

```typescript
---
import { handleZodErrors } from "./utils/errorHandler";
```

```
const result = userSchema.safeParse(data);

if (!result.success) {
  const formattedErrors =
handleZodErrors(result.error.errors);
  // Use formattedErrors as needed
}
```

Explanation:

- By centralizing error formatting, you ensure that all parts of your application handle errors uniformly.

b. Provide Meaningful and Actionable Feedback

Ensure that error messages are clear and guide users on how to correct their input.

Example:

- Instead of: `"invalid_type"`
- Use: `"Email must be a valid email address."`

Implementation:

Define custom error messages in your Zod schemas to provide clarity.

```typescript
---
const userSchema = z.object({
  name: z.string().nonempty({ message: "Name is required."
}),
  age: z.number().min(18, { message: "Age must be at least
18." }),
  email: z.string().email({ message: "Please enter a valid
email address." }),
});
```

Explanation:

- Custom messages replace generic error codes, making feedback more user-friendly.

c. Log Errors for Monitoring and Debugging

Maintain logs of validation errors to monitor application health and identify recurring issues.

Step-by-Step Implementation:

1. **Define a Logging Function:**

```typescript
---
function logValidationErrors(errors: z.ZodIssue[]): void {
  errors.forEach((error) => {
    console.error(`Validation Error - Path:
${error.path.join(".")}, Message: ${error.message}`);
  });
}
```

2. **Integrate Logging into Error Handling:**

```typescript
---
const result = userSchema.safeParse(data);

if (!result.success) {
  logValidationErrors(result.error.errors);
  // Additional error handling
}
```

Explanation:

- Logging provides insights into common validation failures, aiding in proactive issue resolution.

d. Avoid Overloading Users with Errors

Present errors in a clear and concise manner without overwhelming users.

Implementation Tips:

- **Prioritize Errors:** Display the most critical errors first.
- **Group Related Errors:** Organize errors by form sections or data categories.
- **Use Visual Cues:** Highlight fields with errors using colors or icons.

Example:

```typescript
---
// Display errors in a grouped format
const groupedErrors = formattedErrors.reduce((acc, err) => {
  const [field, message] = err.split(": ");
  if (!acc[field]) acc[field] = [];
  acc[field].push(message);
  return acc;
}, {} as Record<string, string[]>);

for (const field in groupedErrors) {
  console.log(`Errors for ${field}:`);
  groupedErrors[field].forEach((msg) => console.log(`-
${msg}`));
}
```

Explanation:

- Grouping errors by field makes it easier for users to identify and correct issues without feeling overwhelmed.

---

6. My Insight: Streamlining Error Management

In my experience, effective error management significantly enhances both the developer workflow and the end-user experience. Initially, handling validation errors was a tedious process, often involving repetitive code and unclear error messages. Integrating Zod streamlined this process by providing detailed error information and flexible handling methods. By adopting centralized error handling utilities and customizing error messages, I was able to reduce redundancy and present clearer feedback to users. This not only improved the application's reliability but also made the codebase more maintainable and easier to work with for the entire development team.

Conclusion

Managing validation errors effectively is a pivotal aspect of building robust and user-friendly applications. By leveraging Zod's comprehensive error handling features alongside TypeScript's type safety, you can create applications that gracefully handle invalid data inputs and provide meaningful feedback to users. Implementing strategies such as centralized error handling, meaningful feedback, and thoughtful error presentation ensures that your application remains resilient and maintains a high standard of reliability and usability. As you continue to integrate TypeScript and Zod into your development workflow, these error management practices will play a crucial role in enhancing both your development experience and the overall quality of your applications.

In the next chapter, we'll explore real-world applications of TypeScript and Zod integration, showcasing how these tools work together in various scenarios to build type-safe and reliable systems. Let's continue building a strong foundation for your development projects!

Chapter 5: Advanced Zod Techniques

As you become more comfortable with the basics of Zod and its integration with TypeScript, it's time to explore some of its advanced features. These techniques will empower you to handle more complex data structures, implement dynamic validation logic, and optimize performance for large-scale applications. In this chapter, we'll delve into building complex schemas, utilizing conditional and recursive schemas, creating custom validators and transformations, and implementing performance tips for efficient validation.

5.1 Building Complex Schemas: Nested Objects and Arrays

In real-world applications, data structures are rarely flat. Often, data includes nested objects and arrays that represent complex relationships and hierarchies. Zod excels at handling these intricate structures, allowing developers to define comprehensive schemas that ensure data integrity across all levels. This section explores how to build complex schemas with nested objects and arrays using Zod, providing clear explanations and practical, step-by-step examples to enhance your understanding.

1. Understanding Nested Objects and Arrays

Before diving into implementation, it's essential to grasp what nested objects and arrays entail:

- **Nested Objects:** These are objects within objects, representing hierarchical data. For instance, a user object might contain an address object.
- **Arrays:** Collections of items, all adhering to a specific type. Arrays can contain primitive types or complex objects.

Combining these allows you to model sophisticated data structures accurately.

2. Building Nested Object Schemas

Nested objects are common in applications that manage related data entities. Zod makes it straightforward to define schemas that reflect these relationships.

Step 1: Define Subschemas

Start by defining schemas for the nested objects. This promotes reusability and clarity.

```typescript
---
import { z } from "zod";

// Address subschema
const addressSchema = z.object({
  street: z.string(),
  city: z.string(),
  zipCode: z.string().length(5, { message: "Zip Code must be
exactly 5 characters long" }),
});
```

Explanation:

- **z.object({...})**: Creates a schema for an object.
- **Field Definitions:**
  - street and city are simple string fields.
  - zipCode is a string with a constraint enforcing exactly 5 characters.

Step 2: Integrate Subschemas into Parent Schemas

Use the subschema within a larger schema to represent nested data structures.

```typescript
---
// User schema with nested address
const userSchema = z.object({
  name: z.string(),
  age: z.number().min(18, { message: "Age must be at least
18" }),
```

```
  email: z.string().email({ message: "Invalid email address"
}),
  address: addressSchema, // Nested address object
});
```

Explanation:

- **address: addressSchema:** Embeds the previously defined
  addressSchema within the userSchema, establishing a hierarchical
  relationship.

Step 3: Validate Nested Data

Ensure that the nested data conforms to the defined schemas.

```typescript
---
const userData = {
  name: "Alice",
  age: 30,
  email: "alice@example.com",
  address: {
    street: "123 Main St",
    city: "Wonderland",
    zipCode: "12345",
  },
};

const validatedUser = userSchema.parse(userData);
console.log(validatedUser);
// Output: Validated user object with nested address
```

Explanation:

- **userSchema.parse(userData):** Validates userData against the
  userSchema. If valid, it returns the parsed object; otherwise, it throws
  a ZodError.

3. Building Array Schemas

Arrays are essential for handling collections of data. Zod provides robust
methods to define and validate arrays of various types.

Step 1: Define an Array Schema

Specify the type of elements within the array using `z.array()`.

```typescript
---
// Schema for an array of strings (tags)
const tagsSchema = z.array(z.string()).min(1, { message: "At
least one tag is required" });
```

Explanation:

- **`z.array(z.string())`:** Defines an array where each element must be a string.
- **`.min(1)`:** Enforces that the array contains at least one element.

Step 2: Define Complex Array Schemas

Arrays can contain complex objects, allowing you to model more intricate data structures.

```typescript
---
// Product schema with tags array
const productSchema = z.object({
  name: z.string(),
  price: z.number().positive({ message: "Price must be a
positive number" }),
  tags: tagsSchema, // Array of strings
});
```

Explanation:

- **`tags: tagsSchema`:** Integrates the previously defined `tagsSchema` into the `productSchema`.

Step 3: Validate Array Data

Ensure that the array data meets the defined constraints.

```typescript
---
const productData = {
  name: "Smartphone",
  price: 699.99,
  tags: ["electronics", "mobile"],
```

```
};

const validatedProduct = productSchema.parse(productData);
console.log(validatedProduct);
// Output: Validated product object with tags array
```

Explanation:

- **productSchema.parse(productData):** Validates `productData` against the `productSchema`. Successful validation returns the parsed object.

---

4. Combining Nested Objects and Arrays

Complex applications often require schemas that combine nested objects and arrays to accurately represent data relationships.

Step 1: Define Subschemas for Nested Structures

Define schemas for each nested entity to maintain modularity.

```typescript
---
// Comment subschema for nested comments
const commentSchema = z.object({
  author: z.string(),
  content: z.string(),
  replies: z.array(z.lazy(() => commentSchema)).optional(),
// Recursive nesting
});
```

Explanation:

- **z.lazy(() => commentSchema):** Allows for recursive schemas, enabling comments to have their own replies, which are also comments.
- **.optional():** Makes the `replies` array optional.

Step 2: Integrate Subschemas into Parent Schemas

Combine the subschemas to form a comprehensive schema.

```typescript
```

113

```
---
// BlogPost schema with nested comments
const blogPostSchema = z.object({
  title: z.string(),
  content: z.string(),
  author: z.string(),
  comments: z.array(commentSchema).optional(), // Array of
nested comments
});
```

Explanation:

- **comments: z.array(commentSchema).optional()**: Defines an optional array of comments, each adhering to the commentSchema.

Step 3: Validate Complex Nested Data

Ensure that deeply nested structures are correctly validated.

```typescript
---
const blogPostData = {
  title: "Understanding Zod and TypeScript",
  content: "Zod is a TypeScript-first schema validation
library...",
  author: "Bob",
  comments: [
    {
      author: "Alice",
      content: "Great article!",
      replies: [
        {
          author: "Charlie",
          content: "I agree with Alice.",
        },
      ],
    },
  ],
};

const validatedBlogPost = blogPostSchema.parse(blogPostData);
console.log(validatedBlogPost);
// Output: Validated blog post object with nested comments
and replies
```

Explanation:

- **`blogPostSchema.parse(blogPostData)`:** Validates the entire `blogPostData`, including nested comments and their replies.

---

5. Best Practices for Building Complex Schemas

Creating complex schemas requires thoughtful structuring to maintain readability and efficiency. Here are some best practices to follow:

a. Modularize Subschemas

Define subschemas in separate files or modules to promote reusability and maintainability.

```typescript
---
// schemas/addressSchema.ts
import { z } from "zod";

export const addressSchema = z.object({
  street: z.string(),
  city: z.string(),
  zipCode: z.string().length(5, { message: "Zip Code must be
exactly 5 characters long" }),
});
```
```typescript
---
// schemas/userSchema.ts
import { z } from "zod";
import { addressSchema } from "./addressSchema";

export const userSchema = z.object({
  name: z.string(),
  age: z.number().min(18, { message: "Age must be at least
18" }),
  email: z.string().email({ message: "Invalid email address"
}),
  address: addressSchema,
});
```

Explanation:

- **Separation of Concerns:** Keeping subschemas in their own modules prevents clutter and enhances clarity.

- **Reusability:** Allows multiple parent schemas to use the same subschema without duplication.

b. Use z.lazy for Recursive Structures

When dealing with self-referential data, use z.lazy to defer schema evaluation, preventing infinite loops and ensuring correct validation.

```typescript
---
const commentSchema: z.ZodType<any> = z.lazy(() =>
  z.object({
    author: z.string(),
    content: z.string(),
    replies: z.array(commentSchema).optional(),
  })
);
```

Explanation:

- **z.lazy:** Defers the evaluation of commentSchema until it's needed, enabling recursion.

c. Apply Constraints Thoughtfully

Add only necessary constraints to maintain flexibility while ensuring data integrity.

```typescript
---
const productSchema = z.object({
  name: z.string(),
  price: z.number().positive({ message: "Price must be a
positive number" }),
  tags: z.array(z.string()).min(1, { message: "At least one
tag is required" }),
});
```

Explanation:

- **Selective Constraints:** Enforce rules that are essential for your application's logic without overcomplicating schemas.

d. Document Your Schemas

Add comments to explain the purpose and constraints of each part of your schema. This enhances readability and aids future maintenance.

```typescript
---
// User schema with nested address
const userSchema = z.object({
  name: z.string(), // User's full name
  age: z.number().min(18, { message: "Age must be at least
18" }), // Must be an adult
  email: z.string().email({ message: "Invalid email address"
}), // Must be a valid email
  address: addressSchema, // User's physical address
});
```

Explanation:

- **Clarity:** Comments help others (and your future self) understand the intent behind each schema field.

---

6. Personal Insight: Streamlining Complex Data Validation

Managing complex data structures can quickly become overwhelming, especially as applications scale. Early in my experience, I found that tightly coupling validation logic with TypeScript types often led to redundancy and increased maintenance overhead. By leveraging Zod's ability to define nested schemas and infer TypeScript types directly from them, I achieved a more streamlined and maintainable codebase. This approach not only reduced duplication but also ensured consistency between type definitions and validation rules, making the development process more efficient and error-resistant.

Conclusion

Building complex schemas with nested objects and arrays is a fundamental skill for any developer working with TypeScript and Zod. By defining clear, modular schemas and leveraging Zod's powerful validation capabilities, you can accurately model intricate data relationships and ensure data integrity throughout your application. Adopting best practices such as modularization, thoughtful constraint application, and thorough documentation will enhance the maintainability and scalability of your schemas. As you continue to master these techniques, you'll find that managing complex data structures becomes more intuitive and efficient, allowing you to focus on building robust and feature-rich applications.

In the next section, we'll explore conditional and recursive schemas, enabling you to implement dynamic validation logic and handle self-referential data structures effectively. Let's continue advancing your Zod expertise!

5.2 Conditional and Recursive Schemas

As applications grow in complexity, so does the data they handle. Often, data structures need to adapt based on certain conditions or exhibit self-referential patterns. Zod provides powerful tools to create **conditional schemas** and **recursive schemas**, enabling developers to model complex and dynamic data structures effectively. This section delves into these advanced schema techniques, offering clear explanations and practical, step-by-step examples to help you leverage Zod's full potential.

1. Conditional Schemas

Conditional schemas allow you to apply different validation rules based on the values of certain fields within your data. This is particularly useful when the validity of one field depends on the value of another.

a. Understanding Conditional Schemas

In many scenarios, certain fields should only be present or adhere to specific rules based on the value of another field. For example, in a payment system, the fields required for a credit card payment differ from those required for a PayPal payment.

Example Scenario:

- If the payment method is "credit_card," then the `cardNumber` and `expiryDate` fields are required.

- If the payment method is "paypal," then the `paypalId` field is required.

b. Implementing Conditional Schemas with Zod

Zod facilitates conditional validation using methods like `.refine()`, `.superRefine()`, and discriminated unions. Below, we explore how to implement conditional schemas using these techniques.

Step 1: Define the Base Schema

Start by defining a base schema that includes all possible fields, marking optional fields as needed.

```typescript
---
import { z } from "zod";

const paymentSchema = z.object({
  method: z.enum(["credit_card", "paypal"]),
  cardNumber: z.string().optional(),
  expiryDate: z.string().optional(),
  paypalId: z.string().optional(),
});
```

Explanation:

- `method`: A required field that determines the payment method.
- `cardNumber` and `expiryDate`: Optional fields relevant only for credit card payments.
- `paypalId`: An optional field relevant only for PayPal payments.

Step 2: Apply Conditional Validation with `.refine()`

Use the `.refine()` method to enforce conditional rules based on the `method` field.

```typescript
---
const conditionalPaymentSchema = paymentSchema.refine((data)
=> {
  if (data.method === "credit_card") {
    return data.cardNumber !== undefined && data.expiryDate
!== undefined;
  } else if (data.method === "paypal") {
    return data.paypalId !== undefined;
```

119

```
    }
    return false;
}, {
    message: "Required fields are missing based on the payment
method",
    path: ["cardNumber", "expiryDate", "paypalId"],
});
```

Explanation:

- The `.refine()` method adds custom validation logic.
- The function checks:
  - If `method` is "credit_card," both `cardNumber` and `expiryDate` must be present.
  - If `method` is "paypal," `paypalId` must be present.
- The `message` provides a generic error message, and `path` indicates which fields are affected.

Step 3: Validate Data with Conditional Rules

Test the schema with different data inputs to ensure conditional validation works as expected.

```typescript
---
const creditCardPayment = {
  method: "credit_card",
  cardNumber: "1234-5678-9012-3456",
  expiryDate: "12/24",
};

const paypalPayment = {
  method: "paypal",
  paypalId: "user@paypal.com",
};

const invalidPayment = {
  method: "credit_card",
  cardNumber: "1234-5678-9012-3456",
  // Missing expiryDate
};

try {
  conditionalPaymentSchema.parse(creditCardPayment);
  console.log("Credit card payment is valid.");
} catch (e) {
  console.error(e.errors);
}
```

```
try {
  conditionalPaymentSchema.parse(paypalPayment);
  console.log("PayPal payment is valid.");
} catch (e) {
  console.error(e.errors);
}

try {
  conditionalPaymentSchema.parse(invalidPayment);
} catch (e) {
  console.error("Invalid payment:", e.errors);
}
```

Explanation:

- **Valid Inputs:**
  - `creditCardPayment` includes all required fields for a credit card payment.
  - `paypalPayment` includes the required field for a PayPal payment.
- **Invalid Input:**
  - `invalidPayment` is missing the `expiryDate` for a credit card payment, triggering a validation error.

Alternative Approach: Discriminated Unions

Zod also supports **discriminated unions**, which can simplify conditional schemas by separating them into distinct schemas based on a discriminant field.

```typescript
---
const creditCardSchema = z.object({
  method: z.literal("credit_card"),
  cardNumber: z.string(),
  expiryDate: z.string(),
});

const paypalSchema = z.object({
  method: z.literal("paypal"),
  paypalId: z.string(),
});

const paymentUnionSchema = z.union([creditCardSchema,
paypalSchema]);
```

Explanation:

- **creditCardSchema and paypalSchema:** Define separate schemas for each payment method.
- **paymentUnionSchema:** Combines the two schemas into a union, automatically handling the discrimination based on the `method` field.

Validation:

```typescript
---
const paymentData = {
  method: "paypal",
  paypalId: "user@paypal.com",
};

const validatedPayment =
paymentUnionSchema.parse(paymentData);
console.log(validatedPayment);
// Output: { method: "paypal", paypalId: "user@paypal.com" }
```

Advantages:

- **Clarity:** Each schema clearly defines the required fields for its respective payment method.
- **Simplicity:** Reduces the complexity of conditional logic within a single schema.

---

2. Recursive Schemas

Recursive schemas are essential for modeling self-referential data structures, such as trees, nested comments, or organizational hierarchies. Zod handles recursion gracefully using the `z.lazy()` method, which allows schemas to reference themselves without causing infinite loops during evaluation.

a. Understanding Recursive Schemas

A recursive schema is one that includes a reference to itself within its own definition. This is useful for representing data structures where elements can contain nested instances of the same type.

Example Scenario:

- A comment system where each comment can have replies, which are themselves comments.

b. Implementing Recursive Schemas with Zod

Below is a step-by-step guide to creating and using recursive schemas in Zod.

Step 1: Define the Recursive Schema Using `z.lazy()`

Use `z.lazy()` to defer the evaluation of the schema until it is needed, preventing immediate self-referencing that could lead to infinite recursion.

```typescript
---
const commentSchema: z.ZodType<any> = z.lazy(() => z.object({
  author: z.string(),
  content: z.string(),
  replies: z.array(commentSchema).optional(), // Recursive
reference
}));
```

Explanation:

- **`z.lazy(() => ...)`:** Defers the evaluation of the schema, allowing commentSchema to reference itself.
- **replies:** An optional array of commentSchema, enabling nested comments.

Step 2: Integrate the Recursive Schema into a Parent Schema

Embed the recursive schema within a larger schema to represent complex, nested data structures.

```typescript
---
const postSchema = z.object({
  title: z.string(),
  content: z.string(),
  comments: z.array(commentSchema).optional(), // Array of
nested comments
});
```

Explanation:

- **comments:** An optional array of comments, each adhering to the commentSchema, which can themselves contain nested replies.

Step 3: Validate Recursive Data Structures

Ensure that deeply nested data structures are correctly validated against the recursive schema.

```typescript
---
const blogPost = {
  title: "Understanding Recursive Schemas",
  content: "Recursive schemas allow for self-referential data
structures...",
  comments: [
    {
      author: "Alice",
      content: "Great explanation!",
      replies: [
        {
          author: "Bob",
          content: "I agree with Alice.",
        },
      ],
    },
    {
      author: "Charlie",
      content: "Very insightful.",
    },
  ],
};

const validatedPost = postSchema.parse(blogPost);
console.log(validatedPost);
// Output: Validated blog post object with nested comments
and replies
```

Explanation:

- **Nested Comments:** The comments array contains comments, some of which have their own replies arrays, demonstrating recursion.
- **Validation:** Zod ensures that every level of the nested structure adheres to the defined schemas.

c. Practical Use Cases for Recursive Schemas

Recursive schemas are invaluable in scenarios where data naturally forms hierarchical or nested structures.

Common Use Cases:

- **Comment Systems:** Each comment can have replies, which are themselves comments.
- **Organizational Hierarchies:** Employees can have managers, who are also employees.
- **File Systems:** Directories contain files and subdirectories, which follow the same structure.

Example: Organizational Hierarchy

```typescript
---
const employeeSchema: z.ZodType<any> = z.lazy(() =>
z.object({
  name: z.string(),
  position: z.string(),
  manager: employeeSchema.optional(), // Recursive reference
}));

const companySchema = z.object({
  name: z.string(),
  employees: z.array(employeeSchema),
});
```

Explanation:

- **manager:** An optional field referencing another `employeeSchema`, allowing for nested managerial relationships.
- **employees:** An array of employees within the company, each potentially having their own managers.

Validation Example:

```typescript
---
const companyData = {
  name: "Tech Corp",
  employees: [
    {
      name: "Alice",
      position: "CEO",
    },
```

```
    {
      name: "Bob",
      position: "CTO",
      manager: {
        name: "Alice",
        position: "CEO",
      },
    },
    {
      name: "Charlie",
      position: "Engineer",
      manager: {
        name: "Bob",
        position: "CTO",
      },
    },
  ],
};

const validatedCompany = companySchema.parse(companyData);
console.log(validatedCompany);
// Output: Validated company object with nested employee-
manager relationships
```

Explanation:

- **Hierarchical Structure:** The `employees` array includes employees with nested `manager` fields, forming an organizational hierarchy.
- **Validation:** Zod validates each employee and their respective managers, ensuring consistency throughout the structure.

---

3. Best Practices for Conditional and Recursive Schemas

To maximize the effectiveness and maintainability of your conditional and recursive schemas, consider the following best practices:

a. Keep Schemas Modular

- **Separation of Concerns:** Define reusable subschemas in separate modules or files.
- **Reusability:** Allows multiple parent schemas to incorporate the same subschemas without duplication.

Example:

```typescript
---
// schemas/addressSchema.ts
import { z } from "zod";

export const addressSchema = z.object({
  street: z.string(),
  city: z.string(),
  zipCode: z.string().length(5, { message: "Zip Code must be
exactly 5 characters long" }),
});
```
```typescript
---
// schemas/userSchema.ts
import { z } from "zod";
import { addressSchema } from "./addressSchema";

export const userSchema = z.object({
  name: z.string(),
  age: z.number().min(18, { message: "Age must be at least
18" }),
  email: z.string().email({ message: "Invalid email address"
}),
  address: addressSchema,
});
```

b. Use Descriptive Field Names and Custom Messages

- **Clarity:** Helps in debugging and provides clear feedback to users.
- **Maintainability:** Easier for team members to understand the purpose of each field.

Example:

```typescript
---
const userSchema = z.object({
  name: z.string().nonempty({ message: "Name is required."
}),
  age: z.number().min(18, { message: "Age must be at least
18." }),
  email: z.string().email({ message: "Please enter a valid
email address." }),
});
```

c. Optimize Recursive Schemas with z.lazy()

- **Avoid Infinite Loops:** Ensures that recursive references do not cause infinite recursion during schema evaluation.
- **Performance:** Enhances the efficiency of schema parsing and validation.

Example:

```typescript
---
const commentSchema: z.ZodType<any> = z.lazy(() =>
  z.object({
    author: z.string(),
    content: z.string(),
    replies: z.array(commentSchema).optional(),
  })
);
```

d. Leverage Discriminated Unions for Clear Conditional Logic

- **Simplify Conditions:** Use discriminated unions to handle mutually exclusive schema variations based on a specific field.
- **Enhance Readability:** Makes the schema definitions more intuitive and easier to manage.

Example:

```typescript
---
const creditCardSchema = z.object({
  method: z.literal("credit_card"),
  cardNumber: z.string(),
  expiryDate: z.string(),
});

const paypalSchema = z.object({
  method: z.literal("paypal"),
  paypalId: z.string(),
});

const paymentSchema = z.union([creditCardSchema,
paypalSchema]);
```

4. Summary

Conditional and recursive schemas are powerful tools in Zod that enable developers to model complex and dynamic data structures accurately. By understanding and implementing these advanced techniques, you can ensure that your applications handle diverse data scenarios robustly and efficiently. Remember to keep your schemas modular, use clear and descriptive validations, and optimize recursive schemas to maintain performance and readability. Leveraging these practices will enhance the reliability and maintainability of your TypeScript and Zod-powered applications.

In the next section, we'll explore **Custom Validators and Schema Transformations**, further expanding your ability to tailor Zod schemas to meet specific application requirements. Let's continue advancing your mastery of Zod's advanced features!

5.3 Custom Validators and Schema Transformations

While Zod offers a comprehensive set of built-in validators and transformation methods, there are scenarios where you need more tailored validation logic or wish to manipulate data during the validation process. Custom validators and schema transformations empower you to extend Zod's capabilities, allowing for precise control over how data is validated and transformed. This section delves into creating custom validators and applying schema transformations using Zod, complete with step-by-step examples to illustrate these advanced techniques.

1. Understanding Custom Validators and Schema Transformations

Before diving into implementation, it's essential to grasp what custom validators and schema transformations are and why they are useful:

- **Custom Validators:** These allow you to define bespoke validation logic that goes beyond Zod's built-in validators. They are particularly useful for enforcing complex business rules or validating data against external criteria.
- **Schema Transformations:** These enable you to modify or transform data as it passes through the validation process. Transformations can include formatting strings, calculating derived values, or sanitizing inputs to ensure consistency and correctness.

129

2. Creating Custom Validators

Custom validators are indispensable when you need to enforce rules that aren't covered by Zod's standard validation methods. Zod provides the `.refine()` and `.superRefine()` methods to implement custom validation logic.

a. Using `.refine()` for Simple Custom Validation

The `.refine()` method allows you to add a simple custom validation rule to a schema. It takes a validation function and an optional configuration object for error messaging.

Step-by-Step Implementation:

1. **Define a Schema with a Custom Validator:**

    Suppose you want to validate that a username contains only alphanumeric characters and underscores.

```typescript
---
import { z } from "zod";

const usernameSchema = z.string().min(3).max(20).refine((val)
=> /^[a-zA-Z0-9_]+$/.test(val), {
  message: "Username can only contain letters, numbers, and
underscores.",
});
```

Explanation:

- o   `z.string().min(3).max(20)`: Ensures the username is a string between 3 and 20 characters.
- o   `.refine(...)`: Adds a custom rule to allow only alphanumeric characters and underscores.

2. **Validate Data Using the Schema:**

```typescript
---
const validUsername = "user_123";
const invalidUsername = "user-123";
```

```
try {
  usernameSchema.parse(validUsername);
  console.log("Valid username.");
} catch (e) {
  if (e instanceof z.ZodError) {
    console.error(e.errors);
  }
}

try {
  usernameSchema.parse(invalidUsername);
} catch (e) {
  if (e instanceof z.ZodError) {
    console.error("Invalid username:", e.errors);
  }
}
```

Explanation:

- The first parse succeeds, printing "Valid username."
- The second parse fails, logging the custom error message.

b. Using `.superRefine()` for Complex Validation

The `.superRefine()` method is suitable for more intricate validation logic, especially when multiple fields are interdependent. It provides access to the entire data object, allowing for comprehensive validation.

Step-by-Step Implementation:

1. **Define a Schema with Interdependent Fields:**

   Consider a scenario where a user must provide either a phone number or an email address, but not both.

```typescript
---
const contactSchema = z.object({
  phone: z.string().optional(),
  email: z.string().email().optional(),
}).superRefine((data, ctx) => {
  if (!data.phone && !data.email) {
    ctx.addIssue({
      code: z.ZodIssueCode.custom,
      message: "At least one contact method (phone or email)
must be provided.",
```

```
    });
  }

  if (data.phone && data.email) {
    ctx.addIssue({
      code: z.ZodIssueCode.custom,
      message: "Provide either phone or email, not both.",
    });
  }
});
```

Explanation:

- ○ `z.object({...})`: Defines the contact fields as optional.
- ○ `.superRefine(...)`: Adds complex validation rules:
  - Ensures that at least one contact method is provided.
  - Prevents both phone and email from being provided simultaneously.

2. **Validate Data Using the Schema:**

```typescript
---
const validContact1 = { phone: "123-456-7890" };
const validContact2 = { email: "user@example.com" };
const invalidContact1 = {};
const invalidContact2 = { phone: "123-456-7890", email:
"user@example.com" };

// Valid Contact 1
try {
  contactSchema.parse(validContact1);
  console.log("Valid contact 1.");
} catch (e) {
  if (e instanceof z.ZodError) {
    console.error(e.errors);
  }
}

// Valid Contact 2
try {
  contactSchema.parse(validContact2);
  console.log("Valid contact 2.");
} catch (e) {
  if (e instanceof z.ZodError) {
    console.error(e.errors);
  }
}

// Invalid Contact 1
```

```
try {
  contactSchema.parse(invalidContact1);
} catch (e) {
  if (e instanceof z.ZodError) {
    console.error("Invalid contact 1:", e.errors);
  }
}

// Invalid Contact 2
try {
  contactSchema.parse(invalidContact2);
} catch (e) {
  if (e instanceof z.ZodError) {
    console.error("Invalid contact 2:", e.errors);
  }
}
```

Explanation:

- Valid contacts pass validation.
- Invalid contacts trigger custom error messages defined in `.superRefine()`.

---

3. Applying Schema Transformations

Schema transformations allow you to modify or manipulate data during the validation process. This can include formatting strings, converting data types, or deriving new fields based on existing data.

a. Using `.transform()` to Modify Data

The `.transform()` method applies a transformation function to the validated data, enabling you to alter its shape or format.

Step-by-Step Implementation:

1. **Define a Schema with a Transformation:**

   Suppose you want to ensure that email addresses are stored in lowercase and trimmed of whitespace.

```
typescript
---
```

133

```typescript
const emailSchema = z.string().email().transform((val) =>
val.trim().toLowerCase());
```

Explanation:

- o `z.string().email()`: Validates that the input is a properly formatted email address.
- o `.transform(...)`: Trims whitespace and converts the email to lowercase.

2. **Validate and Transform Data:**

```typescript
---
const userEmail = "  User@Example.COM ";

const validatedEmail = emailSchema.parse(userEmail);
console.log(validatedEmail);
// Output: "user@example.com"
```

Explanation:

- o The input email is validated and transformed according to the defined rules, resulting in a clean, standardized format.

b. Deriving New Fields with `.transform()`

Transformations can also be used to derive new fields based on existing data, enhancing the utility of your schemas.

Step-by-Step Implementation:

1. **Define a Schema with Derived Fields:**

    Suppose you want to create a `fullName` field by combining `firstName` and `lastName`.

```typescript
---
const userSchema = z.object({
  firstName: z.string(),
  lastName: z.string(),
}).transform((data) => ({
  ...data,
  fullName: `${data.firstName} ${data.lastName}`,
}));
```

134

Explanation:

- o `z.object({...})`: Defines the basic user fields.
- o `.transform(...)`: Adds a new `fullName` field by concatenating `firstName` and `lastName`.

2. **Validate and Transform Data:**

```typescript
---
const userData = {
  firstName: "Jane",
  lastName: "Doe",
};

const validatedUser = userSchema.parse(userData);
console.log(validatedUser);
// Output: { firstName: "Jane", lastName: "Doe", fullName:
"Jane Doe" }
```

Explanation:

- o The transformation enriches the validated data with the `fullName` field, derived from existing properties.

c. Custom Transformation Functions

For more complex transformations, you can define custom functions to process data as needed.

Step-by-Step Implementation:

1. **Define a Custom Transformation Function:**

Create a function that performs a specific transformation, such as normalizing a phone number.

```typescript
---
function normalizePhoneNumber(phone: string): string {
  return phone.replace(/\D/g, ""); // Removes all non-digit
characters
}
```

2. **Apply the Custom Transformation:**

Use `.transform()` to apply the custom function during validation.

```typescript
---
const phoneSchema =
z.string().min(10).max(15).transform(normalizePhoneNumber);
```

Explanation:

- o `z.string().min(10).max(15)`: Validates that the phone number is between 10 and 15 characters.
- o `.transform(normalizePhoneNumber)`: Cleans the phone number by removing non-digit characters.

3. **Validate and Transform Data:**

```typescript
---
const rawPhone = "(123) 456-7890";

const validatedPhone = phoneSchema.parse(rawPhone);
console.log(validatedPhone);
// Output: "1234567890"
```

Explanation:

- o The input phone number is validated for length and transformed to a standardized numeric format.

---

4. Combining Custom Validators and Transformations

Often, you'll need to apply both custom validation logic and transformations within a single schema. Zod allows you to chain these methods to create sophisticated validation pipelines.

Step-by-Step Implementation:

1. **Define a Schema with Both Validation and Transformation:**

Suppose you want to validate a password for strength and then hash it before storing.

```typescript
```

```
---
import { z } from "zod";
import bcrypt from "bcryptjs";

const passwordSchema = z.string()
  .min(8, { message: "Password must be at least 8 characters
long." })
  .refine((val) => /[A-Z]/.test(val), { message: "Password
must contain at least one uppercase letter." })
  .refine((val) => /[0-9]/.test(val), { message: "Password
must contain at least one number." })
  .transform(async (val) => {
    const salt = await bcrypt.genSalt(10);
    const hash = await bcrypt.hash(val, salt);
    return hash;
  });
```

Explanation:

- Multiple `.refine()` methods enforce password strength rules.
- `.transform(async ...)`: Hashes the password asynchronously using `bcrypt`.

2. **Validate and Transform Data Asynchronously:**

Since the transformation is asynchronous, use `parseAsync` to handle the validation.

```typescript
---
const rawPassword = "SecurePass123";

async function validateAndHashPassword(password: string) {
  try {
    const hashedPassword = await
passwordSchema.parseAsync(password);
    console.log("Hashed Password:", hashedPassword);
    // Proceed with storing the hashed password
  } catch (e) {
    if (e instanceof z.ZodError) {
      console.error("Validation errors:", e.errors);
    }
  }
}

validateAndHashPassword(rawPassword);
```

Explanation:

- o `parseAsync` handles the asynchronous transformation.
- o Successful validation returns the hashed password.
- o Validation failures provide detailed error messages.

---

5. Best Practices for Custom Validators and Transformations

To effectively utilize custom validators and schema transformations, consider the following best practices:

a. Keep Validation Logic Clear and Concise

- **Single Responsibility:** Each custom validator should focus on a single aspect of validation.
- **Readable Code:** Ensure that your validation functions are easy to understand and maintain.

b. Reuse Transformation Functions

- **Modularity:** Define transformation functions separately if they are used across multiple schemas.
- **Consistency:** Reusing transformations ensures consistent data handling throughout your application.

c. Handle Asynchronous Transformations Appropriately

- **Use `parseAsync`:** When applying asynchronous transformations, always use `parseAsync` to handle the validation process.
- **Error Handling:** Ensure that asynchronous errors are properly caught and managed to prevent application crashes.

d. Provide Meaningful Error Messages

- **User-Friendly:** Craft error messages that are clear and actionable for end-users.
- **Developer-Friendly:** Include enough detail to aid in debugging without exposing sensitive information.

e. Document Custom Logic

- **Comments:** Add comments to explain the purpose and functionality of custom validators and transformations.
- **Documentation:** Maintain comprehensive documentation for complex validation and transformation logic to aid team members and future maintenance.

---

6. Personal Insight: Enhancing Data Integrity with Custom Logic

Incorporating custom validators and transformations has significantly improved data integrity in my projects. Initially, relying solely on built-in validators limited the flexibility needed to enforce specific business rules. By implementing custom validation logic, I could tailor the validation process to meet precise requirements, such as enforcing password complexity or ensuring conditional data fields. Additionally, schema transformations streamlined data processing by automating tasks like data normalization and derivation, reducing the need for manual data handling and minimizing errors. This combination not only enhanced the reliability of the application but also streamlined the development workflow, allowing for more efficient and maintainable codebases.

Conclusion

Custom validators and schema transformations are powerful features in Zod that extend its validation capabilities beyond standard checks. By implementing custom validation logic, you can enforce complex business rules and ensure that your data adheres to specific requirements. Schema transformations enable you to manipulate and enrich data during the validation process, enhancing data consistency and reducing the need for additional processing steps. Combining these techniques allows for the creation of sophisticated, reliable, and maintainable schemas that cater to the nuanced demands of real-world applications.

Adopting best practices such as keeping validation logic clear, reusing transformation functions, handling asynchronous operations appropriately, and providing meaningful error messages will further enhance the effectiveness of your validation strategy. As you integrate these advanced techniques into your TypeScript and Zod workflows, you'll find that managing complex data scenarios becomes more intuitive and efficient, paving the way for building robust and scalable applications.

In the next section, we'll explore performance optimization tips for large-scale validation, ensuring that your application remains responsive and efficient even as data complexity and volume grow. Let's continue advancing your expertise in Zod's advanced features!

5.4 Performance Tips for Large-Scale Validation

As applications grow, so does the volume and complexity of the data they handle. Ensuring efficient validation in large-scale systems is crucial to maintain responsiveness and scalability. Zod, while powerful and flexible, can encounter performance bottlenecks when dealing with extensive or deeply nested schemas. This section provides actionable performance optimization strategies for large-scale validation using Zod, complete with step-by-step implementations and best practices to ensure your application remains fast and efficient.

---

1. Optimize Schema Definitions

Efficient schema definitions are the foundation of performant validations. Streamlining your schemas reduces the computational overhead during validation, leading to faster execution times.

a. Reuse Subschemas

Defining reusable subschemas avoids duplication and minimizes the size of your overall schema. This not only enhances maintainability but also improves performance by reducing the number of unique schema objects that Zod needs to process.

Step-by-Step Implementation:

1. **Define Reusable Subschemas:**

Create subschemas for common data structures used across multiple parent schemas.

```typescript
---
// schemas/addressSchema.ts
import { z } from "zod";

export const addressSchema = z.object({
  street: z.string(),
  city: z.string(),
  zipCode: z.string().length(5, { message: "Zip Code must be
exactly 5 characters long" }),
});
```

2. **Integrate Subschemas into Parent Schemas:**

Use the defined subschemas within larger schemas to promote reuse.

```typescript
---
// schemas/userSchema.ts
import { z } from "zod";
import { addressSchema } from "./addressSchema";

export const userSchema = z.object({
  name: z.string(),
  age: z.number().min(18, { message: "Age must be at least
18" }),
  email: z.string().email({ message: "Invalid email address"
}),
  address: addressSchema, // Reused subschema
});
```

Explanation:

- **Reusability:** By defining `addressSchema` separately, you can reuse it in multiple parent schemas without redefining it each time.
- **Maintainability:** Changes to the `addressSchema` propagate to all parent schemas, ensuring consistency and reducing maintenance effort.

b. Minimize Deep Nesting

Excessive nesting of schemas can lead to increased validation times due to the recursive nature of validation logic. Strive to keep your schemas as flat as possible without compromising the representation of your data structures.

Best Practices:

141

- **Flatten Hierarchies:** Where feasible, avoid deeply nested objects. Instead, reference related data through identifiers or flatter structures.
- **Limit Recursion Depth:** For recursive schemas, impose a maximum depth to prevent excessive validation cycles.

Example:

Instead of nesting comments indefinitely, limit the depth of replies.

```typescript
---
const commentSchema: z.ZodType<any> = z.lazy(() =>
  z.object({
    author: z.string(),
    content: z.string(),
    replies: z.array(commentSchema).max(3, { message:
"Maximum of 3 replies allowed" }).optional(),
  })
);
```

Explanation:

- `.max(3)`: Restricts the number of nested replies, preventing uncontrolled recursion and reducing validation time.

---

2. Lazy Evaluation for Recursive Schemas

Recursive schemas, such as those used for comments or organizational hierarchies, can introduce performance challenges if not handled properly. Zod's `z.lazy()` method allows for deferred schema evaluation, which optimizes recursion handling.

a. Implementing `z.lazy()` Correctly

Ensure that recursive references are properly encapsulated within `z.lazy()` to prevent unnecessary evaluations and infinite loops.

Step-by-Step Implementation:

1. **Define the Recursive Schema with `z.lazy()`:**

```typescript
```

```
---
// schemas/commentSchema.ts
import { z } from "zod";

export const commentSchema: z.ZodType<any> = z.lazy(() =>
  z.object({
    author: z.string(),
    content: z.string(),
    replies: z.array(commentSchema).max(5, { message:
"Maximum of 5 replies allowed" }).optional(),
  })
);
```

2. **Integrate the Recursive Schema into a Parent Schema:**

```
typescript
---
// schemas/postSchema.ts
import { z } from "zod";
import { commentSchema } from "./commentSchema";

export const postSchema = z.object({
  title: z.string(),
  content: z.string(),
  comments: z.array(commentSchema).max(100, { message:
"Maximum of 100 comments allowed" }).optional(),
});
```

Explanation:

- **`z.lazy(() => ...)`:** Defers the evaluation of `commentSchema`, allowing it to reference itself without immediate execution.
- **`.max(5)`:** Limits the number of nested replies, controlling recursion depth and enhancing performance.

b. Avoiding Infinite Recursion

Infinite recursion can occur if recursive schemas are not properly bounded. Always set limits on recursion depth or the number of nested elements to prevent stack overflows and excessive validation times.

Example:

Setting a maximum depth for nested comments.

```
typescript
```

```
---
const commentSchema: z.ZodType<any> = z.lazy(() =>
  z.object({
    author: z.string(),
    content: z.string(),
    replies: z.array(commentSchema).max(3, { message:
"Maximum of 3 replies allowed" }).optional(),
  })
);
```

Explanation:

- **Recursion Control:** By setting `.max(3)`, you limit the number of nested replies, preventing infinite loops during validation.

---

3. Batch Validation

Validating large datasets individually can be inefficient. Zod allows for batch validation, enabling you to validate multiple data entries in a single operation, which can significantly improve performance.

a. Define Batch Schemas Using `z.array`

Batch schemas are designed to validate arrays of similar objects efficiently.

Step-by-Step Implementation:

1. **Define the Individual Schema:**

```typescript
---
// schemas/userSchema.ts
import { z } from "zod";

export const userSchema = z.object({
  name: z.string(),
  age: z.number().min(18, { message: "Age must be at least
18" }),
  email: z.string().email({ message: "Invalid email address"
}),
});
```

2. **Create a Batch Schema:**

Use `z.array()` to define a schema that validates an array of `userSchema` objects.

```typescript
---
// schemas/usersBatchSchema.ts
import { z } from "zod";
import { userSchema } from "./userSchema";

export const usersBatchSchema = z.array(userSchema).min(1, {
message: "At least one user is required" });
```

3. **Validate Data in Batches:**

```typescript
---
const usersData = [
  { name: "Alice", age: 30, email: "alice@example.com" },
  { name: "Bob", age: 25, email: "bob@example.com" },
  // ...additional user objects
];

try {
  const validatedUsers = usersBatchSchema.parse(usersData);
  console.log("All users are valid:", validatedUsers);
} catch (e) {
  if (e instanceof z.ZodError) {
    console.error("Batch validation failed:", e.errors);
  }
}
```

Explanation:

- **Efficiency:** Validating multiple entries in a single `z.array` call reduces the number of validation operations, enhancing performance.
- **Error Handling:** Zod provides detailed error reports for each invalid entry within the batch, allowing for comprehensive error management.

b. Parallel Processing for Independent Validations

When dealing with independent validation tasks, leveraging parallel processing can further optimize performance. This approach is particularly useful when validating large arrays asynchronously.

Step-by-Step Implementation:

145

1. Define Asynchronous Validation Functions:

```typescript
---
import { z } from "zod";

const userSchema = z.object({
  name: z.string(),
  age: z.number().min(18, { message: "Age must be at least
18" }),
  email: z.string().email({ message: "Invalid email address"
}),
});

type User = z.infer<typeof userSchema>;

async function validateUser(user: unknown): Promise<{
success: boolean; data?: User; errors?: z.ZodIssue[] }> {
  const result = userSchema.safeParse(user);
  if (result.success) {
    return { success: true, data: result.data };
  } else {
    return { success: false, errors: result.error.errors };
  }
}
```

2. Validate Multiple Users in Parallel:

```typescript
---
const usersData = [
  { name: "Alice", age: 30, email: "alice@example.com" },
  { name: "Bob", age: 25, email: "bob@example.com" },
  // ...additional user objects
];

async function validateUsersInParallel(users: unknown[]) {
  const validationPromises = users.map((user) =>
validateUser(user));
  const results = await Promise.all(validationPromises);

  const validUsers = results.filter(result =>
result.success).map(result => result.data);
  const invalidUsers = results.filter(result =>
!result.success).map(result => result.errors);

  console.log("Valid Users:", validUsers);
  console.log("Invalid Users:", invalidUsers);
}
```

```
validateUsersInParallel(usersData);
```

Explanation:

- **Parallel Execution:** Using `Promise.all`, multiple validations run concurrently, reducing total validation time.
- **Scalability:** This method efficiently handles large datasets by distributing validation tasks across multiple asynchronous operations.

---

4. Asynchronous Validation

In scenarios where validation depends on external resources, such as database lookups or API calls, asynchronous validation becomes necessary. Zod supports asynchronous operations, enabling you to perform validations without blocking the main execution thread.

a. Implement Asynchronous Custom Validators

Custom validators that require asynchronous operations can be integrated using `.refine()` with asynchronous functions.

Step-by-Step Implementation:

1. **Define the Asynchronous Validation Function:**

Suppose you need to check if a username is unique by querying a database.

```typescript
---
import { z } from "zod";

async function isUsernameUnique(username: string):
Promise<boolean> {
  // Simulate a database check with a delay
  await new Promise(resolve => setTimeout(resolve, 100));
  const existingUsernames = ["existingUser", "admin",
"user123"];
  return !existingUsernames.includes(username);
}
```

2. **Define the Schema with Asynchronous Custom Validator:**

```typescript
---
const usernameSchema = z.string().min(3).max(20).refine(async
(username) => {
  return await isUsernameUnique(username);
}, {
  message: "Username is already taken.",
});
```

3. **Validate Data Asynchronously:**

Use `parseAsync` to handle the asynchronous validation.

```typescript
---
const newUser = "newUser";

async function validateUsername(username: string) {
  try {
    const validUsername = await
usernameSchema.parseAsync(username);
    console.log("Username is valid and unique:",
validUsername);
  } catch (e) {
    if (e instanceof z.ZodError) {
      console.error("Validation failed:", e.errors);
    }
  }
}

validateUsername(newUser);
```

Explanation:

- **Asynchronous Refinement:** `.refine(async (username) => ...)` allows integrating asynchronous checks within the schema.
- **parseAsync:** Facilitates the handling of asynchronous validation without blocking the execution flow.

b. Batch Asynchronous Validations

When validating multiple entries that require asynchronous operations, batching can optimize performance by reducing the number of external calls.

Step-by-Step Implementation:

1. Define the Schema with Asynchronous Validators:

```typescript
const emailSchema = z.string().email();

const userSchema = z.object({
  name: z.string(),
  email: emailSchema.refine(async (email) => {
    // Simulate an asynchronous check, e.g., verifying email uniqueness
    await new Promise(resolve => setTimeout(resolve, 100));
    const existingEmails = ["alice@example.com", "bob@example.com"];
    return !existingEmails.includes(email);
  }, {
    message: "Email is already registered.",
  }),
});
```

2. Validate Multiple Users Asynchronously:

```typescript
const usersData = [
  { name: "Alice", email: "alice@example.com" },
  { name: "Bob", email: "bob_new@example.com" },
  { name: "Charlie", email: "charlie@example.com" },
];

async function validateUsers(users: unknown[]) {
  const validationPromises = users.map(user =>
userSchema.parseAsync(user).then(
    data => ({ success: true, data }),
    err => ({ success: false, errors: err.errors })
  ));

  const results = await Promise.all(validationPromises);

  const validUsers = results.filter(result =>
result.success).map(result => result.data);
  const invalidUsers = results.filter(result =>
!result.success).map(result => result.errors);

  console.log("Valid Users:", validUsers);
  console.log("Invalid Users:", invalidUsers);
}

validateUsers(usersData);
```

Explanation:

- **Efficient Processing:** By batching asynchronous validations, you minimize the total validation time compared to sequential processing.
- **Structured Results:** Collecting both valid and invalid users allows for comprehensive handling of validation outcomes.

---

5. Profiling and Benchmarking

Regularly profiling and benchmarking your validation logic helps identify performance bottlenecks and areas for optimization. Implementing these practices ensures that your application remains responsive as data complexity and volume increase.

a. Use Profiling Tools

Utilize profiling tools to monitor the performance of your validation schemas.

Recommended Tools:

- **Node.js Profiler:** Built-in profiling capabilities for server-side applications.
- **Chrome DevTools:** Useful for profiling client-side validations in browser environments.
- **Benchmark.js:** A robust library for benchmarking JavaScript code.

Example with Benchmark.js:

1. **Install Benchmark.js:**

```bash
---
npm install benchmark
```

2. **Set Up Benchmark Tests:**

```typescript
---
import Benchmark from "benchmark";
import { userSchema } from "./schemas/userSchema";
```

```
const suite = new Benchmark.Suite;

const validUser = { name: "Alice", age: 30, email:
"alice@example.com" };
const invalidUser = { name: "Bob", age: 17, email: "bob-at-
example.com" };

suite
  .add('Valid User Validation', () => {
    userSchema.parse(validUser);
  })
  .add('Invalid User Validation', () => {
    try {
      userSchema.parse(invalidUser);
    } catch {}
  })
  .on('complete', function () {
    this.forEach(function (bench) {
      console.log(`${bench.name}: ${bench.hz.toFixed(2)}
ops/sec`);
    });
  })
  .run({ 'async': true });
```

Explanation:

- **Benchmarking:** Measures the number of operations per second for validating both valid and invalid user data.
- **Performance Insights:** Helps identify which validation scenarios are more resource-intensive, guiding optimization efforts.

b. Identify and Optimize Hotspots

Focus on optimizing the parts of your schemas or validation logic that consume the most resources.

Step-by-Step Implementation:

1. **Analyze Benchmark Results:**

   Determine which validation operations have the lowest throughput or highest latency.

2. **Refine Schemas:**

- o **Simplify Complex Rules:** Break down intricate validation logic into simpler, more efficient steps.
- o **Reduce Redundant Validations:** Avoid unnecessary checks that don't contribute to data integrity.
3. **Optimize Custom Validators:**
   - o **Efficient Logic:** Ensure that custom validation functions are optimized for performance, avoiding heavy computations where possible.
   - o **Caching Results:** If certain validation outcomes are repetitive, consider caching results to prevent redundant operations.

Example:

Caching results of unique username checks to avoid repeated database queries.

```typescript
---
const usernameCache = new Set<string>();

async function isUsernameUnique(username: string):
Promise<boolean> {
  if (usernameCache.has(username)) {
    return false; // Assume already taken
  }
  // Simulate database check
  await new Promise(resolve => setTimeout(resolve, 100));
  const existingUsernames = ["existingUser", "admin",
"user123"];
  const isUnique = !existingUsernames.includes(username);
  if (!isUnique) {
    usernameCache.add(username);
  }
  return isUnique;
}

const usernameSchema = z.string().min(3).max(20).refine(async
(username) => {
  return await isUsernameUnique(username);
}, {
  message: "Username is already taken.",
});
```

Explanation:

- **Caching:** By storing already checked usernames in `usernameCache`, you reduce the number of database queries for duplicate checks, enhancing performance.

c. Continuously Monitor Performance

Incorporate performance monitoring into your development workflow to catch and address issues promptly.

Best Practices:

- **Automated Testing:** Include performance benchmarks in your CI/CD pipeline to detect regressions.
- **Real-Time Monitoring:** Use monitoring tools to track validation performance in production environments.
- **Feedback Loops:** Regularly review performance metrics and iterate on optimization strategies based on findings.

---

6. Best Practices for Large-Scale Validation

Adhering to best practices ensures that your validation logic remains efficient, maintainable, and scalable as your application evolves.

a. Modularize Your Schemas

Breaking down schemas into smaller, reusable modules enhances both performance and maintainability.

Implementation Tips:

- **Separate Concerns:** Define related schemas in separate files or modules.
- **Reuse Subschemas:** Import and use subschemas across multiple parent schemas to avoid duplication.

b. Limit Validation Scope

Avoid validating unnecessary fields or data that doesn't impact your application's core functionality.

153

Implementation Tips:

- **Selective Validation:** Only include fields that are essential for your application logic within your schemas.
- **Prune Extraneous Data:** Use Zod's `.strict()` method to prevent validation of unknown fields, reducing overhead.

```typescript
---
const strictUserSchema = z.object({
  name: z.string(),
  age: z.number().min(18),
  email: z.string().email(),
}).strict();
```

Explanation:

- `.strict()`: Ensures that no additional unexpected fields are present, streamlining validation.

c. Utilize Schema Inference

Leverage Zod's ability to infer TypeScript types from schemas to maintain consistency and reduce redundancy.

Implementation Tips:

- **Type Inference:** Use `z.infer` to derive TypeScript types directly from Zod schemas.
- **Avoid Manual Typing:** Refrain from manually defining TypeScript interfaces that mirror Zod schemas, preventing inconsistencies.

```typescript
---
import { z } from "zod";

const userSchema = z.object({
  name: z.string(),
  age: z.number().min(18),
  email: z.string().email(),
});

type User = z.infer<typeof userSchema>;
```

Explanation:

- **Consistency:** Ensures that TypeScript types and Zod schemas are always in sync, enhancing type safety.

d. Asynchronous Operations Cautiously

While asynchronous validators are powerful, they can introduce performance complexities. Use them judiciously and optimize their implementation to prevent bottlenecks.

Best Practices:

- **Batch External Calls:** When possible, batch external validations to minimize the number of asynchronous operations.
- **Optimize Async Logic:** Ensure that asynchronous functions are as efficient as possible, avoiding unnecessary delays.

---

7. Personal Insight: Balancing Complexity and Performance

In my experience, achieving optimal performance in large-scale validation requires a balance between schema complexity and efficiency. Initially, handling vast and deeply nested schemas without optimization led to sluggish validation times and unresponsive applications. By implementing strategies such as reusing subschemas, minimizing deep nesting, leveraging `z.lazy()` for recursive schemas, and employing batch validations, I was able to significantly enhance validation performance. Additionally, regularly profiling and refining schemas based on performance insights ensured that the application remained scalable and efficient as data complexity grew. This proactive approach to performance optimization not only improved application responsiveness but also contributed to a smoother and more enjoyable development experience.

Conclusion

Optimizing performance for large-scale validation is essential for maintaining responsive and scalable applications. By implementing the strategies outlined in this section—such as reusing subschemas, minimizing deep nesting, leveraging `z.lazy()` for recursive schemas, performing batch validations, and carefully managing asynchronous operations—you can ensure that your Zod validations remain efficient even as your data structures grow in complexity and volume. Additionally, regularly profiling and monitoring your validation logic allows you to identify and address performance bottlenecks proactively.

Adhering to these best practices not only enhances the performance of your application but also contributes to a more maintainable and scalable codebase. As you continue to develop and refine your schemas, keep these optimization techniques in mind to build robust and high-performing TypeScript applications with Zod.

Chapter 6: Practical Applications

As you become proficient with TypeScript and Zod, the next logical step is to apply these tools to real-world scenarios. This chapter explores practical applications of TypeScript and Zod across different layers of software development, including frontend and backend environments, as well as full-stack integrations. By understanding how to implement Zod in various contexts, you can build robust, type-safe, and maintainable applications that leverage the strengths of both TypeScript and Zod.

6.1 Frontend Development

In frontend development, ensuring that user inputs are valid is essential for maintaining data integrity and providing a seamless user experience. Integrating Zod with TypeScript enhances form validation by offering type-safe, declarative schemas that streamline validation logic. This section explores two key applications of Zod in frontend development: form validation with React and Zod, and integrating Zod in Next.js projects.

Form Validation with React and Zod

Form validation is a critical aspect of frontend development. It ensures that users provide the necessary and correctly formatted data before submission, reducing errors and enhancing user experience. Combining React with Zod enables developers to implement robust, type-safe form validations efficiently.

1. Setting Up the Project

Before diving into form validation, set up a React project with TypeScript and install the necessary dependencies.

Step 1: Initialize a New React Project with TypeScript

Use `create-react-app` to initialize a new React project with TypeScript support.

```bash
---
npx create-react-app react-zod-form --template typescript
cd react-zod-form
```

Step 2: Install Zod and React Hook Form

React Hook Form is a popular library for handling form state and validations in React. Install it along with Zod.

```bash
---
npm install zod @hookform/resolvers react-hook-form
```

- `zod`: For schema validation.
- `@hookform/resolvers`: Integrates Zod with React Hook Form.
- `react-hook-form`: For managing form state and validation.

2. Defining Zod Schemas

Define a Zod schema that outlines the structure and validation rules for your form data.

Step 1: Create a Schema for User Registration

Create a `schemas` directory and add a `userSchema.ts` file.

```typescript
---
// src/schemas/userSchema.ts
import { z } from "zod";

export const userSchema = z.object({
  username: z.string().min(3, { message: "Username must be at
least 3 characters long." }),
  email: z.string().email({ message: "Please enter a valid
email address." }),
  password: z.string()
    .min(8, { message: "Password must be at least 8
characters long." })
    .refine((val) => /[A-Z]/.test(val), { message: "Password
must contain at least one uppercase letter." })
    .refine((val) => /[0-9]/.test(val), { message: "Password
must contain at least one number." }),
});
```

Explanation:

- **username**: Must be a string with a minimum length of 3.
- **email**: Must be a valid email format.
- **password**: Must be at least 8 characters long, contain at least one uppercase letter and one number.

Step 2: Infer TypeScript Types from Zod Schema

Using Zod's `z.infer`, derive TypeScript types directly from the schema to ensure type safety.

```typescript
---
// src/types/user.ts
import { z } from "zod";
import { userSchema } from "../schemas/userSchema";

export type User = z.infer<typeof userSchema>;
```

Explanation:

- `User` type now accurately reflects the structure defined in `userSchema`.

3. Integrating Zod with React Hook Form

React Hook Form simplifies form state management and integrates seamlessly with Zod for validation.

Step 1: Create the Registration Form Component

Create a `components` directory and add a `RegistrationForm.tsx` file.

```typescript
---
// src/components/RegistrationForm.tsx
import React from "react";
import { useForm } from "react-hook-form";
import { zodResolver } from "@hookform/resolvers/zod";
import { userSchema } from "../schemas/userSchema";

type User = z.infer<typeof userSchema>;

const RegistrationForm: React.FC = () => {
```

```
  const { register, handleSubmit, formState: { errors } } =
useForm<User>({
    resolver: zodResolver(userSchema),
  });

  const onSubmit = async (data: User) => {
    try {
      const response = await fetch("/api/register", {
        method: "POST",
        headers: {
          "Content-Type": "application/json",
        },
        body: JSON.stringify(data),
      });

      if (!response.ok) {
        const errorData = await response.json();
        console.error("Registration failed:", errorData);
      } else {
        console.log("Registration successful!");
      }
    } catch (error) {
      console.error("An unexpected error occurred:", error);
    }
  };

  return (
    <form onSubmit={handleSubmit(onSubmit)}>
      <div>
        <label>Username:</label>
        <input {...register("username")} />
        {errors.username &&
<span>{errors.username.message}</span>}
      </div>

      <div>
        <label>Email:</label>
        <input {...register("email")} />
        {errors.email && <span>{errors.email.message}</span>}
      </div>

      <div>
        <label>Password:</label>
        <input type="password" {...register("password")} />
        {errors.password &&
<span>{errors.password.message}</span>}
      </div>

      <button type="submit">Register</button>
    </form>
  );
```

```
};

export default RegistrationForm;
```

Explanation:

- **useForm<User>**: Initializes the form with the `User` type inferred from Zod schema.
- **zodResolver(userSchema)**: Connects Zod schema with React Hook Form for validation.
- **register("fieldName")**: Connects input fields to the form state.
- **errors.fieldName**: Displays validation errors if present.

Step 2: Integrate the Form Component into the Application

Modify the `App.tsx` to include the `RegistrationForm`.

```typescript
---
// src/App.tsx
import React from "react";
import RegistrationForm from "./components/RegistrationForm";

function App() {
  return (
    <div className="App">
      <h1>User Registration</h1>
      <RegistrationForm />
    </div>
  );
}

export default App;
```

Explanation:

- **App Component**: Renders the `RegistrationForm` component within the application.

4. Handling Validation Results and Errors

React Hook Form, combined with Zod, provides structured error handling and feedback mechanisms.

Step 1: Displaying Validation Errors

In the `RegistrationForm` component, validation errors are accessed via `errors` and displayed conditionally next to each input field.

```jsx
---
{errors.username && <span>{errors.username.message}</span>}
```

Explanation:

- **Conditional Rendering**: Checks if there is an error for the `username` field and displays the corresponding error message.

Step 2: Managing Form Submission

Upon successful validation, the `onSubmit` function is called with the validated data.

```typescript
---
const onSubmit = async (data: User) => {
  try {
    const response = await fetch("/api/register", {
      method: "POST",
      headers: {
        "Content-Type": "application/json",
      },
      body: JSON.stringify(data),
    });

    if (!response.ok) {
      const errorData = await response.json();
      console.error("Registration failed:", errorData);
    } else {
      console.log("Registration successful!");
    }
  } catch (error) {
    console.error("An unexpected error occurred:", error);
  }
};
```

Explanation:

- **Form Data Handling**: After validation, you can proceed with actions such as sending data to an API, updating the application state, or navigating to another page.

5. Best Practices for Frontend Form Validation

To ensure efficient and maintainable form validation in frontend applications, adhere to the following best practices:

- **Centralize Schemas:** Define Zod schemas in a dedicated directory to promote reuse and maintainability.
- **Leverage Type Inference:** Use `z.infer` to derive TypeScript types directly from Zod schemas, ensuring consistency.
- **Provide Clear Feedback:** Display user-friendly error messages to guide users in correcting their inputs.
- **Minimize Re-renders:** Optimize React components to prevent unnecessary re-renders during form interactions.
- **Secure Sensitive Data:** Handle sensitive information, like passwords, securely by minimizing exposure in the frontend.

Integrating Zod in Next.js Projects

Next.js is a powerful React framework that supports server-side rendering, static site generation, and robust API routes. Integrating Zod within Next.js projects ensures that both client-side and server-side data validations are consistent and type-safe, enhancing the overall reliability and maintainability of your applications.

1. Setting Up the Next.js Project

Begin by setting up a new Next.js project with TypeScript support and installing necessary dependencies.

Step 1: Initialize a New Next.js Project with TypeScript

Use `create-next-app` to set up a new Next.js project.

```bash
---
npx create-next-app@latest next-zod-integration --typescript
cd next-zod-integration
```

Step 2: Install Zod and Related Dependencies

```bash
```

```
---
npm install zod @hookform/resolvers react-hook-form
```

- `zod`: For schema validation.
- `@hookform/resolvers`: Integrates Zod with React Hook Form.
- `react-hook-form`: For managing form state and validation.

2. Defining Shared Zod Schemas

To maintain consistency between frontend and backend, define shared Zod schemas that can be imported by both parts of the application.

Step 1: Create a `schemas` Directory

Organize your schemas in a dedicated directory.

```bash
---
mkdir src/schemas
```

Step 2: Define a Shared User Schema

```typescript
---
// src/schemas/userSchema.ts
import { z } from "zod";

export const userSchema = z.object({
  username: z.string().min(3, { message: "Username must be at
least 3 characters long." }),
  email: z.string().email({ message: "Please enter a valid
email address." }),
  password: z.string()
    .min(8, { message: "Password must be at least 8
characters long." })
    .refine((val) => /[A-Z]/.test(val), { message: "Password
must contain at least one uppercase letter." })
    .refine((val) => /[0-9]/.test(val), { message: "Password
must contain at least one number." }),
});
```

Explanation:

- **Consistency:** By defining schemas in a shared directory, both frontend and backend can reference the same validation rules, eliminating duplication.

3. Integrating Zod in Frontend Forms

Use Zod schemas with React Hook Form to validate user inputs on the client side, ensuring immediate feedback and reducing unnecessary server requests.

Step 1: Create a Registration Form Component

```typescript
---
// src/components/RegistrationForm.tsx
import React from "react";
import { useForm } from "react-hook-form";
import { zodResolver } from "@hookform/resolvers/zod";
import { userSchema } from "../schemas/userSchema";

type User = z.infer<typeof userSchema>;

const RegistrationForm: React.FC = () => {
  const { register, handleSubmit, formState: { errors } } =
useForm<User>({
    resolver: zodResolver(userSchema),
  });

  const onSubmit = async (data: User) => {
    try {
      const response = await fetch("/api/register", {
        method: "POST",
        headers: {
          "Content-Type": "application/json",
        },
        body: JSON.stringify(data),
      });

      if (!response.ok) {
        const errorData = await response.json();
        console.error("Registration failed:", errorData);
      } else {
        console.log("Registration successful!");
      }
    } catch (error) {
      console.error("An unexpected error occurred:", error);
    }
  };

  return (
    <form onSubmit={handleSubmit(onSubmit)}>
      <div>
        <label>Username:</label>
        <input {...register("username")} />
        {errors.username &&
<span>{errors.username.message}</span>}
      </div>
```

```typescript
      <div>
        <label>Email:</label>
        <input {...register("email")} />
        {errors.email && <span>{errors.email.message}</span>}
      </div>

      <div>
        <label>Password:</label>
        <input type="password" {...register("password")} />
        {errors.password &&
<span>{errors.password.message}</span>}
      </div>

      <button type="submit">Register</button>
    </form>
  );
};

export default RegistrationForm;
```

Explanation:

- **Shared Schema:** Uses userSchema for consistent validation.
- **Form Handling:** Leverages React Hook Form with Zod for efficient validation.
- **Error Display:** Shows validation errors adjacent to respective fields.
- **Form Submission:** Sends validated data to the backend API.

Step 2: Use the Form Component in a Page

```typescript
---
// src/pages/register.tsx
import React from "react";
import RegistrationForm from
"../components/RegistrationForm";

const RegisterPage: React.FC = () => {
  return (
    <div>
      <h1>User Registration</h1>
      <RegistrationForm />
    </div>
  );
};

export default RegisterPage;
```

166

Explanation:

- **Page Integration:** Embeds the `RegistrationForm` within the `/register` page.

4. Implementing Server-Side Validation in API Routes

Next.js API routes serve as backend endpoints. Implementing Zod validation within these routes ensures that data received from frontend forms adheres to expected formats and rules.

Step 1: Create an API Route for Registration

```typescript
---
// src/pages/api/register.ts
import { NextApiRequest, NextApiResponse } from "next";
import { userSchema } from "../../schemas/userSchema";

export default async function handler(req: NextApiRequest,
res: NextApiResponse) {
  if (req.method !== "POST") {
    return res.status(405).json({ error: "Method Not Allowed"
});
  }

  try {
    // Validate the request body using Zod
    const validatedData = userSchema.parse(req.body);

    // Proceed with registration logic, e.g., saving to a
database
    // For demonstration, we'll just return the validated
data
    res.status(200).json({ message: "Registration
successful", data: validatedData });
  } catch (e) {
    if (e instanceof z.ZodError) {
      // Return validation errors to the client
      return res.status(400).json({ errors: e.errors });
    }

    // Handle other errors
    res.status(500).json({ error: "Internal Server Error" });
  }
}
```

Explanation:

- **Method Check:** Ensures only POST requests are handled.
- **Validation:** Uses `userSchema` to validate incoming data.
- **Error Handling:**
    - **Zod Errors:** Returns detailed validation errors with a 400 status code.
    - **Other Errors:** Returns a generic 500 error for unexpected issues.
- **Registration Logic:** Placeholder for actual registration processes like database interactions.

5. Ensuring Consistency Across Frontend and Backend

Maintaining consistent validation rules across frontend forms and backend API routes is crucial for data integrity and reducing bugs.

Step 1: Share Schemas Between Frontend and Backend

By defining Zod schemas in a shared directory, both frontend components and backend API routes can import and use the same validation logic.

Example Structure:

```
src/
  schemas/
    userSchema.ts
  types/
    user.ts
  components/
    RegistrationForm.tsx
  pages/
    register.tsx
    api/
      register.ts
```

Explanation:

- **Single Source of Truth:** Schemas defined once are reused across different parts of the application, ensuring consistency.
- **Type Inference:** Using `z.infer` keeps TypeScript types synchronized with validation schemas, enhancing type safety.

6. Best Practices for Integrating Zod in Next.js Frontend

To maximize the benefits of integrating Zod in Next.js frontend development, consider the following best practices:

- **Define Shared Schemas:** Centralize schema definitions to promote reuse and maintain consistency between frontend and backend.
- **Leverage Type Inference:** Use `z.infer` to derive TypeScript types from Zod schemas, ensuring type safety and reducing duplication.
- **Handle Validation Errors Gracefully:** Provide clear and user-friendly error messages to guide users in correcting input mistakes.
- **Secure Sensitive Data:** Ensure that sensitive information, such as passwords, is handled securely, avoiding exposure in frontend code.
- **Optimize Form Performance:** Utilize React Hook Form's performance optimizations to manage large forms efficiently.

Conclusion

Frontend development demands robust validation mechanisms to ensure that user inputs are accurate and consistent. Integrating Zod with React and Next.js elevates form validation by providing type-safe, declarative schemas that align seamlessly with TypeScript's type system. By defining shared Zod schemas, leveraging React Hook Form for efficient state management, and implementing server-side validation within Next.js API routes, you can build applications that are both user-friendly and maintainable. Adhering to best practices in schema reuse, type inference, and error handling further enhances the reliability and efficiency of your frontend validations. As you continue to develop frontend applications, the synergy between TypeScript and Zod will prove invaluable in maintaining data integrity and delivering exceptional user experiences.

6.2 Backend Development

Backend development is the backbone of any application, handling data processing, business logic, and interactions with databases and external services. Ensuring that the data received and processed by the backend is valid and consistent is crucial for application stability, security, and reliability. Integrating Zod with TypeScript in backend environments empowers developers to implement robust validation mechanisms, streamline error handling, and maintain type safety across the entire application stack. This section delves into two primary areas of backend validation: **API Payload Validation in Node.js** and **Schema Validation for REST and GraphQL APIs**. Each subsection provides a comprehensive analysis accompanied by practical, step-by-step code examples to illustrate effective implementation strategies.

API Payload Validation in Node.js

Validating API payloads is essential to ensure that the data your server receives adheres to the expected formats and business rules. Proper validation prevents malformed data from causing unexpected behaviors, enhances security by mitigating injection attacks, and improves overall application robustness.

1. Setting Up the Node.js Project

Before implementing payload validation, set up a Node.js project with TypeScript and install the necessary dependencies.

Step 1: Initialize a New Node.js Project with TypeScript

Use npm to initialize a new project and install TypeScript.

```bash
---
mkdir node-zod-validation
cd node-zod-validation
npm init -y
npm install typescript ts-node @types/node --save-dev
npx tsc --init
```

Step 2: Install Zod and Express

Express is a minimal and flexible Node.js web application framework that provides a robust set of features for web and mobile applications. Install it along with Zod for validation.

```bash
---
npm install express zod
npm install @types/express --save-dev
```

Step 3: Configure TypeScript

Ensure that your `tsconfig.json` is set up correctly for a Node.js environment. Key settings include:

```json
{
  "compilerOptions": {
    "target": "ES6",
    "module": "commonjs",
    "rootDir": "./src",
    "outDir": "./dist",
    "strict": true,
    "esModuleInterop": true
  }
}
```

2. Defining Zod Schemas for API Payloads

Define Zod schemas that represent the structure and validation rules of the data your API expects. This approach centralizes validation logic and ensures consistency across different parts of your application.

Step 1: Create a `schemas` Directory and Define Schemas

Organize your schemas in a dedicated directory for better maintainability.

```bash
mkdir src/schemas
```

Example: User Registration Schema

```typescript
// src/schemas/userSchema.ts
import { z } from "zod";

export const userRegistrationSchema = z.object({
  username: z.string().min(3, { message: "Username must be at
least 3 characters long." }),
  email: z.string().email({ message: "Please enter a valid
email address." }),
  password: z.string()
    .min(8, { message: "Password must be at least 8
characters long." })
```

```typescript
    .refine((val) => /[A-Z]/.test(val), { message: "Password
must contain at least one uppercase letter." })
    .refine((val) => /[0-9]/.test(val), { message: "Password
must contain at least one number." }),
});
```

Explanation:

- **username**: Must be a string with a minimum length of 3.
- **email**: Must be a valid email format.
- **password**: Must be at least 8 characters long, contain at least one uppercase letter, and one number.

3. Implementing API Routes with Validation

Integrate Zod schemas into your Express routes to validate incoming API requests. This ensures that only well-formed data is processed by your application logic.

Step 1: Create the Express Server

Set up a basic Express server with TypeScript support.

```typescript
---
// src/server.ts
import express, { Request, Response } from "express";
import { userRegistrationSchema } from
"./schemas/userSchema";

const app = express();
app.use(express.json());

app.post("/api/register", async (req: Request, res: Response)
=> {
  try {
    // Validate the request body against the Zod schema
    const validatedData =
userRegistrationSchema.parse(req.body);

    // Proceed with registration logic (e.g., saving to a
database)
    // For demonstration, we'll return the validated data
    res.status(200).json({
      message: "Registration successful",
      data: validatedData,
    });
```

```
  } catch (error) {
    if (error instanceof z.ZodError) {
      // Extract and format validation errors
      const formattedErrors = error.errors.map(err => ({
        field: err.path.join("."),
        message: err.message,
      }));

      return res.status(400).json({
        message: "Validation failed",
        errors: formattedErrors,
      });
    }

    // Handle other unexpected errors
    res.status(500).json({
      message: "Internal Server Error",
    });
  }
});

const PORT = process.env.PORT || 5000;
app.listen(PORT, () => {
  console.log(`Server running on port ${PORT}`);
});
```

Explanation:

- **Express Setup:** Initializes an Express application and configures it to parse JSON request bodies.
- **API Route (`/api/register`):**
  - **Validation:** Uses `userRegistrationSchema.parse(req.body)` to validate incoming data.
  - **Success Response:** Returns a success message along with the validated data.
  - **Error Handling:**
    - **Zod Errors:** Catches `ZodError`, formats the errors, and sends a 400 response with detailed error messages.
    - **Other Errors:** Sends a generic 500 Internal Server Error response for unexpected issues.

Step 2: Run the Server

Use `ts-node` to run your TypeScript server without compiling it first.

173

```bash
---
npx ts-node src/server.ts
```

Explanation:

- **Server Execution:** Starts the Express server on the specified port, ready to handle incoming API requests.

4. Testing the API Payload Validation

Ensure that your validation logic works as intended by testing different payloads.

Step 1: Valid Registration Request

```json
---
POST /api/register
Content-Type: application/json

{
  "username": "john_doe",
  "email": "john@example.com",
  "password": "SecurePass1"
}
```

Expected Response:

```json
---
{
  "message": "Registration successful",
  "data": {
    "username": "john_doe",
    "email": "john@example.com",
    "password": "SecurePass1"
  }
}
```

Step 2: Invalid Registration Request (Missing Password Number)

```json
---
POST /api/register
Content-Type: application/json
```

```
{
  "username": "jd",
  "email": "john@example.com",
  "password": "securepass"
}
```

Expected Response:

```
json
---
{
  "message": "Validation failed",
  "errors": [
    {
      "field": "username",
      "message": "Username must be at least 3 characters
long."
    },
    {
      "field": "password",
      "message": "Password must contain at least one
uppercase letter."
    },
    {
      "field": "password",
      "message": "Password must contain at least one number."
    }
  ]
}
```

Explanation:

- **Successful Validation:** Returns the validated data when all fields meet the schema requirements.
- **Failed Validation:** Provides detailed error messages indicating which fields failed and why.

5. Best Practices for API Payload Validation

To maintain efficient and reliable backend systems, adhere to the following best practices when implementing API payload validation with Zod and TypeScript:

- **Centralize Validation Schemas:**
  - o Keep all Zod schemas in a dedicated directory (`src/schemas`) to promote reuse and maintainability.
- **Leverage Type Inference:**

- o Use `z.infer` to derive TypeScript types directly from Zod schemas, ensuring type consistency across your application.

```typescript
---
import { z } from "zod";
import { userRegistrationSchema } from "./userSchema";

type UserRegistration = z.infer<typeof
userRegistrationSchema>;
```

- **Handle Errors Gracefully:**
  - o Provide clear and actionable error messages to clients, specifying which fields failed validation and why.
  - o Log unexpected errors for debugging while avoiding exposure of sensitive information to clients.
- **Reuse Subschemas:**
  - o Define reusable subschemas for common data structures (e.g., address, profile) to avoid duplication and ensure consistency.
- **Limit Schema Complexity:**
  - o Keep schemas as simple and flat as possible to enhance performance, especially for APIs handling large volumes of requests.
- **Implement Security Measures:**
  - o Validate all incoming data rigorously to prevent injection attacks and other security vulnerabilities.
  - o Sanitize inputs as necessary, especially for fields that will be stored or processed further.
- **Automate Testing:**
  - o Write automated tests for your schemas to ensure that validation rules work as expected and to prevent regressions.
- **Documentation:**
  - o Document your schemas and validation logic to aid team members in understanding data requirements and validation rules.

Schema Validation for REST and GraphQL APIs

Different API architectures, such as REST and GraphQL, have unique validation requirements. Zod's flexibility allows it to integrate seamlessly with both, ensuring that your APIs enforce consistent and reliable data validation.

1. REST API Validation

REST APIs typically handle data through various HTTP methods and endpoints. Validating request parameters, query strings, headers, and body data is essential to ensure that the API functions correctly and securely.

Step 1: Define Schemas for Different Parts of the Request

Create separate Zod schemas for request bodies, query parameters, and headers as needed.

Example: Validating Query Parameters

```typescript
---
// src/schemas/querySchema.ts
import { z } from "zod";

export const paginationSchema = z.object({
  page: z.string().optional().transform(val => val ?
parseInt(val, 10) : 1).refine(val => val > 0, { message:
"Page must be a positive number." }),
  limit: z.string().optional().transform(val => val ?
parseInt(val, 10) : 10).refine(val => val > 0, { message:
"Limit must be a positive number." }),
});
```

Explanation:

- **page and limit:** Optional query parameters that default to 1 and 10, respectively, if not provided. They are transformed from strings to integers and validated to ensure they are positive numbers.

Step 2: Implement Validation Middleware

Create middleware functions to validate different parts of the request using the defined schemas.

Example: Validation Middleware for Query Parameters

```typescript
---
```

```typescript
// src/middleware/validatePagination.ts
import { Request, Response, NextFunction } from "express";
import { paginationSchema } from "../schemas/querySchema";

export const validatePagination = (req: Request, res:
Response, next: NextFunction) => {
  try {
    const validatedQuery = paginationSchema.parse(req.query);
    req.query = validatedQuery; // Overwrite with validated
and transformed data
    next();
  } catch (error) {
    if (error instanceof z.ZodError) {
      const formattedErrors = error.errors.map(err => ({
        field: err.path.join("."),
        message: err.message,
      }));
      return res.status(400).json({
        message: "Invalid query parameters",
        errors: formattedErrors,
      });
    }

    res.status(500).json({ message: "Internal Server Error"
});
  }
};
```

Explanation:

- **parse(req.query):** Validates and transforms the query parameters.
- **Error Handling:** Returns detailed error messages if validation fails.

Step 3: Apply Middleware to Routes

Use the validation middleware in your Express routes to enforce data integrity.

```typescript
typescript
---
// src/routes/userRoutes.ts
import express, { Request, Response } from "express";
import { validatePagination } from
"../middleware/validatePagination";
import { userRegistrationSchema } from
"../schemas/userSchema";

const router = express.Router();
```

178

```
router.post("/register", async (req: Request, res: Response)
=> {
  try {
    const validatedData =
userRegistrationSchema.parse(req.body);
    // Proceed with registration logic
    res.status(201).json({ message: "User registered
successfully", data: validatedData });
  } catch (error) {
    if (error instanceof z.ZodError) {
      const formattedErrors = error.errors.map(err => ({
        field: err.path.join("."),
        message: err.message,
      }));
      return res.status(400).json({ message: "Validation
failed", errors: formattedErrors });
    }

    res.status(500).json({ message: "Internal Server Error"
});
  }
});

router.get("/users", validatePagination, (req: Request, res:
Response) => {
  const { page, limit } = req.query;
  // Fetch users based on pagination
  res.status(200).json({ message: "Users fetched
successfully", page, limit });
});

export default router;
```

Explanation:

- **POST /register:** Validates the request body using
  userRegistrationSchema.
- **GET /users:** Applies validatePagination middleware to validate
  query parameters before handling the request.

2. GraphQL API Validation

GraphQL APIs handle data through queries and mutations, with a strong
emphasis on type safety and flexible data retrieval. Validating inputs in
GraphQL ensures that clients send correctly structured data, preventing
errors and enhancing security.

Step 1: Define GraphQL Schemas and Resolvers

When using GraphQL with Node.js, libraries like `Apollo Server` facilitate schema definition and resolver implementation. Integrate Zod within resolvers to validate input arguments.

Step 2: Install Apollo Server and Related Dependencies

```bash
---
npm install apollo-server graphql
npm install @types/graphql --save-dev
```

Step 3: Define Zod Schemas for GraphQL Inputs

Create Zod schemas corresponding to your GraphQL input types.

```typescript
---
// src/schemas/graphqlSchema.ts
import { z } from "zod";

export const createUserInputSchema = z.object({
  username: z.string().min(3, { message: "Username must be at
least 3 characters long." }),
  email: z.string().email({ message: "Please enter a valid
email address." }),
  password: z.string()
    .min(8, { message: "Password must be at least 8
characters long." })
    .refine((val) => /[A-Z]/.test(val), { message: "Password
must contain at least one uppercase letter." })
    .refine((val) => /[0-9]/.test(val), { message: "Password
must contain at least one number." }),
});
```

Step 4: Implement Apollo Server with Zod Validation

Integrate Zod schemas within your GraphQL resolvers to validate input data.

```typescript
---
// src/server.ts
import { ApolloServer, gql } from "apollo-server";
import { createUserInputSchema } from
"./schemas/graphqlSchema";
import { z } from "zod";

// Define GraphQL type definitions
```

```
const typeDefs = gql`
  type User {
    username: String!
    email: String!
  }

  type Mutation {
    createUser(username: String!, email: String!, password:
String!): User!
  }

  type Query {
    users: [User!]!
  }
`;

// In-memory user store for demonstration purposes
const users: { username: string; email: string }[] = [];

// Define resolvers with Zod validation
const resolvers = {
  Query: {
    users: () => users,
  },
  Mutation: {
    createUser: async (_: any, args: any) => {
      try {
        // Validate input arguments using Zod
        const validatedInput =
createUserInputSchema.parse(args);

        // Proceed with user creation logic
        users.push({
          username: validatedInput.username,
          email: validatedInput.email,
        });

        return {
          username: validatedInput.username,
          email: validatedInput.email,
        };
      } catch (error) {
        if (error instanceof z.ZodError) {
          // Format and throw GraphQL-friendly validation
errors
          throw new Error(error.errors.map(err =>
err.message).join(", "));
        }

        throw new Error("Internal Server Error");
      }
```

```
    },
  },
};

// Initialize Apollo Server
const server = new ApolloServer({
  typeDefs,
  resolvers,
});

// Start the server
server.listen().then(({ url }) => {
  console.log(` 🚀 Server ready at ${url}`);
});
```

Explanation:

- **Type Definitions:** Defines User type, createUser mutation, and users query.
- **Resolvers:**
  - **Mutation createUser:** Validates input using createUserInputSchema. On success, adds the user to an in-memory store and returns the user data. On failure, throws a formatted error.
  - **Query users:** Returns the list of registered users.
- **Error Handling:** Converts Zod validation errors into GraphQL-friendly error messages.

Step 5: Testing the GraphQL API

Use tools like Apollo Studio or GraphQL Playground to interact with your GraphQL API.

Example: Valid Mutation Request

```graphql
---
mutation {
  createUser(username: "jane_doe", email: "jane@example.com",
password: "SecurePass1") {
    username
    email
  }
}
```

Expected Response:

```
json
---
{
  "data": {
    "createUser": {
      "username": "jane_doe",
      "email": "jane@example.com"
    }
  }
}
```

Example: Invalid Mutation Request (Short Password)

```
graphql
---
mutation {
  createUser(username: "jd", email: "jane@example.com",
password: "pass") {
    username
    email
  }
}
```

Expected Response:

```
json
---
{
  "errors": [
    {
      "message": "Username must be at least 3 characters
long., Password must be at least 8 characters long., Password
must contain at least one uppercase letter., Password must
contain at least one number.",
      "locations": [{ "line": 2, "column": 3 }],
      "path": ["createUser"]
    }
  ],
  "data": null
}
```

Explanation:

- **Successful Mutation:** Returns the created user data when all inputs are valid.
- **Failed Mutation:** Provides a consolidated error message detailing all validation failures.

3. Best Practices for Backend Schema Validation

Implementing effective schema validation in backend environments requires adherence to best practices that promote security, performance, and maintainability.

- **Centralize Schemas:**
    - o Keep all Zod schemas in a dedicated directory (`src/schemas`) to promote reuse and maintain consistency across different parts of the backend.
- **Leverage Type Inference:**
    - o Use `z.infer` to derive TypeScript types from Zod schemas, ensuring that types remain synchronized and reducing the risk of type mismatches.

```typescript
---
import { z } from "zod";
import { userRegistrationSchema } from "./userSchema";

type UserRegistration = z.infer<typeof
userRegistrationSchema>;
```

- **Implement Modular Middleware:**
    - o Create reusable middleware functions for different types of validations (e.g., body, query, headers) to streamline request processing and validation logic.
- **Handle Errors Gracefully:**
    - o Provide clear and actionable error messages to clients, specifying which fields failed validation and why.
    - o Log detailed error information on the server for debugging purposes without exposing sensitive details to clients.
- **Reuse Subschemas:**
    - o Define common subschemas for shared data structures (e.g., address, profile) to avoid duplication and ensure consistency.
- **Optimize Performance:**
    - o Keep schemas as simple and flat as possible to enhance validation performance, especially for APIs handling high traffic.
    - o Limit the use of deeply nested or overly complex schemas unless necessary for your application's logic.
- **Secure Sensitive Data:**

- o Validate and sanitize all incoming data to protect against injection attacks and other security vulnerabilities.
  - o Handle sensitive information, such as passwords and personal data, with care, ensuring they are not exposed or logged inadvertently.
- **Automate Testing:**
  - o Write unit and integration tests for your schemas to ensure that validation rules work as intended and to prevent regressions.
- **Documentation:**
  - o Document your schemas and validation logic thoroughly to aid team members in understanding data requirements and validation rules.

Conclusion

Backend development demands rigorous data validation to ensure that the server processes only well-structured and valid data. By integrating Zod with TypeScript in Node.js environments, developers can implement robust, type-safe validation mechanisms that enhance application security, reliability, and maintainability. Whether validating API payloads in Express or enforcing schema rules in GraphQL APIs, Zod provides the flexibility and power needed to handle diverse validation scenarios effectively.

Adhering to best practices—such as centralizing schemas, leveraging type inference, handling errors gracefully, and optimizing performance—ensures that your backend validation logic remains efficient and scalable as your application grows. By mastering these validation techniques, you lay a solid foundation for building secure and resilient backend systems that can handle complex data interactions with confidence.

6.3 Full-Stack Integration

Full-stack development encompasses building both the frontend and backend of an application, ensuring seamless interaction between the two. Achieving end-to-end type safety across the entire stack enhances reliability, reduces errors, and streamlines development workflows. By leveraging TypeScript and Zod together, developers can maintain consistent validation rules and type definitions from the client side to the server side. This section explores strategies for integrating TypeScript and Zod in full-stack applications, focusing on shared schemas, automated type inference, and maintaining consistency across different layers of the application.

---

1. Introduction to Full-Stack Type Safety

Ensuring type safety across the full stack of an application involves maintaining consistent data structures and validation rules between the frontend and backend. This consistency minimizes the risk of runtime errors, enhances developer productivity, and improves overall application stability. TypeScript provides static type checking, while Zod offers runtime validation, both of which can be harmoniously integrated to achieve comprehensive type safety.

Key Benefits:

- **Consistency:** Shared schemas ensure that data structures are uniformly defined and validated across the entire application.
- **Reduced Redundancy:** Defining schemas once and reusing them across frontend and backend prevents duplication and discrepancies.
- **Enhanced Developer Experience:** Type inference and shared types streamline the development process, providing immediate feedback and reducing the likelihood of type-related bugs.
- **Improved Maintainability:** Centralized schema definitions make it easier to update and maintain validation logic as the application evolves.

---

2. Defining Shared Zod Schemas

Centralizing schema definitions allows both the frontend and backend to reference the same validation rules and TypeScript types. This approach ensures that data exchanged between the client and server adheres to consistent standards, reducing the likelihood of mismatches and errors.

a. Setting Up a Shared Schema Directory

Organize your project to include a shared directory for schemas and types that can be accessed by both frontend and backend components.

Project Structure Example:

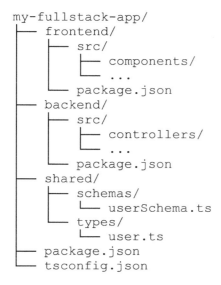

```
my-fullstack-app/
├── frontend/
│   ├── src/
│   │   ├── components/
│   │   │   └── ...
│   └── package.json
├── backend/
│   ├── src/
│   │   ├── controllers/
│   │   │   └── ...
│   └── package.json
├── shared/
│   ├── schemas/
│   │   └── userSchema.ts
│   └── types/
│       └── user.ts
├── package.json
└── tsconfig.json
```

Explanation:

- **shared/schemas/**: Contains Zod schemas shared across frontend and backend.
- **shared/types/**: Contains TypeScript type definitions inferred from Zod schemas.

b. Creating a Shared User Schema

Define a Zod schema that represents the structure and validation rules for user-related data. This schema will be used by both the frontend forms and backend API endpoints.

```typescript
---
// shared/schemas/userSchema.ts
import { z } from "zod";

export const userSchema = z.object({
  username: z.string().min(3, { message: "Username must be at
least 3 characters long." }),
```

```
  email: z.string().email({ message: "Please enter a valid
email address." }),
  password: z.string()
    .min(8, { message: "Password must be at least 8
characters long." })
    .refine((val) => /[A-Z]/.test(val), { message: "Password
must contain at least one uppercase letter." })
    .refine((val) => /[0-9]/.test(val), { message: "Password
must contain at least one number." }),
});
```

Explanation:

- **username**: Must be a string with a minimum length of 3 characters.
- **email**: Must follow a valid email format.
- **password**: Must be at least 8 characters long and include at least one uppercase letter and one number.

c. Inferring TypeScript Types from Zod Schemas

Use Zod's `z.infer` to derive TypeScript types directly from the schemas. This ensures that the types remain synchronized with the validation rules.

```typescript
---
// shared/types/user.ts
import { z } from "zod";
import { userSchema } from "../schemas/userSchema";

export type User = z.infer<typeof userSchema>;
```

Explanation:

- **User Type**: Represents the structure defined in `userSchema`, ensuring type consistency across the application.

---

3. Integrating Shared Schemas in Frontend

Incorporate the shared Zod schemas into frontend components to validate user inputs and manage form state effectively.

a. Setting Up the Frontend Project

188

Assuming a React-based frontend, ensure that it has access to the shared schemas and types.

Step 1: Initialize a React Project with TypeScript

```bash
---
npx create-react-app frontend --template typescript
cd frontend
```

Step 2: Install Necessary Dependencies

```bash
---
npm install zod @hookform/resolvers react-hook-form
```

- **zod**: For runtime validation.
- **@hookform/resolvers**: To integrate Zod with React Hook Form.
- **react-hook-form**: For managing form state and validation.

b. Creating the Registration Form Component

Implement a registration form that utilizes the shared `userSchema` for validation.

```typescript
---
// frontend/src/components/RegistrationForm.tsx
import React from "react";
import { useForm } from "react-hook-form";
import { zodResolver } from "@hookform/resolvers/zod";
import { userSchema } from "../../shared/schemas/userSchema";
import { User } from "../../shared/types/user";

const RegistrationForm: React.FC = () => {
  const { register, handleSubmit, formState: { errors } } =
useForm<User>({
    resolver: zodResolver(userSchema),
  });

  const onSubmit = async (data: User) => {
    try {
      const response = await fetch("/api/register", {
        method: "POST",
        headers: {
          "Content-Type": "application/json",
        },
```

```
        body: JSON.stringify(data),
      });

      if (!response.ok) {
        const errorData = await response.json();
        console.error("Registration failed:", errorData);
      } else {
        console.log("Registration successful!");
      }
    } catch (error) {
      console.error("An unexpected error occurred:", error);
    }
  };

  return (
    <form onSubmit={handleSubmit(onSubmit)}>
      <div>
        <label>Username:</label>
        <input {...register("username")} />
        {errors.username &&
<span>{errors.username.message}</span>}
      </div>

      <div>
        <label>Email:</label>
        <input {...register("email")} />
        {errors.email && <span>{errors.email.message}</span>}
      </div>

      <div>
        <label>Password:</label>
        <input type="password" {...register("password")} />
        {errors.password &&
<span>{errors.password.message}</span>}
      </div>

      <button type="submit">Register</button>
    </form>
  );
};

export default RegistrationForm;
```

Explanation:

- **useForm<User>**: Initializes the form with the User type inferred from the shared schema.
- **zodResolver(userSchema)**: Connects the Zod schema with React Hook Form for validation.

- **register("fieldName")**: Binds input fields to the form state.
- **errors.fieldName**: Displays validation errors adjacent to the respective input fields.
- **onSubmit**: Handles form submission by sending validated data to the backend API.

c. Incorporating the Form into a Page

Embed the `RegistrationForm` component within a page to render it in the application.

```typescript
---
// frontend/src/pages/RegisterPage.tsx
import React from "react";
import RegistrationForm from
"../components/RegistrationForm";

const RegisterPage: React.FC = () => {
  return (
    <div>
      <h1>User Registration</h1>
      <RegistrationForm />
    </div>
  );
};

export default RegisterPage;
```

Explanation:

- **RegisterPage Component**: Renders the `RegistrationForm` within the page, providing users with a registration interface.

---

4. Integrating Shared Schemas in Backend

Incorporate the shared Zod schemas into backend API routes to validate incoming requests, ensuring that the server processes only well-structured and valid data.

a. Setting Up the Backend Project

Assuming a Node.js backend using Express, configure the project to utilize the shared schemas and types.

Step 1: Initialize a Node.js Project with TypeScript

```bash
---
mkdir backend
cd backend
npm init -y
npm install typescript ts-node @types/node @types/express --save-dev
npx tsc --init
```

Step 2: Install Dependencies

```bash
---
npm install express zod
```

- **express**: Web framework for Node.js.
- **zod**: For runtime validation.

b. Creating the Registration API Route

Implement an API endpoint that validates incoming registration data using the shared `userSchema`.

```typescript
---
// backend/src/server.ts
import express, { Request, Response } from "express";
import { userSchema } from "../../shared/schemas/userSchema";
import { z } from "zod";

const app = express();
app.use(express.json());

app.post("/api/register", async (req: Request, res: Response)
=> {
  try {
    // Validate the request body against the shared Zod
schema
    const validatedData = userSchema.parse(req.body);

    // Proceed with registration logic (e.g., saving to a
database)
```

```
      // For demonstration, respond with the validated data
      res.status(200).json({
        message: "Registration successful",
        data: validatedData,
      });
  } catch (error) {
    if (error instanceof z.ZodError) {
      // Format and send validation errors to the client
      const formattedErrors = error.errors.map(err => ({
        field: err.path.join("."),
        message: err.message,
      }));

      return res.status(400).json({
        message: "Validation failed",
        errors: formattedErrors,
      });
    }

    // Handle other unexpected errors
    res.status(500).json({
      message: "Internal Server Error",
    });
  }
});

const PORT = process.env.PORT || 5000;
app.listen(PORT, () => {
  console.log(`Backend server running on port ${PORT}`);
});
```

Explanation:

- **Express Setup:** Initializes an Express application and configures it to parse JSON request bodies.
- **POST** `/api/register`:
  - **Validation:** Uses the shared `userSchema` to validate incoming registration data.
  - **Success Response:** Returns a success message along with the validated data.
  - **Error Handling:**
    - **Zod Errors:** Formats and sends detailed validation errors with a 400 status code.
    - **Other Errors:** Returns a generic 500 Internal Server Error response for unexpected issues.

c. Running the Backend Server

Use `ts-node` to run the TypeScript-based Express server without prior compilation.

```bash
bash
---
npx ts-node src/server.ts
```

Explanation:

- **Server Execution:** Starts the backend server on the specified port, ready to handle incoming API requests.

---

5. Automating Type Synchronization

Maintaining consistency between frontend and backend types is crucial for type safety and preventing runtime errors. Automating type synchronization ensures that any changes in the shared schemas are immediately reflected across the entire application.

a. Using Monorepo Tools

Monorepo tools like **Lerna** or **Yarn Workspaces** facilitate the management of shared packages and dependencies within a single repository.

Step 1: Initialize a Monorepo with Yarn Workspaces

```bash
bash
---
# At the root of your project
npm install --global yarn
yarn init -y
```

Step 2: Configure `package.json` for Workspaces

```json
json
---
// package.json
{
  "name": "my-fullstack-app",
  "private": true,
  "workspaces": [
    "frontend",
    "backend",
```

```
    "shared"
  ],
  "dependencies": {}
}
```

Step 3: Create the Shared Package

```bash
---
mkdir shared
cd shared
yarn init -y
```

Explanation:

- **Workspaces Configuration:** Defines `frontend`, `backend`, and `shared` as separate workspaces within the monorepo.
- **Shared Package:** The `shared` workspace houses schemas and types that are accessible by both `frontend` and `backend`.

b. Sharing Schemas and Types

Ensure that both frontend and backend can import and use the shared schemas and types seamlessly.

Step 1: Configure TypeScript Paths

Adjust the `tsconfig.json` in both frontend and backend to recognize the shared directory.

```json
---
// frontend/tsconfig.json and backend/tsconfig.json
{
  "compilerOptions": {
    // ...other settings
    "baseUrl": "./",
    "paths": {
      "@shared/*": ["../shared/*"]
    }
  }
}
```

Step 2: Import Shared Schemas and Types

Use the configured paths to import schemas and types in frontend and backend projects.

```typescript
---
// frontend/src/components/RegistrationForm.tsx
import { userSchema } from "@shared/schemas/userSchema";
import { User } from "@shared/types/user";

// backend/src/server.ts
import { userSchema } from "@shared/schemas/userSchema";
import { User } from "@shared/types/user";
```

Explanation:

- **Path Aliasing:** Simplifies imports and ensures that both frontend and backend reference the exact same schemas and types.
- **Consistency:** Any updates to the shared schemas automatically propagate to both frontend and backend, maintaining type synchronization.

---

6. Best Practices for Full-Stack Type Safety

Adhering to best practices ensures that your full-stack integration remains efficient, maintainable, and scalable.

a. Centralize Schema Definitions

- **Single Source of Truth:** Maintain all Zod schemas in the shared directory to prevent duplication and ensure consistency.
- **Modularization:** Organize schemas logically, grouping related schemas together for better maintainability.

b. Leverage Type Inference and Shared Types

- **Use z.infer:** Derive TypeScript types from Zod schemas to maintain synchronization between validation logic and type definitions.
- **Shared Types Directory:** Store inferred types in the shared `types` directory for easy access across the application.

c. Implement Consistent Error Handling

- **Uniform Error Responses:** Ensure that both frontend and backend handle validation errors consistently, providing clear and actionable feedback to users.
- **Logging:** Log detailed error information on the backend for debugging purposes while avoiding exposing sensitive details to the frontend.

d. Automate Testing for Shared Schemas

- **Unit Tests:** Write tests for your Zod schemas to verify that they enforce the intended validation rules.
- **Integration Tests:** Test the interaction between frontend forms and backend API endpoints to ensure that data flows correctly and validation is consistently applied.

e. Optimize Performance with Shared Schemas

- **Reusability:** Reuse schemas wherever possible to reduce validation overhead and improve performance.
- **Simplify Schemas:** Keep schemas as simple and flat as possible, avoiding unnecessary complexity that can impact validation speed.

Conclusion

Integrating TypeScript and Zod across the full stack of an application ensures that data structures and validation rules are consistently defined and enforced from the client side to the server side. By centralizing schema definitions, leveraging type inference, and maintaining consistent validation logic, developers can build robust, type-safe applications that minimize runtime errors and enhance maintainability. Automating type synchronization through monorepo tools and adhering to best practices further streamline the development process, making it easier to manage and scale applications as they grow in complexity.

Embracing end-to-end type safety not only improves the reliability of your application but also enhances the developer experience by providing clear, immediate feedback and reducing the likelihood of type-related bugs. As you continue to develop full-stack applications, the synergy between TypeScript and Zod will prove invaluable in maintaining data integrity and delivering high-quality software solutions.

Chapter 7: Testing and Debugging

Ensuring that your TypeScript and Zod implementations function correctly is paramount for building reliable and maintainable applications. Testing and debugging are integral components of the development lifecycle, helping developers identify and rectify issues early, enforce code quality, and maintain confidence in the software's behavior. This chapter delves into effective strategies for testing TypeScript code with Jest, writing comprehensive tests for Zod schemas, and debugging common validation and typing issues. By mastering these techniques, you can enhance the robustness and stability of your applications.

7.1 Testing TypeScript Code with Jest

Testing is a fundamental aspect of software development, ensuring that your code behaves as expected and facilitating the maintenance of high-quality applications. When working with TypeScript, integrating a robust testing framework like Jest can significantly enhance your development workflow. This section provides a comprehensive guide to setting up and using Jest for testing TypeScript code, complete with detailed explanations and step-by-step instructions.

1. Introduction to Jest and Its Integration with TypeScript

Jest is a widely-adopted testing framework developed by Facebook, renowned for its simplicity, speed, and powerful features. It offers an all-in-one solution for writing and running tests, making it an excellent choice for TypeScript projects. Key features of Jest include:

- **Zero Configuration:** Jest works out of the box for most JavaScript projects, requiring minimal setup.
- **Snapshot Testing:** Allows you to capture and compare the rendered output of components.
- **Mocking Capabilities:** Facilitates the mocking of functions, modules, and timers to isolate tests.
- **Code Coverage:** Generates detailed reports on how much of your code is covered by tests.

- **Parallel Test Execution:** Runs tests concurrently to speed up the testing process.

Integrating Jest with TypeScript ensures type safety within your tests, leveraging TypeScript's static type checking to catch errors early in the development cycle.

---

2. Setting Up the Project

Before writing tests, you need to set up a TypeScript project and install Jest along with the necessary dependencies.

Step 1: Initialize a New Node.js Project

Start by creating a new directory for your project and initializing it with `npm`.

```bash
---
mkdir typescript-jest-testing
cd typescript-jest-testing
npm init -y
```

Explanation:

- `mkdir typescript-jest-testing`: Creates a new directory named `typescript-jest-testing`.
- `cd typescript-jest-testing`: Navigates into the newly created directory.
- `npm init -y`: Initializes a new Node.js project with default settings.

Step 2: Install TypeScript

Install TypeScript as a development dependency.

```bash
---
npm install typescript --save-dev
```

Explanation:

- `typescript`: The TypeScript compiler.

- `--save-dev`: Adds TypeScript to the `devDependencies` section in `package.json`.

Step 3: Initialize TypeScript Configuration

Generate a `tsconfig.json` file to configure TypeScript settings.

```bash
---
npx tsc --init
```

Explanation:

- `npx tsc --init`: Creates a `tsconfig.json` file with default TypeScript compiler options.

Step 4: Install Jest and Related Dependencies

Install Jest, its TypeScript preprocessor, and type definitions.

```bash
---
npm install jest ts-jest @types/jest --save-dev
```

Explanation:

- `jest`: The Jest testing framework.
- `ts-jest`: A Jest transformer that allows Jest to understand TypeScript.
- `@types/jest`: TypeScript type definitions for Jest, enabling type safety in tests.

---

3. Configuring Jest for TypeScript

Proper configuration ensures that Jest can interpret and execute TypeScript files seamlessly.

Step 1: Initialize Jest Configuration

Use `ts-jest` to create a Jest configuration file tailored for TypeScript.

```bash
---
npx ts-jest config:init
```

Explanation:

- `npx ts-jest config:init`: Generates a `jest.config.js` file with recommended settings for TypeScript projects.

Step 2: Review and Modify `jest.config.js`

Open the generated `jest.config.js` file to understand and adjust configurations as needed.

```javascript
---
// jest.config.js
module.exports = {
  preset: 'ts-jest',
  testEnvironment: 'node',
  // Optionally, specify paths or additional settings
};
```

Explanation:

- `preset: 'ts-jest'`: Instructs Jest to use `ts-jest` for processing TypeScript files.
- `testEnvironment: 'node'`: Sets the testing environment to Node.js. Change to `'jsdom'` if testing browser-specific code.

Optional Configuration Adjustments:

- **Coverage Reporting:** Enable coverage reports by adding the following:

  ```javascript
  ---
  collectCoverage: true,
  coverageDirectory: 'coverage',
  ```

- **Module Name Mapping:** If using path aliases, configure `moduleNameMapper` to resolve them correctly.

  ```javascript
  ---
  ```

```
moduleNameMapper: {
  '^@src/(.*)$': '<rootDir>/src/$1',
},
```

4. Writing Tests in TypeScript with Jest

With Jest configured, you can now write tests for your TypeScript code. This process involves creating test files, writing test cases, and running them to verify functionality.

Step 1: Create a Source File to Test

For demonstration, create a simple TypeScript module with functions to be tested.

```bash
---
mkdir src
typescript
---
// src/math.ts
export const add = (a: number, b: number): number => a + b;

export const subtract = (a: number, b: number): number => a -
b;
```

Explanation:

- add: Adds two numbers.
- subtract: Subtracts the second number from the first.

Step 2: Create a Test File

Jest conventionally looks for test files with .test.ts or .spec.ts extensions. Create a test file for the math.ts module.

```bash
---
mkdir __tests__
typescript
---
// __tests__/math.test.ts
import { add, subtract } from '../src/math';

describe('Math Functions', () => {
```

```
describe('add', () => {
  it('should correctly add two positive numbers', () => {
    expect(add(2, 3)).toBe(5);
  });

  it('should correctly add two negative numbers', () => {
    expect(add(-2, -3)).toBe(-5);
  });

  it('should correctly add a positive and a negative
number', () => {
    expect(add(5, -3)).toBe(2);
  });
});

describe('subtract', () => {
  it('should correctly subtract two positive numbers', ()
=> {
    expect(subtract(5, 3)).toBe(2);
  });

  it('should correctly subtract two negative numbers', ()
=> {
    expect(subtract(-5, -3)).toBe(-2);
  });

  it('should correctly subtract a positive and a negative
number', () => {
    expect(subtract(5, -3)).toBe(8);
  });
});
});
```

Explanation:

- **Import Statements:** Imports the add and subtract functions from the math.ts module.
- **describe Blocks:** Organize tests into groups for better readability and structure.
- **it Blocks:** Define individual test cases with descriptive names.
- **expect Statements:** Assert that the function outputs match expected values.

Step 3: Configure Test Script in package.json

Add a test script to your package.json to run Jest easily.

```json
json
```

```
---
// package.json
{
  // ... other configurations
  "scripts": {
    "test": "jest"
  },
  // ... other configurations
}
```

Explanation:

- "test": "jest": Allows you to run tests using npm test.

Step 4: Run the Tests

Execute the test script to run your tests.

```bash
---
npm test
```

Expected Output:

```bash
---
> typescript-jest-testing@1.0.0 test
> jest

 PASS  __tests__/math.test.ts
  Math Functions
    add
      ✓ should correctly add two positive numbers (5 ms)
      ✓ should correctly add two negative numbers
      ✓ should correctly add a positive and a negative number
    subtract
      ✓ should correctly subtract two positive numbers
      ✓ should correctly subtract two negative numbers
      ✓ should correctly subtract a positive and a negative
number

Test Suites: 1 passed, 1 total
Tests:       6 passed, 6 total
Snapshots:   0 total
Time:        1.234 s
Ran all test suites.
```

Explanation:

- **PASS Status:** Indicates that all tests have passed successfully.
- **Test Details:** Shows each test case with its corresponding status and execution time.

---

5. Advanced Testing Techniques

Once you're comfortable with basic testing, you can explore more advanced techniques to enhance your test suite's robustness and coverage.

a. Mocking Functions and Modules

Mocking allows you to isolate the unit of code being tested by replacing dependencies with controlled implementations.

Example: Mocking a Dependency

Suppose you have a module that fetches data from an external API. You can mock this module in your tests to avoid making real API calls.

```typescript
---
// src/api.ts
export const fetchData = async (url: string): Promise<any> =>
{
  const response = await fetch(url);
  return response.json();
};
```
```typescript
---
// src/service.ts
import { fetchData } from './api';

export const getProcessedData = async (url: string):
Promise<any> => {
  const data = await fetchData(url);
  // Process data...
  return data;
};
```

Test with Mocking:

```typescript
---
// __tests__/service.test.ts
import { getProcessedData } from '../src/service';
import { fetchData } from '../src/api';

jest.mock('../src/api');

const mockedFetchData = fetchData as
jest.MockedFunction<typeof fetchData>;

describe('getProcessedData', () => {
  it('should process fetched data correctly', async () => {
    const mockData = { key: 'value' };
    mockedFetchData.mockResolvedValue(mockData);

    const result = await
getProcessedData('https://api.example.com/data');


expect(fetchData).toHaveBeenCalledWith('https://api.example.com/data');
    expect(result).toEqual(mockData);
  });
});
```

Explanation:

- **`jest.mock('../src/api')`:** Mocks the entire `api` module.
- **`mockedFetchData`:** Casts the mocked `fetchData` to a Jest mock function.
- **`mockResolvedValue`:** Defines the resolved value of the mocked function.
- **Assertions:** Verifies that `fetchData` was called with the correct arguments and that `getProcessedData` returns the expected result.

b. Snapshot Testing

Snapshot testing captures the output of a component or function and compares it against a stored snapshot to detect unexpected changes.

Example: Snapshot Testing a Component

```typescript
---
// src/components/Greeting.tsx
import React from 'react';
```

```typescript
interface GreetingProps {
  name: string;
}

const Greeting: React.FC<GreetingProps> = ({ name }) =>
<h1>Hello, {name}!</h1>;

export default Greeting;
typescript
---
// __tests__/Greeting.test.tsx
import React from 'react';
import renderer from 'react-test-renderer';
import Greeting from '../src/components/Greeting';

test('Greeting component renders correctly', () => {
  const tree = renderer.create(<Greeting name="John Doe"
/>).toJSON();
  expect(tree).toMatchSnapshot();
});
```

Explanation:

- **react-test-renderer:** Renders React components to pure JavaScript objects without depending on the DOM.
- **toMatchSnapshot():** Compares the rendered output with the stored snapshot, flagging any discrepancies.

Running Snapshot Tests:

```bash
bash
---
npm test
```

Initial Snapshot Creation:

On the first run, Jest creates a snapshot file. Subsequent runs compare against this snapshot to detect changes.

c. Code Coverage

Measuring code coverage helps identify untested parts of your codebase, ensuring comprehensive test coverage.

Step 1: Enable Coverage Reporting

Modify the test script in `package.json` to include coverage reporting.

```json
// package.json
{
  // ... other configurations
  "scripts": {
    "test": "jest --coverage"
  },
  // ... other configurations
}
```

Step 2: Run Tests with Coverage

Execute the test script to generate coverage reports.

```bash
npm test
```

6. Best Practices for Testing TypeScript Code with Jest

Adhering to best practices enhances the effectiveness and maintainability of your test suite. Consider the following guidelines to optimize your testing strategy with Jest and TypeScript:

a. Organize Test Files Clearly

- **Mirrored Directory Structure:** Place test files alongside their corresponding source files or in a dedicated __tests__ directory.

```bash
src/
  components/
    Header.tsx
    __tests__/
      Header.test.tsx
```

- **Consistent Naming Conventions:** Use `.test.ts` or `.spec.ts` suffixes for test files to ensure Jest recognizes and runs them automatically.

b. Utilize Type Inference

- **Leverage `z.infer`:** Derive TypeScript types directly from Zod schemas to maintain consistency between types and validation logic.

```typescript
---
import { z } from "zod";
import { userSchema } from "./userSchema";

type User = z.infer<typeof userSchema>;
```

- **Avoid Manual Type Definitions:** Let TypeScript infer types to prevent discrepancies and reduce redundancy.

c. Write Descriptive Test Cases

- **Clear Descriptions:** Ensure that `describe` and `it` blocks have descriptive names that convey the purpose of the tests.

```typescript
---
describe('add', () => {
  it('should correctly add two positive numbers', () => {
    // Test implementation
  });
});
```

- **Granular Testing:** Focus on testing one behavior or condition per test case to isolate issues effectively.

d. Mock External Dependencies

- **Isolate Units of Code:** Use Jest's mocking capabilities to replace external dependencies, such as API calls or database interactions, ensuring that tests focus solely on the unit being tested.

```typescript
---
jest.mock('../src/api');
```

- **Control Test Environment:** Mock functions to return predictable results, facilitating the testing of different scenarios.

e. Maintain High Test Coverage

- **Comprehensive Testing:** Aim to cover all critical paths and edge cases in your codebase to minimize the risk of undetected bugs.
- **Regularly Review Coverage Reports:** Use Jest's coverage reports to identify untested areas and prioritize writing tests for them.

f. Integrate Continuous Testing

- **Automate Test Execution:** Incorporate Jest tests into your Continuous Integration (CI) pipeline to run tests automatically on code commits and pull requests.
- **Prevent Regressions:** Automated testing helps catch regressions early, maintaining the stability of your application over time.

g. Optimize Test Performance

- **Avoid Heavy Computations:** Keep tests lightweight to ensure quick execution times, enabling faster feedback loops.
- **Run Tests in Parallel:** Leverage Jest's ability to run tests concurrently, speeding up the overall testing process.

h. Document Your Tests

- **Inline Comments:** Add comments to explain complex test logic or non-obvious assertions.
- **Test Documentation:** Maintain documentation that outlines testing strategies, conventions, and guidelines for your team.

Conclusion

Testing TypeScript code with Jest is a powerful combination that leverages TypeScript's type safety and Jest's robust testing features to create reliable and maintainable applications. By following this guide, you can set up a TypeScript project with Jest, write effective tests, and adhere to best practices that enhance your testing strategy. Comprehensive testing not only ensures that your code functions correctly but also facilitates easier maintenance and scalability as your project grows. Embracing these testing methodologies will lead to higher-quality software, reduced bugs, and a more efficient development workflow.

In the next section, **7.2 Writing Tests for Zod Schemas**, we will explore how to create and structure tests specifically for Zod schemas, ensuring that your data validation logic is both accurate and resilient. Let's continue building on this foundation to master the art of testing and debugging in TypeScript and Zod-powered applications.

7.2 Writing Tests for Zod Schemas

Ensuring that your data validation logic is robust and reliable is crucial for maintaining the integrity of your application. Zod schemas play a pivotal role in defining and enforcing the structure and constraints of your data. Testing these schemas guarantees that they behave as expected, effectively catching invalid data and preventing potential runtime errors. This section provides a comprehensive guide on writing tests for Zod schemas, offering in-depth analysis, best practices, and practical implementations to help you build dependable validation logic.

---

1. Importance of Testing Zod Schemas

Testing Zod schemas is essential for several reasons:

- **Validation Accuracy:** Ensures that schemas correctly accept valid data and reject invalid data based on defined rules.
- **Prevent Regression:** Detects unintended changes to schemas that might break existing validations.
- **Confidence in Data Integrity:** Provides assurance that your data structures remain consistent and reliable throughout the application lifecycle.
- **Facilitate Refactoring:** Allows safe modifications to schemas with immediate feedback on the impact of changes.

By systematically testing your Zod schemas, you can maintain high standards of data integrity and application stability.

---

2. Setting Up the Testing Environment

Before writing tests for your Zod schemas, set up a testing environment using Jest, a popular testing framework that integrates seamlessly with TypeScript and Zod.

Step 1: Initialize the Project

Assuming you have a Node.js project set up with TypeScript and Zod, proceed to install Jest and its TypeScript support.

```bash
---
npm install --save-dev jest ts-jest @types/jest
```

- **jest:** The testing framework.
- **ts-jest:** A Jest transformer that allows Jest to understand TypeScript.
- **@types/jest:** Type definitions for Jest, enabling type safety in tests.

Step 2: Configure Jest for TypeScript

Initialize Jest configuration using `ts-jest` to handle TypeScript files.

```bash
---
npx ts-jest config:init
```

This command creates a `jest.config.js` file with the necessary configurations.

Example `jest.config.js`:

```javascript
---
module.exports = {
  preset: 'ts-jest',
  testEnvironment: 'node',
  roots: ['<rootDir>/tests'],
  moduleFileExtensions: ['ts', 'tsx', 'js', 'jsx', 'json',
'node'],
  transform: {
    '^.+\\.tsx?$': 'ts-jest',
  },
};
```

Explanation:

- **preset:** Specifies the use of `ts-jest` for handling TypeScript files.
- **testEnvironment:** Sets the testing environment to Node.js.
- **roots:** Defines the root directory for test files.
- **moduleFileExtensions:** Lists file extensions Jest will recognize.
- **transform:** Instructs Jest to use `ts-jest` for transforming `.ts` and `.tsx` files.

Step 3: Organize Test Files

Create a `tests` directory to house all your test files.

```bash
---
mkdir tests
```

Organize your test files to mirror the structure of your source code for better maintainability.

```
project-root/
├── src/
│   ├── schemas/
│   │   └── userSchema.ts
│   └── ...
├── tests/
│   └── schemas/
│       └── userSchema.test.ts
├── jest.config.js
├── package.json
└── tsconfig.json
```

3. Writing Tests for Zod Schemas

With the testing environment set up, you can now write tests to validate the behavior of your Zod schemas.

Step 1: Define the Zod Schema

Assume you have a `userSchema.ts` that defines the structure and validation rules for user data.

```typescript
---
// src/schemas/userSchema.ts
import { z } from 'zod';
```

```typescript
export const userSchema = z.object({
  username: z.string().min(3, { message: 'Username must be at
least 3 characters long.' }),
  email: z.string().email({ message: 'Please enter a valid
email address.' }),
  password: z.string()
    .min(8, { message: 'Password must be at least 8
characters long.' })
    .refine((val) => /[A-Z]/.test(val), { message: 'Password
must contain at least one uppercase letter.' })
    .refine((val) => /[0-9]/.test(val), { message: 'Password
must contain at least one number.' }),
});
```

Explanation:

- **username:** Must be a string with a minimum length of 3 characters.
- **email:** Must follow a valid email format.
- **password:** Must be at least 8 characters long, contain at least one uppercase letter, and one number.

Step 2: Create the Test File

Create a corresponding test file userSchema.test.ts in the tests/schemas directory.

```typescript
---
// tests/schemas/userSchema.test.ts
import { userSchema } from '../../src/schemas/userSchema';
import { ZodError } from 'zod';

describe('User Schema Validation', () => {
  it('should validate a correct user object', () => {
    const validUser = {
      username: 'john_doe',
      email: 'john@example.com',
      password: 'SecurePass1',
    };

    expect(() => userSchema.parse(validUser)).not.toThrow();
  });

  it('should fail validation when username is too short', ()
=> {
    const invalidUser = {
      username: 'jd',
```

214

```
      email: 'john@example.com',
      password: 'SecurePass1',
    };

    expect(() =>
userSchema.parse(invalidUser)).toThrow(ZodError);
  });

  it('should fail validation when email is invalid', () => {
    const invalidUser = {
      username: 'john_doe',
      email: 'johnexample.com',
      password: 'SecurePass1',
    };

    expect(() =>
userSchema.parse(invalidUser)).toThrow(ZodError);
  });

  it('should fail validation when password is too short', ()
=> {
    const invalidUser = {
      username: 'john_doe',
      email: 'john@example.com',
      password: 'Short1',
    };

    expect(() =>
userSchema.parse(invalidUser)).toThrow(ZodError);
  });

  it('should fail validation when password lacks uppercase
letters', () => {
    const invalidUser = {
      username: 'john_doe',
      email: 'john@example.com',
      password: 'securepass1',
    };

    expect(() =>
userSchema.parse(invalidUser)).toThrow(ZodError);
  });

  it('should fail validation when password lacks numbers', ()
=> {
    const invalidUser = {
      username: 'john_doe',
      email: 'john@example.com',
      password: 'SecurePass',
    };
```

```
      expect(() =>
userSchema.parse(invalidUser)).toThrow(ZodError);
  });

  it('should collect all validation errors', () => {
    const invalidUser = {
      username: 'jd',
      email: 'johnexample.com',
      password: 'pass',
    };

    try {
      userSchema.parse(invalidUser);
    } catch (e) {
      if (e instanceof ZodError) {
        expect(e.errors.length).toBe(4);
        expect(e.errors).toEqual(
          expect.arrayContaining([
            expect.objectContaining({ path: ['username'],
message: 'Username must be at least 3 characters long.' }),
            expect.objectContaining({ path: ['email'],
message: 'Please enter a valid email address.' }),
            expect.objectContaining({ path: ['password'],
message: 'Password must be at least 8 characters long.' }),
            expect.objectContaining({ path: ['password'],
message: 'Password must contain at least one uppercase
letter.' }),
            expect.objectContaining({ path: ['password'],
message: 'Password must contain at least one number.' }),
          ])
        );
      }
    }
  });
});
```

Explanation:

- **Test Cases:**
    - **Valid User:** Ensures that a correctly structured user object passes validation without errors.
    - **Invalid Username:** Checks that usernames shorter than 3 characters fail validation.
    - **Invalid Email:** Verifies that improperly formatted emails are rejected.
    - **Invalid Password Length:** Ensures that passwords shorter than 8 characters are invalid.

- Password Without Uppercase Letters: Checks that passwords lacking uppercase letters fail validation.
    - **Password Without Numbers:** Ensures that passwords without numbers are invalid.
    - **Multiple Validation Errors:** Confirms that all relevant validation errors are captured when multiple fields are invalid.
- **Assertions:**
    - `toThrow(ZodError):` Expects the schema parsing to throw a `ZodError` for invalid inputs.
    - **Error Message Matching:** Verifies that specific error messages are returned for each invalid field.
    - **Error Count:** Ensures that all expected validation errors are present when multiple validations fail.

Step 3: Run the Tests

Execute the tests using the Jest test runner.

```bash
---
npm test
```

4. Best Practices for Testing Zod Schemas

To ensure that your tests for Zod schemas are effective and maintainable, follow these best practices:

a. Cover All Validation Rules

Ensure that each validation rule defined in your Zod schemas is thoroughly tested. This includes:

- **Field-Level Validations:** Test individual fields for their specific constraints (e.g., string length, format).
- **Interdependent Validations:** If certain fields depend on others (e.g., conditional fields), write tests to cover these scenarios.
- **Custom Refinements:** If you use `.refine()` or `.superRefine()` for complex validations, ensure these are tested comprehensively.

b. Test Both Positive and Negative Cases

For every validation rule, write tests that confirm:

- **Positive Cases:** Valid data passes validation without errors.
- **Negative Cases:** Invalid data triggers appropriate validation errors.

This dual approach ensures that your schemas correctly enforce the intended constraints.

c. Isolate Schema Tests

Keep schema tests focused solely on validation logic without involving other parts of the application. This isolation simplifies debugging and ensures that tests are specific to the schema's behavior.

d. Use Descriptive Test Names

Craft clear and descriptive names for your test cases to convey their purpose. Well-named tests enhance readability and make it easier to identify failing tests.

```typescript
---
it('should fail validation when email is invalid', () => { /*
... */ });
```

e. Incorporate Edge Cases

Identify and test edge cases that may challenge your validation logic, such as:

- **Boundary Values:** Test values at the limits of validation rules (e.g., minimum and maximum lengths).
- **Unexpected Data Types:** Attempt to pass incorrect data types to ensure type guards are effective.
- **Special Characters:** Include special characters in string fields to test format validations.

f. Automate Schema Testing

Integrate schema tests into your Continuous Integration (CI) pipeline to ensure that validation logic remains consistent and correct as the application evolves.

g. Maintain High Test Coverage

Use Jest's coverage reporting to monitor the extent of your test coverage. Strive for high coverage to ensure that all parts of your schemas are tested.

Enable Coverage Reporting:

Modify the test script in `package.json` to include coverage reporting.

```json
---
"scripts": {
  "test": "jest --coverage"
}
```

Run Tests with Coverage:

```bash
---
npm test
```

Interpret Coverage Reports:

- **Statements:** Percentage of executable statements covered by tests.
- **Branches:** Coverage of conditional branches (e.g., `if` statements).
- **Functions:** Percentage of functions tested.
- **Lines:** Coverage of individual lines of code.

Aim for comprehensive coverage to ensure that your schemas are fully validated.

---

5. Handling Complex Schemas and Nested Objects

As your application grows, your Zod schemas may become more complex, featuring nested objects and intricate validation rules. Testing these complex schemas requires additional strategies to maintain clarity and effectiveness.

a. Testing Nested Objects

Ensure that nested objects within your schemas are validated correctly by writing tests that target each nested level.

Example: Address Schema

```typescript
---
// src/schemas/addressSchema.ts
import { z } from 'zod';

export const addressSchema = z.object({
  street: z.string().min(1, { message: 'Street is required.'
}),
  city: z.string().min(1, { message: 'City is required.' }),
  zipCode: z.string().length(5, { message: 'Zip Code must be
exactly 5 characters long.' }),
});
```
User Schema with Nested Address:
```typescript
---
// src/schemas/userSchema.ts
import { z } from 'zod';
import { addressSchema } from './addressSchema';

export const userSchema = z.object({
  username: z.string().min(3, { message: 'Username must be at
least 3 characters long.' }),
  email: z.string().email({ message: 'Please enter a valid
email address.' }),
  password: z.string()
    .min(8, { message: 'Password must be at least 8
characters long.' })
    .refine((val) => /[A-Z]/.test(val), { message: 'Password
must contain at least one uppercase letter.' })
    .refine((val) => /[0-9]/.test(val), { message: 'Password
must contain at least one number.' }),
  address: addressSchema,
});
```

Test Cases for Nested Objects:

```typescript
---
// tests/schemas/userSchema.test.ts
import { userSchema } from '../../src/schemas/userSchema';
import { ZodError } from 'zod';

describe('User Schema Validation with Nested Address', () =>
{
  it('should validate a correct user object with address', ()
=> {
    const validUser = {
      username: 'jane_doe',
      email: 'jane@example.com',
      password: 'SecurePass1',
```

220

```
      address: {
        street: '123 Main St',
        city: 'Anytown',
        zipCode: '12345',
      },
    };

    expect(() => userSchema.parse(validUser)).not.toThrow();
  });

  it('should fail validation when address is missing', () =>
{
    const invalidUser = {
      username: 'jane_doe',
      email: 'jane@example.com',
      password: 'SecurePass1',
      // address is missing
    };

    expect(() =>
userSchema.parse(invalidUser)).toThrow(ZodError);
  });

  it('should fail validation when address fields are
invalid', () => {
    const invalidUser = {
      username: 'jane_doe',
      email: 'jane@example.com',
      password: 'SecurePass1',
      address: {
        street: '',
        city: 'Anytown',
        zipCode: '1234', // Invalid zipCode length
      },
    };

    try {
      userSchema.parse(invalidUser);
    } catch (e) {
      if (e instanceof ZodError) {
        expect(e.errors.length).toBe(2);
        expect(e.errors).toEqual(
          expect.arrayContaining([
            expect.objectContaining({ path: ['address',
'street'], message: 'Street is required.' }),
            expect.objectContaining({ path: ['address',
'zipCode'], message: 'Zip Code must be exactly 5 characters
long.' }),
          ])
        );
      }
```

```
    }
  });
});
```

Explanation:

- **Valid User with Address:** Confirms that a user object with a correctly structured address passes validation.
- **Missing Address:** Ensures that omitting the `address` field triggers a validation error.
- **Invalid Address Fields:** Checks that specific issues within the nested `address` object (e.g., empty street, incorrect zip code length) are correctly identified and reported.

b. Testing Conditional Validations

If your schemas include conditional validations—where the presence or value of one field affects the validation of another—ensure that these scenarios are thoroughly tested.

Example: User Schema with Conditional Field

```typescript
---
// src/schemas/userSchema.ts
import { z } from 'zod';
import { addressSchema } from './addressSchema';

export const userSchema = z.object({
  username: z.string().min(3, { message: 'Username must be at
least 3 characters long.' }),
  email: z.string().email({ message: 'Please enter a valid
email address.' }),
  password: z.string()
    .min(8, { message: 'Password must be at least 8
characters long.' })
    .refine((val) => /[A-Z]/.test(val), { message: 'Password
must contain at least one uppercase letter.' })
    .refine((val) => /[0-9]/.test(val), { message: 'Password
must contain at least one number.' }),
  address: z.object({
    street: z.string().min(1, { message: 'Street is
required.' }),
    city: z.string().min(1, { message: 'City is required.'
}),
    zipCode: z.string().length(5, { message: 'Zip Code must
be exactly 5 characters long.' }),
```

```typescript
    })).optional(),
}).refine((data) => data.address ||
data.email.endsWith('@example.com'), {
  message: 'Address is required if email is not from
example.com.',
  path: ['address'],
});
```

Explanation:

- **Conditional Rule:** The `address` field is optional unless the user's email does not end with `@example.com`. In such cases, `address` becomes required.

Test Cases for Conditional Validations:

```typescript
---
// tests/schemas/userSchema.test.ts
import { userSchema } from '../../src/schemas/userSchema';
import { ZodError } from 'zod';

describe('User Schema Validation with Conditional Address
Requirement', () => {
  it('should validate without address when email is from
example.com', () => {
    const validUser = {
      username: 'jane_doe',
      email: 'jane@example.com',
      password: 'SecurePass1',
      // address is optional here
    };

    expect(() => userSchema.parse(validUser)).not.toThrow();
  });

  it('should require address when email is not from
example.com', () => {
    const invalidUser = {
      username: 'jane_doe',
      email: 'jane@anotherdomain.com',
      password: 'SecurePass1',
      // address is missing
    };

    expect(() =>
userSchema.parse(invalidUser)).toThrow(ZodError);
  });
```

```
  it('should validate when address is provided even if email
is not from example.com', () => {
    const validUser = {
      username: 'jane_doe',
      email: 'jane@anotherdomain.com',
      password: 'SecurePass1',
      address: {
        street: '456 Elm St',
        city: 'Othertown',
        zipCode: '67890',
      },
    };

    expect(() => userSchema.parse(validUser)).not.toThrow();
  });

  it('should fail when email is not from example.com and
address is invalid', () => {
    const invalidUser = {
      username: 'jane_doe',
      email: 'jane@anotherdomain.com',
      password: 'SecurePass1',
      address: {
        street: '',
        city: 'Othertown',
        zipCode: '6789', // Invalid zipCode length
      },
    };

    try {
      userSchema.parse(invalidUser);
    } catch (e) {
      if (e instanceof ZodError) {
        expect(e.errors.length).toBe(3);
        expect(e.errors).toEqual(
          expect.arrayContaining([
            expect.objectContaining({ path: ['address',
'street'], message: 'Street is required.' }),
            expect.objectContaining({ path: ['address',
'zipCode'], message: 'Zip Code must be exactly 5 characters
long.' }),
            expect.objectContaining({ path: ['address'],
message: 'Address is required if email is not from
example.com.' }),
          ])
        );
      }
    }
  });
});
```

Explanation:

- **Email from `example.com` without Address:** Validates that the user can omit the `address` field when the email domain is `example.com`.
- **Email Not from `example.com` without Address:** Ensures that omitting the `address` field triggers a validation error when the email domain is different.
- **Email Not from `example.com` with Valid Address:** Confirms that providing a valid `address` satisfies the conditional requirement.
- **Email Not from `example.com` with Invalid Address:** Checks that multiple validation errors are reported when both the conditional requirement and nested address validations fail.

---

6. Automating and Enhancing Tests

To further enhance the effectiveness of your schema tests, consider incorporating additional testing strategies and tools.

a. Parameterized Testing

Parameterized tests allow you to run the same test logic with different inputs, reducing code duplication and increasing test coverage.

Example: Parameterized Tests for Username Validation

```typescript
---
// tests/schemas/userSchema.test.ts
import { userSchema } from '../../src/schemas/userSchema';
import { ZodError } from 'zod';

describe('User Schema Username Validation', () => {
  const invalidUsernames = ['ab', '', 'a', '12'];

  invalidUsernames.forEach((username) => {
    it(`should fail validation when username is
"${username}"`, () => {
      const invalidUser = {
        username,
        email: 'john@example.com',
        password: 'SecurePass1',
      };
```

```typescript
      expect(() =>
userSchema.parse(invalidUser)).toThrow(ZodError);
    });
  });
});
```

Explanation:

- **invalidUsernames Array:** Contains various invalid username inputs.
- **forEach Loop:** Iterates over each invalid username, running the same test logic.
- **Dynamic Test Descriptions:** Each test case clearly indicates which invalid username is being tested.

b. Snapshot Testing with Zod

While Jest's snapshot testing is typically used for UI components, you can leverage it for Zod schemas to capture and compare the shape of validated data.

Example: Snapshot Test for Valid User Data

```typescript
---
// tests/schemas/userSchemaSnapshot.test.ts
import { userSchema } from '../../src/schemas/userSchema';

describe('User Schema Snapshot Testing', () => {
  it('should match the snapshot for a valid user', () => {
    const validUser = {
      username: 'john_doe',
      email: 'john@example.com',
      password: 'SecurePass1',
    };

    const parsedUser = userSchema.parse(validUser);
    expect(parsedUser).toMatchSnapshot();
  });
});
```

Explanation:

- **Snapshot Creation:** The first run creates a snapshot file storing the structure of `parsedUser`.

- **Snapshot Comparison:** Subsequent runs compare the current output against the stored snapshot to detect changes.

Benefits:

- **Detect Structural Changes:** Identifies unintended modifications to the validated data structure.
- **Maintain Consistency:** Ensures that valid data continues to conform to the expected shape.

c. Leveraging Jest's Before and After Hooks

Use Jest's lifecycle hooks to set up and tear down conditions for your tests, ensuring a clean and controlled testing environment.

Example: Setting Up Shared Resources

```typescript
---
// tests/schemas/userSchema.test.ts
import { userSchema } from '../../src/schemas/userSchema';
import { ZodError } from 'zod';

describe('User Schema Validation', () => {
  beforeAll(() => {
    // Setup tasks, e.g., initializing shared resources
  });

  afterAll(() => {
    // Cleanup tasks, e.g., closing database connections
  });

  // Test cases...
});
```

Explanation:

- **beforeAll:** Runs once before all tests in the suite.
- **afterAll:** Runs once after all tests in the suite.
- **Use Cases:** Initialize shared data, mock global functions, or clean up resources after tests.

---

7. Common Pitfalls and How to Avoid Them

When testing Zod schemas, developers may encounter several common issues. Being aware of these pitfalls and understanding how to address them can streamline your testing process.

a. Ignoring Edge Cases

Issue: Failing to test edge cases can result in schemas that overlook specific invalid inputs, leading to potential runtime errors.

Solution: Identify and include tests for boundary conditions and unusual inputs, such as extremely long strings, special characters, or unexpected data types.

b. Overlooking Asynchronous Validations

Issue: Some Zod validations may involve asynchronous operations, which, if not handled correctly, can lead to false positives or negatives in tests.

Solution: Use Jest's asynchronous testing capabilities (`async/await`, `done` callbacks) to properly handle asynchronous schema validations.

Example: Asynchronous Refinement

```typescript
---
// src/schemas/userSchema.ts
import { z } from 'zod';

export const asyncUserSchema = z.object({
  username: z.string().min(3),
  email: z.string().email(),
  password: z.string().min(8),
}).refine(async (data) => {
  // Simulate asynchronous uniqueness check
  const isUnique = await checkUsernameUnique(data.username);
  return isUnique;
}, {
  message: 'Username already exists.',
  path: ['username'],
});

async function checkUsernameUnique(username: string):
Promise<boolean> {
  const existingUsernames = ['existingUser', 'admin'];
  // Simulate database check delay
  await new Promise(resolve => setTimeout(resolve, 100));
```

```typescript
    return !existingUsernames.includes(username);
}
```

Test for Asynchronous Validation:

```typescript
---
// tests/schemas/asyncUserSchema.test.ts
import { asyncUserSchema } from
'../../src/schemas/userSchema';
import { ZodError } from 'zod';

describe('Async User Schema Validation', () => {
  it('should validate a unique username', async () => {
    const validUser = {
      username: 'uniqueUser',
      email: 'unique@example.com',
      password: 'SecurePass1',
    };

    await
expect(asyncUserSchema.parseAsync(validUser)).resolves.toEqual(validUser);
  });

  it('should fail validation for an existing username', async
() => {
    const invalidUser = {
      username: 'admin',
      email: 'admin@example.com',
      password: 'SecurePass1',
    };

    await
expect(asyncUserSchema.parseAsync(invalidUser)).rejects.toThrow(ZodError);
  });
});
```

Explanation:

- **Asynchronous Schema:** Uses `.refine()` with an asynchronous function to check username uniqueness.
- **Async Tests:** Utilizes `parseAsync` and Jest's `async/await` syntax to handle asynchronous validations correctly.

c. Not Utilizing Type Inference Effectively

Issue: Manually defining TypeScript types that mirror Zod schemas can lead to inconsistencies and increased maintenance overhead.

Solution: Use Zod's `z.infer` to derive TypeScript types directly from schemas, ensuring synchronization and reducing redundancy.

Example: Type Inference

```typescript
---
import { z } from 'zod';
import { userSchema } from './userSchema';

type User = z.infer<typeof userSchema>;
```

Explanation:

- **`z.infer`:** Automatically derives the `User` type based on the `userSchema`, ensuring that any changes to the schema are reflected in the type definition.

---

8. Enhancing Test Coverage and Reliability

To maximize the effectiveness of your schema tests, consider adopting additional strategies that enhance coverage and reliability.

a. Continuous Integration (CI) Integration

Integrate your Jest tests into a CI pipeline to automate test execution on code commits and pull requests. Tools like GitHub Actions, Travis CI, or CircleCI can be configured to run tests automatically, ensuring that code changes do not introduce regressions.

Example: GitHub Actions Workflow

```yaml
---
# .github/workflows/ci.yml
name: CI

on:
  push:
```

```
    branches: [ main ]
  pull_request:
    branches: [ main ]

jobs:
  build-and-test:
    runs-on: ubuntu-latest

    steps:
      - uses: actions/checkout@v2

      - name: Set up Node.js
        uses: actions/setup-node@v2
        with:
          node-version: '14'

      - name: Install Dependencies
        run: npm install

      - name: Run Tests
        run: npm test
```

Explanation:

- **Trigger Conditions:** Runs on pushes and pull requests to the `main` branch.
- **Jobs:** Checks out the code, sets up Node.js, installs dependencies, and runs tests.
- **Outcome:** Automatically verifies that new changes pass all tests before merging.

b. Utilizing Test Coverage Reports

Regularly review Jest's coverage reports to identify untested parts of your schemas. Aim to cover all critical validation rules and scenarios to ensure comprehensive testing.

Step 1: Enable Coverage Reporting

Add the `--coverage` flag to your test script in `package.json`.

```json
---
"scripts": {
  "test": "jest --coverage"
}
```

Step 2: Run Tests with Coverage

```bash
---
npm test
```

Step 3: Review Coverage Reports

Jest generates a `coverage` directory with detailed reports. Focus on:

- **Statements:** Percentage of executable statements covered by tests.
- **Branches:** Coverage of conditional branches.
- **Functions:** Percentage of functions tested.
- **Lines:** Coverage of individual lines of code.

Strive for high coverage to ensure that all validation rules are tested.

c. Automating Schema Validation Tests

Automate the execution of schema validation tests as part of your development workflow to catch issues early.

Example: Pre-Commit Hooks with Husky

1. **Install Husky:**

```bash
---
npm install husky --save-dev
npx husky install
```

2. **Add Pre-Commit Hook:**

```bash
---
npx husky add .husky/pre-commit "npm test"
```

Explanation:

- **Husky:** Enables Git hooks in your project.
- **Pre-Commit Hook:** Runs tests before allowing a commit, preventing code with failing tests from being committed.

7.3 Debugging Common Validation and Typing Issues

Even with robust testing practices in place, developers may still encounter validation and typing issues when working with TypeScript and Zod. Effective debugging strategies are essential for identifying and resolving these issues promptly, ensuring the continued reliability and integrity of your applications. This section explores common pitfalls related to validation and typing, provides actionable solutions, and offers practical guidance to streamline the debugging process.

1. Understanding Common Validation and Typing Issues

Before diving into debugging techniques, it's important to recognize the typical challenges that arise when integrating TypeScript with Zod. These issues can stem from various sources, including schema misconfigurations, type mismatches, and complex validation rules. Familiarizing yourself with these common problems can accelerate the debugging process and enhance your ability to maintain clean, error-free code.

Common Issues:

- **Mismatched Types:** Discrepancies between TypeScript types and Zod schemas can lead to validation failures or runtime errors.
- **Missing Required Fields:** Omitting essential fields in data objects causes schemas to reject the data.
- **Overly Permissive Schemas:** Schemas that are too lenient may allow invalid or unexpected data to pass through.
- **Complex Conditional Validations:** Implementing intricate conditional logic can introduce errors if not carefully managed.
- **Recursive Schema Issues:** Defining recursive schemas without proper handling can result in infinite loops or stack overflows.
- **Asynchronous Validation Problems:** Asynchronous refinements or validations may not be correctly handled in tests or application logic.

2. Debugging Strategies for Validation and Typing Issues

233

Effective debugging involves a systematic approach to identifying, isolating, and resolving issues. The following strategies provide a structured methodology for tackling common validation and typing problems in TypeScript and Zod integrations.

a. Leveraging TypeScript's Type Checking

TypeScript's static type checking is a powerful tool for catching type-related issues before they manifest at runtime. Ensuring that your types and schemas are synchronized is fundamental to preventing validation errors.

Strategies:

- **Use z.infer for Type Inference:** Derive TypeScript types directly from Zod schemas using z.infer. This ensures that your TypeScript types always align with your validation schemas.

```typescript
---
import { z } from 'zod';
import { userSchema } from './userSchema';

type User = z.infer<typeof userSchema>;
```

- **Enable Strict Type Checking:** Configure TypeScript's tsconfig.json to enforce strict type checking. Settings like strict, noImplicitAny, and strictNullChecks help catch potential type mismatches early.

```json
---
// tsconfig.json
{
  "compilerOptions": {
    "strict": true,
    "noImplicitAny": true,
    "strictNullChecks": true,
    // ...other settings
  }
}
```

- **Consistent Type Usage:** Avoid manually defining TypeScript types that mirror Zod schemas. Instead, rely on z.infer to maintain consistency and reduce redundancy.

b. Utilizing Descriptive Error Messages

Clear and descriptive error messages are invaluable for quickly pinpointing the source of validation failures. Zod provides detailed error objects that can be leveraged to enhance debugging efficiency.

Strategies:

- **Custom Error Messages:** Define custom error messages within your Zod schemas to provide specific feedback when validation fails.

```typescript
---
const userSchema = z.object({
  username: z.string().min(3, { message: 'Username must be at least 3 characters long.' }),
  email: z.string().email({ message: 'Please enter a valid email address.' }),
  password: z.string()
    .min(8, { message: 'Password must be at least 8 characters long.' })
    .refine((val) => /[A-Z]/.test(val), { message: 'Password must contain at least one uppercase letter.' })
    .refine((val) => /[0-9]/.test(val), { message: 'Password must contain at least one number.' }),
});
```

- **Error Formatting:** Implement consistent error formatting in your application to present validation errors clearly to developers and users.

```typescript
---
try {
  userSchema.parse(data);
} catch (e) {
  if (e instanceof z.ZodError) {
    const formattedErrors = e.errors.map(err => ({
      field: err.path.join('.'),
      message: err.message,
    }));
    console.error('Validation Errors:', formattedErrors);
  }
}
```

- **Logging Detailed Errors:** Log comprehensive error details during development to facilitate easier troubleshooting.

```typescript
---
```

```
catch (e) {
  if (e instanceof z.ZodError) {
    console.error('Validation failed with errors:',
e.errors);
  } else {
    console.error('Unexpected error:', e);
  }
}
```

c. Isolating and Reproducing Issues

Isolating the problematic code segment and reproducing the issue in a controlled environment simplifies the debugging process. This approach allows you to focus on specific parts of your codebase without interference from other components.

Strategies:

- **Create Minimal Reproducible Examples:** Simplify your data and schemas to the smallest version that still produces the issue. This reduces complexity and makes it easier to identify the root cause.

```typescript
---
// Minimal schema example
const simpleSchema = z.object({
  name: z.string(),
});

// Minimal data example
const invalidData = { name: 123 };
```

- **Use Debugging Tools:** Utilize IDE debugging features to set breakpoints and inspect variables during schema parsing and validation.

```typescript
---
// Insert a breakpoint before validation
debugger;
userSchema.parse(data);
```

- **Incremental Testing:** Gradually build up your data and schema complexity, testing at each step to identify when and where the issue arises.

d. Employing Development Tools and Extensions

Various development tools and IDE extensions can enhance your debugging capabilities, making it easier to identify and resolve issues related to TypeScript and Zod.

Tools and Extensions:

- **TypeScript Language Server:** Provides real-time type checking and error highlighting within your code editor.
- **ESLint with TypeScript and Zod Plugins:** Enforces coding standards and catches potential issues before they escalate.
- **Zod Playground:** An online tool to interactively test and visualize Zod schemas.
- **Debugger Integration:** Use built-in debugging tools in editors like VSCode to step through code execution.

Example: Setting Up ESLint for TypeScript and Zod

```bash
---
npm install eslint @typescript-eslint/parser @typescript-eslint/eslint-plugin eslint-plugin-zod --save-dev
```

```javascript
---
// .eslintrc.js
module.exports = {
  parser: '@typescript-eslint/parser',
  plugins: ['@typescript-eslint', 'zod'],
  extends: [
    'eslint:recommended',
    'plugin:@typescript-eslint/recommended',
    // ...other extensions
  ],
  rules: {
    // Define your custom rules here
  },
};
```

Explanation:

- **ESLint Plugins:** Integrate TypeScript and Zod-specific linting rules to catch issues during development.
- **Custom Rules:** Customize linting rules to align with your project's coding standards and validation practices.

e. Reviewing and Refactoring Schemas Regularly

Regularly reviewing and refactoring your Zod schemas ensures that they remain aligned with evolving application requirements and maintain optimal performance.

Strategies:

- **Schema Audits:** Periodically audit your schemas to identify and remove redundant or outdated validation rules.
- **Refactor Complex Schemas:** Simplify overly complex schemas by breaking them down into smaller, reusable subschemas.

```typescript
---
// src/schemas/addressSchema.ts
import { z } from 'zod';

export const addressSchema = z.object({
  street: z.string().min(1, { message: 'Street is required.' }),
  city: z.string().min(1, { message: 'City is required.' }),
  zipCode: z.string().length(5, { message: 'Zip Code must be exactly 5 characters long.' }),
});

// src/schemas/userSchema.ts
import { z } from 'zod';
import { addressSchema } from './addressSchema';

export const userSchema = z.object({
  username: z.string().min(3, { message: 'Username must be at least 3 characters long.' }),
  email: z.string().email({ message: 'Please enter a valid email address.' }),
  password: z.string()
    .min(8, { message: 'Password must be at least 8 characters long.' })
    .refine((val) => /[A-Z]/.test(val), { message: 'Password must contain at least one uppercase letter.' })
    .refine((val) => /[0-9]/.test(val), { message: 'Password must contain at least one number.' }),
  address: addressSchema.optional(),
});
```

- **Performance Optimization:** Optimize schemas by removing unnecessary validations or leveraging Zod's features to enhance performance.

3. Practical Implementations and Code Examples

To illustrate effective debugging techniques, let's walk through some practical scenarios where common validation and typing issues occur. Each example includes a step-by-step approach to identify and resolve the issue.

a. Resolving Mismatched Types Between TypeScript and Zod Schemas

Scenario:

You have a TypeScript interface and a corresponding Zod schema. Despite appearing identical, a type mismatch causes validation failures.

Step 1: Define the TypeScript Interface and Zod Schema

```typescript
---
// src/types/user.ts
export interface User {
  username: string;
  email: string;
  age: number;
}
```
```typescript
---
// src/schemas/userSchema.ts
import { z } from 'zod';

export const userSchema = z.object({
  username: z.string(),
  email: z.string().email(),
  // age is defined as a string instead of number
  age: z.string(),
});
```

Issue:

The `age` field is defined as a `number` in the TypeScript interface but as a `string` in the Zod schema. This discrepancy causes validation failures when parsing user data.

Step 2: Write a Test Case to Identify the Issue

```typescript
// tests/schemas/userSchema.test.ts
import { userSchema } from '../../src/schemas/userSchema';
import { ZodError } from 'zod';

describe('User Schema Validation with Type Mismatch', () => {
  it('should fail validation when age is a number instead of
string', () => {
    const invalidUser = {
      username: 'john_doe',
      email: 'john@example.com',
      age: 30, // Should be a string as per schema
    };

    expect(() =>
userSchema.parse(invalidUser)).toThrow(ZodError);
  });
});
```

Step 3: Run the Test and Observe the Failure

```bash
npm test
```

Expected Output:

```csharp
 FAIL  tests/schemas/userSchema.test.ts
  User Schema Validation with Type Mismatch
    X should fail validation when age is a number instead of
string (5 ms)

  ● User Schema Validation with Type Mismatch › should fail
validation when age is a number instead of string

    ZodError: [
      {
        "code": "invalid_type",
        "expected": "string",
        "received": "number",
        "path": ["age"],
        "message": "Expected string, received number"
      }
    ]
```

Step 4: Resolve the Type Mismatch

Update the Zod schema to align with the TypeScript interface.

```typescript
---
// src/schemas/userSchema.ts
import { z } from 'zod';

export const userSchema = z.object({
  username: z.string(),
  email: z.string().email(),
  age: z.number(), // Corrected to number
});
```

Step 5: Re-run the Tests to Confirm Resolution

```bash
---
npm test
```

Expected Output:

```
 PASS  tests/schemas/userSchema.test.ts
  User Schema Validation with Type Mismatch
    ✓ should fail validation when age is a number instead of
string (3 ms)

Test Suites: 1 passed, 1 total
Tests:       1 passed, 1 total
Snapshots:   0 total
Time:        1.234 s
```

Explanation:

By aligning the age field type in the Zod schema with the TypeScript interface, the validation now accurately reflects the intended data structure, and the test passes as expected.

b. Handling Missing Required Fields

Scenario:

A user object is missing a required field, causing validation to fail. You need to identify and address this issue.

Step 1: Define the Zod Schema with a Required Field

241

```typescript
---
// src/schemas/userSchema.ts
import { z } from 'zod';

export const userSchema = z.object({
  username: z.string().min(3, { message: 'Username must be at
least 3 characters long.' }),
  email: z.string().email({ message: 'Please enter a valid
email address.' }),
  password: z.string()
    .min(8, { message: 'Password must be at least 8
characters long.' })
    .refine((val) => /[A-Z]/.test(val), { message: 'Password
must contain at least one uppercase letter.' })
    .refine((val) => /[0-9]/.test(val), { message: 'Password
must contain at least one number.' }),
});
```

Step 2: Write a Test Case for Missing Field

```typescript
---
// tests/schemas/userSchema.test.ts
import { userSchema } from '../../src/schemas/userSchema';
import { ZodError } from 'zod';

describe('User Schema Validation for Missing Fields', () => {
  it('should fail validation when password is missing', () =>
{
    const invalidUser = {
      username: 'john_doe',
      email: 'john@example.com',
      // password is missing
    };

    expect(() =>
userSchema.parse(invalidUser)).toThrow(ZodError);
  });
});
```

Step 3: Run the Test and Analyze the Failure

```bash
---
npm test
```

Step 4: Update the Data Object to Include the Missing Field

Modify the application logic to ensure that all required fields are provided.

```typescript
const validUser = {
  username: 'john_doe',
  email: 'john@example.com',
  password: 'SecurePass1',
};
```

Step 5: Re-run the Test to Confirm the Fix

```bash
npm test
```

c. Addressing Overly Permissive Schemas

Scenario:

Your Zod schema allows additional unexpected fields, potentially leading to data inconsistencies or security vulnerabilities.

Step 1: Define an Overly Permissive Zod Schema

```typescript
// src/schemas/userSchema.ts
import { z } from 'zod';

export const userSchema = z.object({
  username: z.string(),
  email: z.string().email(),
  password: z.string(),
});
```

Issue:

The current schema does not prevent additional unknown fields from being present in the validated data.

Step 2: Write a Test Case to Detect Extra Fields

```typescript
// tests/schemas/userSchema.test.ts
```

```
import { userSchema } from '../../src/schemas/userSchema';
import { ZodError } from 'zod';

describe('User Schema Validation for Extra Fields', () => {
  it('should allow additional fields when not using
.strict()', () => {
    const validUser = {
      username: 'john_doe',
      email: 'john@example.com',
      password: 'SecurePass1',
      age: 30, // Extra field not defined in schema
    };

    expect(() => userSchema.parse(validUser)).not.toThrow();
  });
});
```

Step 3: Run the Test and Observe the Behavior

```bash
npm test
```

Step 4: Refine the Zod Schema to Reject Extra Fields

Use Zod's `.strict()` method to disallow unknown fields.

```typescript
// src/schemas/userSchema.ts
import { z } from 'zod';

export const userSchema = z.object({
  username: z.string(),
  email: z.string().email(),
  password: z.string(),
}).strict();
```

Step 5: Update the Test Case to Reflect the Strict Schema

```typescript
// tests/schemas/userSchema.test.ts
describe('User Schema Validation for Extra Fields', () => {
  it('should fail validation when additional fields are
present with .strict()', () => {
    const invalidUser = {
      username: 'john_doe',
      email: 'john@example.com',
```

```
    password: 'SecurePass1',
    age: 30, // Extra field
  };

  expect(() =>
userSchema.parse(invalidUser)).toThrow(ZodError);
  });
});
```

Step 6: Re-run the Tests to Confirm the Fix

```bash
---
npm test
```

d. Managing Complex Conditional Validations

Scenario:

Your schema includes conditional validations where the validation of one field depends on the value of another. Implementing and debugging such logic can be challenging.

Step 1: Define a Zod Schema with Conditional Validation

```typescript
---
// src/schemas/userSchema.ts
import { z } from 'zod';

export const userSchema = z.object({
  isAdmin: z.boolean(),
  adminCode: z.string().optional(),
}).refine((data) => {
  if (data.isAdmin) {
    return data.adminCode !== undefined &&
data.adminCode.length > 0;
  }
  return true;
}, {
  message: 'adminCode is required when isAdmin is true.',
  path: ['adminCode'],
});
```

Explanation:

- **isAdmin:** A boolean indicating if the user has admin privileges.

245

- **adminCode:** An optional string that becomes required if `isAdmin` is true.
- **refine:** Adds a conditional rule to enforce the presence of `adminCode` based on the value of `isAdmin`.

Step 2: Write Test Cases for Conditional Validation

```typescript
---
// tests/schemas/userSchema.test.ts
import { userSchema } from '../../src/schemas/userSchema';
import { ZodError } from 'zod';

describe('User Schema Conditional Validation', () => {
  it('should validate successfully when isAdmin is false and
adminCode is missing', () => {
    const validUser = {
      isAdmin: false,
      // adminCode is optional here
    };

    expect(() => userSchema.parse(validUser)).not.toThrow();
  });

  it('should validate successfully when isAdmin is true and
adminCode is provided', () => {
    const validUser = {
      isAdmin: true,
      adminCode: 'ADMIN123',
    };

    expect(() => userSchema.parse(validUser)).not.toThrow();
  });

  it('should fail validation when isAdmin is true but
adminCode is missing', () => {
    const invalidUser = {
      isAdmin: true,
      // adminCode is missing
    };

    expect(() =>
userSchema.parse(invalidUser)).toThrow(ZodError);
  });

  it('should fail validation when isAdmin is true but
adminCode is empty', () => {
    const invalidUser = {
      isAdmin: true,
```

```
      adminCode: '',
    };

    expect(() =>
userSchema.parse(invalidUser)).toThrow(ZodError);
  });
});
```

Step 3: Run the Tests and Analyze Results

```bash
---
npm test
```

e. Addressing Recursive Schema Issues

Scenario:

Your application requires validating nested or recursive data structures, such as trees or linked lists. Improper handling can lead to infinite loops or stack overflows.

Step 1: Define a Recursive Zod Schema Using `z.lazy`

```typescript
---
// src/schemas/categorySchema.ts
import { z } from 'zod';

export const categorySchema: z.ZodType<any> = z.lazy(() =>
z.object({
  name: z.string(),
  subcategories: z.array(categorySchema).optional(),
}));
```

Explanation:

- **z.lazy:** Allows the schema to reference itself recursively, enabling the validation of nested structures.
- **subcategories:** An optional array of categorySchema, allowing for recursive nesting of categories.

Step 2: Write Test Cases for Recursive Schemas

```typescript
---
```

```typescript
// tests/schemas/categorySchema.test.ts
import { categorySchema } from
'../../src/schemas/categorySchema';
import { ZodError } from 'zod';

describe('Category Schema Validation with Recursion', () => {
  it('should validate a category without subcategories', ()
=> {
    const validCategory = {
      name: 'Electronics',
    };

    expect(() =>
categorySchema.parse(validCategory)).not.toThrow();
  });

  it('should validate a category with subcategories', () => {
    const validCategory = {
      name: 'Electronics',
      subcategories: [
        { name: 'Computers' },
        {
          name: 'Mobile Phones',
          subcategories: [
            { name: 'Smartphones' },
            { name: 'Feature Phones' },
          ],
        },
      ],
    };

    expect(() =>
categorySchema.parse(validCategory)).not.toThrow();
  });

  it('should fail validation when subcategory name is
missing', () => {
    const invalidCategory = {
      name: 'Electronics',
      subcategories: [
        { name: 'Computers' },
        {
          // name is missing
          subcategories: [
            { name: 'Smartphones' },
          ],
        },
      ],
    };
```

```
    expect(() =>
categorySchema.parse(invalidCategory)).toThrow(ZodError);
  });

  it('should handle deep recursive structures without stack
overflow', () => {
    const deepCategory = {
      name: 'Level 1',
      subcategories: {
        name: 'Level 2',
        subcategories: {
          name: 'Level 3',
          subcategories: {
            name: 'Level 4',
            // Continue nesting as needed
          },
        },
      },
    };

    expect(() =>
categorySchema.parse(deepCategory)).toThrow(ZodError);
  });
});
```

Explanation:

- **Valid Cases:** Tests both shallow and nested categories to ensure proper validation.
- **Invalid Cases:** Checks for missing required fields within nested subcategories.
- **Deep Recursion Handling:** Attempts to parse an excessively deep recursive structure to ensure that the schema handles it gracefully without causing stack overflows.

Step 3: Run the Tests and Address Issues

```bash
---
npm test
```

Note:

Handling deeply nested or infinitely recursive structures may require additional schema constraints or custom validation logic to prevent performance issues or stack overflows.

4. Best Practices for Debugging Validation and Typing Issues

Adopting best practices ensures that debugging remains efficient and that similar issues are less likely to recur in the future. The following guidelines provide a framework for maintaining clean and reliable TypeScript and Zod integrations.

a. Centralize Schema Definitions

- **Single Source of Truth:** Maintain all Zod schemas in a dedicated `schemas` directory. This centralization promotes reuse and ensures consistency across different parts of the application.

```bash
bash
---
project-root/
├── src/
│   ├── schemas/
│   │   └── userSchema.ts
│   └── ...
├── tests/
│   └── schemas/
│       └── userSchema.test.ts
└── ...
```

- **Modular Schemas:** Break down complex schemas into smaller, reusable subschemas. This modular approach simplifies testing and enhances maintainability.

```typescript
typescript
---
// src/schemas/addressSchema.ts
import { z } from 'zod';

export const addressSchema = z.object({
  street: z.string().min(1, { message: 'Street is
required.' }),
  city: z.string().min(1, { message: 'City is
required.' }),
  zipCode: z.string().length(5, { message: 'Zip Code
must be exactly 5 characters long.' }),
});
```

b. Maintain Type Synchronization

- **Use `z.infer`:** Derive TypeScript types from Zod schemas to ensure that types and validation logic remain synchronized.

```typescript
---
import { z } from 'zod';
import { userSchema } from './userSchema';

type User = z.infer<typeof userSchema>;
```

- **Avoid Manual Type Definitions:** Refrain from manually defining TypeScript interfaces or types that duplicate the structure of Zod schemas. This reduces the risk of discrepancies and simplifies maintenance.

c. Write Comprehensive and Focused Tests

- **Cover All Scenarios:** Ensure that your tests cover all possible data scenarios, including valid inputs, invalid inputs, edge cases, and boundary conditions.
- **Isolate Tests:** Focus each test case on a specific aspect of the schema, avoiding overlapping or redundant tests.
- **Descriptive Test Names:** Use clear and descriptive names for your test cases to convey their purpose and facilitate easier debugging.

```typescript
---
it('should fail validation when email is invalid', ()
=> { /* ... */ });
```

d. Utilize Debugging Tools Effectively

- **Integrated Debugging:** Use IDE debugging features to step through schema parsing and validation processes, inspecting variable states and identifying issues in real-time.
- **Logging:** Implement detailed logging within your validation logic to capture error states and facilitate post-mortem analysis.

```typescript
---
try {
  userSchema.parse(data);
} catch (e) {
  if (e instanceof z.ZodError) {
    console.error('Validation Errors:', e.errors);
```

```
    }
  }
```

- **Snapshot Testing:** Leverage Jest's snapshot testing for Zod schemas to monitor changes in validated data structures over time.

e. Regularly Review and Refactor Schemas

- **Schema Audits:** Periodically review your Zod schemas to ensure they align with evolving application requirements and remove any outdated or redundant validations.
- **Simplify Complex Logic:** Break down intricate validation rules into smaller, manageable components to enhance readability and reduce the likelihood of errors.

```typescript
---
// src/schemas/userSchema.ts
import { z } from 'zod';
import { addressSchema } from './addressSchema';

export const userSchema = z.object({
  username: z.string().min(3, { message: 'Username must be at
least 3 characters long.' }),
  email: z.string().email({ message: 'Please enter a valid
email address.' }),
  password: z.string()
    .min(8, { message: 'Password must be at least 8
characters long.' })
    .refine((val) => /[A-Z]/.test(val), { message: 'Password
must contain at least one uppercase letter.' })
    .refine((val) => /[0-9]/.test(val), { message: 'Password
must contain at least one number.' }),
  address: addressSchema.optional(),
});
```

f. Implement Automated Testing Pipelines

- **Continuous Integration (CI):** Integrate your Jest tests into a CI pipeline to automate test execution on code commits and pull requests. This practice ensures that validation logic is consistently enforced and that new changes do not introduce regressions.

Example: GitHub Actions Workflow

```yaml
```

```
---
# .github/workflows/ci.yml
name: CI

on:
  push:
    branches: [ main ]
  pull_request:
    branches: [ main ]

jobs:
  build-and-test:
    runs-on: ubuntu-latest

    steps:
      - uses: actions/checkout@v2

      - name: Set up Node.js
        uses: actions/setup-node@v2
        with:
          node-version: '14'

      - name: Install Dependencies
        run: npm install

      - name: Run Tests
        run: npm test
```

- **Automated Test Coverage Checks:** Configure your CI pipeline to enforce minimum test coverage thresholds, ensuring that critical parts of your schemas are always tested.

Example: Enforce Coverage Thresholds in `jest.config.js`

```javascript
---
// jest.config.js
module.exports = {
  preset: 'ts-jest',
  testEnvironment: 'node',
  collectCoverage: true,
  coverageThreshold: {
    global: {
      branches: 90,
      functions: 90,
      lines: 90,
      statements: 90,
    },
  },
```

```
  // ...other settings
};
```

Explanation:

- ○ **coverageThreshold:** Specifies minimum coverage percentages that must be met. Tests will fail if coverage falls below these thresholds.

g. Document Your Validation Logic

- **Inline Comments:** Add comments within your Zod schemas to explain complex validation rules or the reasoning behind certain constraints. This practice aids in understanding and maintaining schemas.

```typescript
---
const userSchema = z.object({
  // Username must be unique and at least 3 characters long
  username: z.string().min(3, { message: 'Username must be at
least 3 characters long.' }),
  // Email must follow a valid email format
  email: z.string().email({ message: 'Please enter a valid
email address.' }),
  // Password requirements
  password: z.string()
    .min(8, { message: 'Password must be at least 8
characters long.' })
    .refine((val) => /[A-Z]/.test(val), { message: 'Password
must contain at least one uppercase letter.' })
    .refine((val) => /[0-9]/.test(val), { message: 'Password
must contain at least one number.' }),
});
```

- **Schema Documentation:** Maintain separate documentation that outlines the structure and validation rules of each schema. This resource serves as a reference for developers and stakeholders, ensuring clarity and alignment across the team.

---

5. Summary of Debugging Techniques

To effectively debug validation and typing issues in TypeScript and Zod integrations, employ a combination of the following techniques:

1. **Leverage TypeScript's Type Checking:** Use `z.infer` and strict TypeScript settings to ensure type consistency between schemas and interfaces.
2. **Utilize Descriptive Error Messages:** Customize and format error messages to provide clear insights into validation failures.
3. **Isolate and Reproduce Issues:** Create minimal, reproducible examples to pinpoint the root cause of problems.
4. **Employ Development Tools and Extensions:** Use IDE features, linting tools, and online playgrounds to enhance your debugging capabilities.
5. **Regularly Review and Refactor Schemas:** Keep your schemas clean, simple, and aligned with application requirements through periodic audits and refactoring.
6. **Implement Automated Testing Pipelines:** Integrate Jest tests into CI workflows to enforce validation logic and prevent regressions.
7. **Document Your Validation Logic:** Provide clear documentation and inline comments to facilitate understanding and maintenance of schemas.

By systematically applying these strategies, you can efficiently identify and resolve validation and typing issues, ensuring that your TypeScript and Zod-powered applications remain robust and reliable.

Conclusion

Debugging validation and typing issues is an essential skill for developers working with TypeScript and Zod. By understanding common pitfalls, adopting effective debugging strategies, and adhering to best practices, you can maintain high standards of data integrity and application reliability. This section provided a comprehensive overview of typical validation and typing challenges, detailed methods for addressing them, and practical implementations to reinforce your understanding. Embracing these techniques will empower you to build more resilient and maintainable applications, leveraging the full potential of TypeScript and Zod.

Chapter 8: Scaling Type-Safe Applications

Building scalable, type-safe applications requires thoughtful organization, strategic planning, and adherence to best practices. As your application grows in complexity and size, maintaining type safety and data integrity becomes increasingly challenging. Leveraging TypeScript and Zod effectively can help manage this complexity, ensuring that your application remains robust, maintainable, and resilient. This chapter explores essential strategies for scaling type-safe applications, focusing on organizing and modularizing schemas, implementing schema versioning for backward compatibility, and adopting scalable practices for large-scale projects.

8.1 Organizing and Modularizing Schemas

As applications grow in complexity, managing and maintaining data validation logic becomes increasingly challenging. Organizing and modularizing your schemas effectively is essential for ensuring scalability, maintainability, and consistency across your codebase. Leveraging TypeScript and Zod together provides a powerful combination for defining, organizing, and reusing schemas efficiently. This section delves into strategies for organizing and modularizing Zod schemas in TypeScript projects, offering practical guidance and step-by-step implementations to streamline your development workflow.

1. Importance of Organizing and Modularizing Schemas

Proper organization and modularization of schemas offer several key benefits:

- **Maintainability:** Well-structured schemas are easier to manage, update, and debug.
- **Reusability:** Modular schemas promote reuse across different parts of the application, reducing duplication.
- **Scalability:** Organized schemas can scale with the application's growth, accommodating new features and requirements seamlessly.
- **Clarity:** Clear separation of concerns enhances code readability and developer collaboration.

By adopting effective organizational strategies, developers can ensure that their validation logic remains robust and adaptable as the application evolves.

2. Structuring the Project Directory

A logical and consistent directory structure is foundational to organizing schemas effectively. Below is a recommended project structure that separates schemas, types, and other related components:

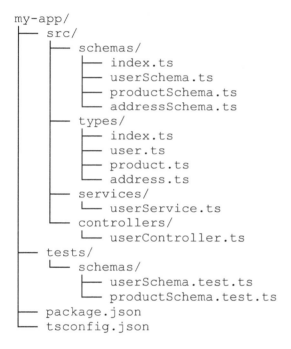

```
my-app/
├── src/
│   ├── schemas/
│   │   ├── index.ts
│   │   ├── userSchema.ts
│   │   ├── productSchema.ts
│   │   └── addressSchema.ts
│   ├── types/
│   │   ├── index.ts
│   │   ├── user.ts
│   │   ├── product.ts
│   │   └── address.ts
│   ├── services/
│   │   └── userService.ts
│   └── controllers/
│       └── userController.ts
├── tests/
│   └── schemas/
│       ├── userSchema.test.ts
│       └── productSchema.test.ts
├── package.json
└── tsconfig.json
```

Explanation:

- **src/schemas/**: Contains all Zod schema definitions, organized by feature or domain.
- **src/types/**: Houses TypeScript type definitions inferred from Zod schemas, ensuring type consistency.
- **src/services/** and **src/controllers/**: Represent application logic layers that utilize schemas and types.
- **tests/schemas/**: Contains test files corresponding to each schema, facilitating organized testing.

3. Creating Reusable Subschemas

Reusability is a cornerstone of modular schema design. By defining subschemas for common data structures, you can avoid duplication and ensure consistency across your application.

Step 1: Define Base Subschemas

Identify common structures used across multiple schemas and define them as separate subschemas.

```typescript
---
// src/schemas/addressSchema.ts
import { z } from 'zod';

export const addressSchema = z.object({
  street: z.string().min(1, { message: 'Street is required.' }),
  city: z.string().min(1, { message: 'City is required.' }),
  zipCode: z.string().length(5, { message: 'Zip Code must be exactly 5 characters long.' }),
});
```

Explanation:

*   **addressSchema**: Defines a standard address structure with validation rules for each field.

Step 2: Utilize Subschemas in Primary Schemas

Incorporate subschemas into primary schemas using Zod's `.merge()` or `.extend()` methods.

```typescript
---
// src/schemas/userSchema.ts
import { z } from 'zod';
import { addressSchema } from './addressSchema';

export const userSchema = z.object({
  username: z.string().min(3, { message: 'Username must be at least 3 characters long.' }),
```

```
  email: z.string().email({ message: 'Please enter a valid
email address.' }),
  password: z.string()
    .min(8, { message: 'Password must be at least 8
characters long.' })
    .refine((val) => /[A-Z]/.test(val), { message: 'Password
must contain at least one uppercase letter.' })
    .refine((val) => /[0-9]/.test(val), { message: 'Password
must contain at least one number.' }),
}).merge(addressSchema.optional());
```

Explanation:

- **merge(addressSchema.optional())**: Integrates the
  addressSchema as an optional field within the userSchema, allowing
  users to include address information if available.

---

4. Centralizing Schema Exports

Managing multiple schema files can become cumbersome. Centralizing
exports simplifies imports and enhances maintainability.

Step 1: Create an **index.ts** File in the Schemas Directory

```typescript
---
// src/schemas/index.ts
export { userSchema } from './userSchema';
export { productSchema } from './productSchema';
export { addressSchema } from './addressSchema';
```

Explanation:

- **Central Export Point:** Allows other parts of the application to
  import schemas from a single location, reducing import complexity.

Step 2: Import Schemas from the Centralized Export

```typescript
---
// src/services/userService.ts
import { userSchema } from '../schemas';

export const createUser = (data: unknown) => {
```

259

```
  const parsedData = userSchema.parse(data);
  // Proceed with user creation logic
};
```

Explanation:

- **Simplified Imports:** Import schemas directly from `'../schemas'` instead of individual schema files, enhancing code readability.

---

5. Inferring TypeScript Types from Zod Schemas

Maintaining synchronization between schemas and TypeScript types is crucial for type safety. Zod's `z.infer` facilitates automatic type inference from schemas.

Step 1: Define TypeScript Types Using `z.infer`

```typescript
---
// src/types/user.ts
import { z } from 'zod';
import { userSchema } from '../schemas';

export type User = z.infer<typeof userSchema>;
```

Explanation:

- **User Type:** Automatically derives the TypeScript type from the `userSchema`, ensuring consistency between validation rules and type definitions.

Step 2: Utilize Inferred Types in Application Logic

```typescript
---
// src/controllers/userController.ts
import { User } from '../types';

export const handleUserCreation = (userData: User) => {
  // User data is guaranteed to conform to the User type
  // Proceed with controller logic
};
```

Explanation:

- **Type Safety:** Ensures that `handleUserCreation` receives data that adheres to the `User` type, preventing type-related errors.

---

6. Implementing Schema Composition

Schema composition allows for building complex schemas from simpler, reusable components. Zod provides methods like `.merge()` and `.extend()` to facilitate schema composition.

Step 1: Extend Existing Schemas

```typescript
---
// src/schemas/adminUserSchema.ts
import { z } from 'zod';
import { userSchema } from './userSchema';

export const adminUserSchema = userSchema.extend({
  role: z.enum(['admin', 'superadmin'], { required_error:
'Role is required.' }),
  permissions: z.array(z.string()).optional(),
});
```

Explanation:

- **`adminUserSchema`**: Extends the `userSchema` by adding `role` and `permissions` fields specific to admin users.

Step 2: Merge Multiple Schemas

```typescript
---
// src/schemas/productSchema.ts
import { z } from 'zod';
import { addressSchema } from './addressSchema';

export const productSchema = z.object({
  productName: z.string().min(1, { message: 'Product name is
required.' }),
  price: z.number().positive({ message: 'Price must be a
positive number.' }),
  description: z.string().optional(),
```

```
})).merge(addressSchema.optional());
```

Explanation:

- **productSchema**: Incorporates the `addressSchema` as an optional field, allowing products to have an associated address if applicable.

---

7. Best Practices for Organizing and Modularizing Schemas

Adhering to best practices ensures that your schema organization remains effective and scalable as the application evolves.

a. Separation of Concerns

- **Domain-Specific Schemas:** Group schemas based on application domains or features (e.g., user management, product catalog) to maintain clear boundaries and reduce interdependencies.
- **Utility Schemas:** Create utility schemas for common patterns or validations (e.g., address structures, pagination parameters) to promote reuse.

b. Consistent Naming Conventions

- **Descriptive Names:** Use clear and descriptive names for schema files and exports to enhance readability and ease of discovery.

```typescript
---
// Good Naming
export const userSchema = z.object({ /* ... */ });

// Avoid Ambiguous Names
export const schema1 = z.object({ /* ... */ });
```

c. Documentation and Comments

- **Inline Documentation:** Add comments within schema definitions to explain complex validation logic or business rules.

```typescript
---
const userSchema = z.object({
```

```
  // Username must be unique and at least 3 characters long
  username: z.string().min(3, { message: 'Username must be at
least 3 characters long.' }),
  // Email must follow a valid email format
  email: z.string().email({ message: 'Please enter a valid
email address.' }),
  // Password requirements
  password: z.string()
    .min(8, { message: 'Password must be at least 8
characters long.' })
    .refine((val) => /[A-Z]/.test(val), { message: 'Password
must contain at least one uppercase letter.' })
    .refine((val) => /[0-9]/.test(val), { message: 'Password
must contain at least one number.' }),
});
```

- **External Documentation:** Maintain comprehensive documentation that outlines the purpose and structure of each schema, facilitating easier onboarding and collaboration.

d. Avoiding Redundancy

- **DRY Principle (Don't Repeat Yourself):** Reuse subschemas and utility schemas across different primary schemas to minimize duplication and ensure consistency.
- **Schema Inheritance:** Use Zod's composition features to build upon existing schemas rather than redefining similar structures.

e. Testing Each Module Independently

- **Isolated Testing:** Write separate test files for each schema module to ensure that validations are functioning correctly without interference from other modules.

```typescript
---
// tests/schemas/userSchema.test.ts
// tests/schemas/productSchema.test.ts
```

f. Leveraging TypeScript Features

- **Type Inference:** Use `z.infer` to derive TypeScript types from schemas, ensuring that types remain synchronized with validation logic.
- **Strict Typing:** Enable strict TypeScript compiler options to catch type-related issues early in the development process.

8. Conclusion

Organizing and modularizing schemas is a critical practice for building scalable and maintainable type-safe applications. By adopting a structured directory layout, creating reusable subschemas, centralizing schema exports, and leveraging TypeScript's type inference, developers can ensure that their validation logic remains consistent, efficient, and adaptable to evolving application needs. Implementing these strategies not only enhances code readability and maintainability but also fosters a collaborative and efficient development environment. As your application grows, these organizational practices will provide a solid foundation for managing complexity and ensuring the continued robustness of your data validation mechanisms.

8.2 Schema Versioning for Backward Compatibility

As applications evolve, so do their data structures and validation requirements. Managing changes to your schemas without disrupting existing functionalities is crucial, especially in environments where multiple clients or services interact with your APIs. Schema versioning ensures that updates can be introduced smoothly, maintaining backward compatibility and minimizing the risk of breaking existing integrations. This section provides a comprehensive guide on implementing schema versioning using TypeScript and Zod, complete with detailed explanations and step-by-step code examples.

1. Understanding Schema Versioning and Backward Compatibility

Schema Versioning refers to the practice of maintaining multiple versions of data schemas to accommodate changes over time. **Backward Compatibility** ensures that newer versions of schemas remain compatible with older clients or services that depend on previous schema versions.

Why Schema Versioning Matters:

- **Continuous Development:** As features are added or modified, schemas need to adapt without disrupting existing functionalities.

- **Client Diversity:** Different clients may rely on different schema versions, necessitating support for multiple versions concurrently.
- **Data Integrity:** Ensures that data remains consistent and valid across various schema iterations.

Key Objectives:

- **Minimize Disruptions:** Allow existing clients to continue functioning without immediate changes.
- **Facilitate Smooth Upgrades:** Enable gradual migration to newer schema versions.
- **Maintain Data Consistency:** Ensure that data adheres to the correct schema version, preventing validation errors.

---

2. Strategies for Schema Versioning

Implementing schema versioning involves several strategies to manage and maintain multiple schema versions effectively:

1. **Namespace-Based Versioning:**
   - Use distinct namespaces or directories for each schema version.
   - Example: `/schemas/v1/userSchema.ts`, `/schemas/v2/userSchema.ts`
2. **Endpoint-Based Versioning:**
   - Incorporate version information into API endpoints.
   - Example: `POST /api/v1/users`, `POST /api/v2/users`
3. **Header-Based Versioning:**
   - Pass version information through HTTP headers.
   - Example: `X-API-Version: 1`
4. **Content Negotiation:**
   - Utilize the `Accept` header to specify desired schema versions.
   - Example: `Accept: application/vnd.myapp.v1+json`
5. **Schema Composition and Inheritance:**
   - Build new schema versions by extending or merging existing schemas to retain previous validations while introducing new ones.

---

3. Implementing Schema Versioning with TypeScript and Zod

This section demonstrates how to implement schema versioning using TypeScript and Zod through a namespace-based approach. We'll walk through creating versioned schemas, organizing them effectively, and managing validations across different schema versions.

Step 1: Setting Up the Project Structure

Organize your project to accommodate multiple schema versions. Below is a recommended directory structure:

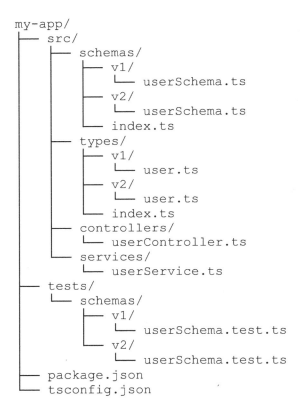

```
my-app/
├── src/
│   ├── schemas/
│   │   ├── v1/
│   │   │   └── userSchema.ts
│   │   ├── v2/
│   │   │   └── userSchema.ts
│   │   └── index.ts
│   ├── types/
│   │   ├── v1/
│   │   │   └── user.ts
│   │   ├── v2/
│   │   │   └── user.ts
│   │   └── index.ts
│   ├── controllers/
│   │   └── userController.ts
│   └── services/
│       └── userService.ts
├── tests/
│   └── schemas/
│       ├── v1/
│       │   └── userSchema.test.ts
│       └── v2/
│           └── userSchema.test.ts
├── package.json
└── tsconfig.json
```

Explanation:

- **src/schemas/**: Contains versioned schema directories (v1, v2, etc.), each housing their respective schema definitions.
- **src/types/**: Holds TypeScript type definitions inferred from each schema version.
- **src/controllers/ & src/services/**: Represent application logic layers that interact with different schema versions.

- **tests/schemas/**: Contains test files for each schema version to ensure validation integrity.

Step 2: Defining Versioned Schemas

Create distinct schema definitions for each version. Let's define userSchema for versions v1 and v2.

Version 1: Basic User Schema

```typescript
---
// src/schemas/v1/userSchema.ts
import { z } from 'zod';

export const userSchemaV1 = z.object({
  username: z.string().min(3, { message: 'Username must be at
least 3 characters long.' }),
  email: z.string().email({ message: 'Please enter a valid
email address.' }),
  password: z.string()
    .min(8, { message: 'Password must be at least 8
characters long.' })
    .refine((val) => /[A-Z]/.test(val), { message: 'Password
must contain at least one uppercase letter.' })
    .refine((val) => /[0-9]/.test(val), { message: 'Password
must contain at least one number.' }),
});
```

Version 2: Enhanced User Schema with Address

```typescript
---
// src/schemas/v2/userSchema.ts
import { z } from 'zod';
import { addressSchemaV2 } from './addressSchema';

export const userSchemaV2 = z.object({
  username: z.string().min(3, { message: 'Username must be at
least 3 characters long.' }),
  email: z.string().email({ message: 'Please enter a valid
email address.' }),
  password: z.string()
    .min(8, { message: 'Password must be at least 8
characters long.' })
    .refine((val) => /[A-Z]/.test(val), { message: 'Password
must contain at least one uppercase letter.' })
```

```typescript
---
    .refine((val) => /[0-9]/.test(val), { message: 'Password
must contain at least one number.' }),
  address: addressSchemaV2.optional(),
});
```

Address Schema for Version 2:

```typescript
---
// src/schemas/v2/addressSchema.ts
import { z } from 'zod';

export const addressSchemaV2 = z.object({
  street: z.string().min(1, { message: 'Street is required.'
}),
  city: z.string().min(1, { message: 'City is required.' }),
  zipCode: z.string().length(5, { message: 'Zip Code must be
exactly 5 characters long.' }),
  country: z.string().min(2, { message: 'Country must be at
least 2 characters long.' }),
});
```

Explanation:

- **userSchemaV1**: Defines the initial user schema with basic fields.
- **userSchemaV2**: Extends v1 by adding an optional address field using addressSchemaV2.
- **addressSchemaV2**: Introduces additional validation for the country field.

Step 3: Inferring TypeScript Types from Schemas

Use Zod's z.infer to derive TypeScript types directly from each schema version, ensuring type consistency.

Type Definitions for Version 1:

```typescript
---
// src/types/v1/user.ts
import { z } from 'zod';
import { userSchemaV1 } from '../../schemas/v1/userSchema';

export type UserV1 = z.infer<typeof userSchemaV1>;
```

Type Definitions for Version 2:

```typescript
---
// src/types/v2/user.ts
import { z } from 'zod';
import { userSchemaV2 } from '../../schemas/v2/userSchema';

export type UserV2 = z.infer<typeof userSchemaV2>;
```

Explanation:

- **UserV1**: Represents the TypeScript type inferred from userSchemaV1.
- **UserV2**: Represents the TypeScript type inferred from userSchemaV2.

Step 4: Centralizing Schema Exports

Create an index.ts file to centralize exports for easier imports across the application.

```typescript
---
// src/schemas/index.ts
export * from './v1/userSchema';
export * from './v2/userSchema';
export * from './v2/addressSchema';
```

Explanation:

- **Central Export Point:** Facilitates importing any schema version from a single location, enhancing code readability and maintainability.

Step 5: Integrating Schema Versions in Application Logic

When implementing API endpoints or services, specify which schema version to use based on the client's requirements or the endpoint's version.

Example: User Controller Handling Multiple Schema Versions

```typescript
---
// src/controllers/userController.ts
import { Request, Response } from 'express';
import { userSchemaV1 } from '../schemas/v1/userSchema';
```

```
import { userSchemaV2 } from '../schemas/v2/userSchema';
import { UserV1 } from '../types/v1/user';
import { UserV2 } from '../types/v2/user';

export const createUser = (req: Request, res: Response) => {
  const apiVersion = req.headers['x-api-version'] || 'v1';

  try {
    if (apiVersion === 'v2') {
      const user: UserV2 = userSchemaV2.parse(req.body);
      // Proceed with v2 user creation logic
      res.status(201).json({ message: 'User created
successfully (v2)', user });
    } else {
      const user: UserV1 = userSchemaV1.parse(req.body);
      // Proceed with v1 user creation logic
      res.status(201).json({ message: 'User created
successfully (v1)', user });
    }
  } catch (error) {
    if (error instanceof z.ZodError) {
      res.status(400).json({ errors: error.errors });
    } else {
      res.status(500).json({ message: 'Internal Server Error'
});
    }
  }
};
```

Explanation:

- **Version Detection:** Determines the API version based on the `x-api-version` header.
- **Schema Parsing:** Parses the request body using the appropriate schema version.
- **Type Safety:** Ensures that the parsed data conforms to the inferred TypeScript type for the specified schema version.
- **Error Handling:** Responds with detailed validation errors if parsing fails.

Step 6: Organizing Tests for Each Schema Version

Maintain separate test files for each schema version to ensure that validations are correctly enforced and that changes in one version do not affect others.

Example: Testing Version 1 User Schema

```typescript
---
// tests/schemas/v1/userSchema.test.ts
import { userSchemaV1 } from
'../../../src/schemas/v1/userSchema';
import { ZodError } from 'zod';

describe('User Schema V1 Validation', () => {
  it('should validate a correct user object', () => {
    const validUser = {
      username: 'john_doe',
      email: 'john@example.com',
      password: 'SecurePass1',
    };

    expect(() =>
userSchemaV1.parse(validUser)).not.toThrow();
  });

  it('should fail validation when username is too short', ()
=> {
    const invalidUser = {
      username: 'jd',
      email: 'john@example.com',
      password: 'SecurePass1',
    };

    expect(() =>
userSchemaV1.parse(invalidUser)).toThrow(ZodError);
  });

  // Additional test cases...
});
```

Example: Testing Version 2 User Schema

```typescript
---
// tests/schemas/v2/userSchema.test.ts
import { userSchemaV2 } from
'../../../src/schemas/v2/userSchema';
import { ZodError } from 'zod';

describe('User Schema V2 Validation', () => {
  it('should validate a correct user object with address', ()
=> {
    const validUser = {
      username: 'jane_doe',
      email: 'jane@example.com',
      password: 'SecurePass1',
```

271

```
      address: {
        street: '123 Main St',
        city: 'Anytown',
        zipCode: '12345',
        country: 'USA',
      },
    };

    expect(() =>
userSchemaV2.parse(validUser)).not.toThrow();
  });

  it('should fail validation when country is missing in
address', () => {
    const invalidUser = {
      username: 'jane_doe',
      email: 'jane@example.com',
      password: 'SecurePass1',
      address: {
        street: '123 Main St',
        city: 'Anytown',
        zipCode: '12345',
        // country is missing
      },
    };

    expect(() =>
userSchemaV2.parse(invalidUser)).toThrow(ZodError);
  });

  // Additional test cases...
});
```

Explanation:

- **Version-Specific Tests:** Each test suite focuses on validating a specific schema version, ensuring that changes in one do not inadvertently affect others.
- **Comprehensive Coverage:** Includes both positive and negative test cases to validate correct behavior and enforce constraints.

---

4. Managing Data Transformations Between Schema Versions

When transitioning from one schema version to another, it's essential to handle data transformations to maintain compatibility. This ensures that data

272

adhering to an older schema can be seamlessly upgraded to the newer version without loss or corruption.

Step 1: Define Transformation Logic

Create utility functions to transform data from one schema version to another. This is particularly useful during migrations or when handling legacy data.

Example: Transforming User Data from V1 to V2

```typescript
---
// src/services/userTransformation.ts
import { UserV1 } from '../types/v1/user';
import { UserV2 } from '../types/v2/user';

export const transformUserV1toV2 = (userV1: UserV1): UserV2
=> {
  return {
    ...userV1,
    address: undefined, // Since address is optional in V2
  };
};
```

Explanation:

- **Data Mapping:** Maps fields from `UserV1` to `UserV2`. Since `address` is optional in `V2`, it can be set to `undefined` or populated based on additional logic.

Step 2: Implement Transformation During Data Handling

Integrate transformation logic within your data handling processes, such as API endpoints or database migrations.

Example: Applying Transformation in User Controller

```typescript
---
// src/controllers/userController.ts
import { Request, Response } from 'express';
import { userSchemaV1 } from '../schemas/v1/userSchema';
import { userSchemaV2 } from '../schemas/v2/userSchema';
import { UserV1 } from '../types/v1/user';
import { UserV2 } from '../types/v2/user';
```

```
import { transformUserV1toV2 } from
'../services/userTransformation';

export const createUser = (req: Request, res: Response) => {
  const apiVersion = req.headers['x-api-version'] || 'v1';

  try {
    if (apiVersion === 'v2') {
      const user: UserV2 = userSchemaV2.parse(req.body);
      // Proceed with v2 user creation logic
      res.status(201).json({ message: 'User created
successfully (v2)', user });
    } else {
      const userV1: UserV1 = userSchemaV1.parse(req.body);
      const userV2: UserV2 = transformUserV1toV2(userV1);
      // Proceed with v2 user creation logic using
transformed data
      res.status(201).json({ message: 'User created
successfully (v1 transformed to v2)', user: userV2 });
    }
  } catch (error) {
    if (error instanceof z.ZodError) {
      res.status(400).json({ errors: error.errors });
    } else {
      res.status(500).json({ message: 'Internal Server Error'
});
    }
  }
};
```

Explanation:

- **Version Detection:** Determines which schema version to use based on the x-api-version header.
- **Data Transformation:** Transforms UserV1 data to UserV2 before proceeding with creation logic.
- **Consistent Response Structure:** Ensures that all responses adhere to the UserV2 type, maintaining consistency across API versions.

---

5. Best Practices for Schema Versioning

Adhering to best practices ensures that schema versioning is implemented effectively, maintaining application stability and facilitating seamless transitions between versions.

a. Semantic Versioning

- **Version Numbers:** Use semantic versioning (e.g., v1.0.0, v1.1.0, v2.0.0) to clearly indicate the nature of changes.
    - **Major Versions (v1 → v2):** Introduce breaking changes.
    - **Minor Versions (v1.0 → v1.1):** Add functionality without breaking existing contracts.
    - **Patch Versions (v1.0.0 → v1.0.1):** Make backward-compatible bug fixes.

b. Maintain Clear Documentation

- **Schema Change Logs:** Document all changes made to each schema version, including added, modified, or deprecated fields.
- **Migration Guides:** Provide guidelines for migrating data and clients from older schema versions to newer ones.
- **API Documentation:** Clearly specify which schema version corresponds to each API endpoint or client.

c. Gradual Deprecation of Older Versions

- **Deprecation Notices:** Inform clients about upcoming deprecations through response headers, API responses, or documentation.
- **Grace Periods:** Allow sufficient time for clients to transition to newer schema versions before retiring older ones.
- **Monitoring Usage:** Track the usage of different schema versions to determine when deprecations can proceed safely.

d. Automated Testing for Multiple Schema Versions

- **Isolated Test Suites:** Maintain separate test suites for each schema version to ensure that validations are correctly enforced.
- **Regression Testing:** Implement regression tests to verify that newer schema versions do not inadvertently affect older versions.

e. Centralized Schema Management

- **Single Repository:** Store all schema versions within a single repository or module to simplify management and version control.
- **Consistent Naming Conventions:** Adopt a consistent naming strategy for schema files and versions to enhance clarity.

6. Summary of Schema Versioning Implementation

Implementing schema versioning with TypeScript and Zod involves:

1. **Organizing Schemas:** Structuring your project to support multiple schema versions, using namespaces or directories.
2. **Defining Versioned Schemas:** Creating distinct schemas for each version, extending or merging as necessary.
3. **Inferring TypeScript Types:** Using `z.infer` to derive TypeScript types from each schema version, ensuring type safety.
4. **Centralizing Exports:** Managing schema exports through centralized files for streamlined imports.
5. **Managing Data Transformations:** Implementing transformation logic to migrate data between schema versions seamlessly.
6. **Adhering to Best Practices:** Following semantic versioning, maintaining clear documentation, and gradually deprecating older versions to ensure backward compatibility.

By systematically applying these strategies, you can effectively manage schema evolution, maintain backward compatibility, and ensure the continued reliability and scalability of your type-safe applications.

Conclusion

Schema versioning is a critical component in the lifecycle of scalable, type-safe applications. By implementing robust versioning strategies using TypeScript and Zod, developers can manage evolving data structures without disrupting existing functionalities. Organized and modular schemas, coupled with clear versioning practices, facilitate seamless transitions, maintain data integrity, and enhance the overall maintainability of applications. Embracing these techniques ensures that your applications remain resilient and adaptable, capable of handling growth and change with confidence.

8.3 Strategies for Large-Scale Applications

Scaling type-safe applications involves addressing increased complexity, ensuring maintainability, and optimizing performance as your project grows.

Leveraging TypeScript and Zod effectively can help manage this complexity, maintain type safety, and streamline development workflows. This section explores key strategies for scaling large-scale applications, providing in-depth analysis and practical, step-by-step implementations to guide you through best practices and advanced techniques.

---

1. Embracing a Modular Architecture

A modular architecture divides your application into distinct, manageable modules or components, each responsible for specific functionalities. This separation of concerns enhances maintainability, facilitates parallel development, and promotes reusability across different parts of the application.

Benefits:

- **Maintainability:** Isolated modules are easier to manage, debug, and update.
- **Reusability:** Common functionalities can be reused across multiple modules, reducing duplication.
- **Scalability:** Modules can be developed and scaled independently, accommodating growth seamlessly.

Implementation Steps:

Step 1: Define Feature-Based Modules

Organize your application based on features or domains. For example, in an e-commerce application, you might have modules for users, products, orders, and payments.

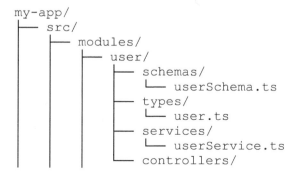

```
my-app/
├── src/
    ├── modules/
        ├── user/
            ├── schemas/
            │   └── userSchema.ts
            ├── types/
            │   └── user.ts
            ├── services/
            │   └── userService.ts
            └── controllers/
```

```
                    └── userController.ts
        ├── product/
        │   ├── schemas/
        │   │   └── productSchema.ts
        │   ├── types/
        │   │   └── product.ts
        │   ├── services/
        │   │   └── productService.ts
        │   └── controllers/
        │       └── productController.ts
        └── ...
    ├── shared/
    │   ├── schemas/
    │   │   └── addressSchema.ts
    │   ├── types/
    │   │   └── address.ts
    │   └── utilities/
    │       └── validationUtils.ts
    └── index.ts
├── tests/
│   ├── modules/
│   │   ├── user/
│   │   │   └── userSchema.test.ts
│   │   ├── product/
│   │   │   └── productSchema.test.ts
│   │   └── ...
│   └── shared/
│       └── schemas/
│           └── addressSchema.test.ts
├── package.json
└── tsconfig.json
```

Explanation:

- **`modules/` Directory:** Contains feature-based modules, each with its own schemas, types, services, and controllers.
- **`shared/` Directory:** Houses schemas, types, and utilities shared across multiple modules, promoting reusability.

Step 2: Create Reusable Subschemas

Extract common data structures into the `shared/schemas/` directory to promote reuse and consistency.

```typescript
---
// src/shared/schemas/addressSchema.ts
import { z } from 'zod';
```

```
export const addressSchema = z.object({
  street: z.string().min(1, { message: 'Street is required.'
}),
  city: z.string().min(1, { message: 'City is required.' }),
  zipCode: z.string().length(5, { message: 'Zip Code must be
exactly 5 characters long.' }),
});
```

Explanation:

- **addressSchema:** A reusable schema for address information, used across different modules like user and product.

Step 3: Integrate Subschemas into Feature Modules

Incorporate the addressSchema into feature-specific schemas using Zod's .merge() or .extend() methods.

```typescript
---
// src/modules/user/schemas/userSchema.ts
import { z } from 'zod';
import { addressSchema } from
'../../shared/schemas/addressSchema';

export const userSchema = z.object({
  username: z.string().min(3, { message: 'Username must be at
least 3 characters long.' }),
  email: z.string().email({ message: 'Please enter a valid
email address.' }),
  password: z.string()
    .min(8, { message: 'Password must be at least 8
characters long.' })
    .refine((val) => /[A-Z]/.test(val), { message: 'Password
must contain at least one uppercase letter.' })
    .refine((val) => /[0-9]/.test(val), { message: 'Password
must contain at least one number.' }),
  address: addressSchema.optional(),
});
```

Explanation:

- **addressSchema.optional():** Incorporates the optional address field from the shared addressSchema, allowing users to provide address information if available.

Step 4: Infer TypeScript Types from Schemas

Use Zod's `z.infer` to derive TypeScript types directly from schemas, ensuring type safety and consistency.

```typescript
---
// src/modules/user/types/user.ts
import { z } from 'zod';
import { userSchema } from '../schemas/userSchema';

export type User = z.infer<typeof userSchema>;
```

Explanation:

- **User Type:** Automatically derived from `userSchema`, ensuring that the TypeScript type remains synchronized with the validation rules.

---

2. Managing Interdependencies Between Schemas

In large-scale applications, schemas often depend on one another. Proper management of these interdependencies is crucial to prevent circular dependencies and maintain a clean architecture.

Strategies:

1. **Use Shared Modules for Common Schemas:**
   o Centralize common schemas in the `shared/schemas/` directory to be imported by multiple feature modules.
2. **Avoid Circular Dependencies:**
   o Design schemas to minimize or eliminate circular references by structuring dependencies hierarchically.
3. **Leverage Zod's `z.lazy` for Recursive Schemas:**
   o Utilize `z.lazy` to define schemas that reference themselves, preventing immediate evaluation and breaking potential circular dependencies.

Implementation Steps:

Step 1: Centralize Common Schemas

Ensure that all shared schemas are placed within the `shared/schemas/` directory, making them easily accessible without creating circular dependencies.

```typescript
---
// src/shared/schemas/categorySchema.ts
import { z } from 'zod';
import { productSchema } from
'../../modules/product/schemas/productSchema';

export const categorySchema = z.object({
  name: z.string().min(1, { message: 'Category name is
required.' }),
  products: z.array(z.lazy(() => productSchema)).optional(),
});
```

Explanation:

- **z.lazy:** Delays the evaluation of `productSchema` to prevent circular dependencies if `productSchema` also references `categorySchema`.

Step 2: Define Recursive Schemas Using `z.lazy`

For schemas that reference themselves or have nested dependencies, use `z.lazy` to enable recursive definitions without causing circular imports.

```typescript
---
// src/shared/schemas/categorySchema.ts
import { z } from 'zod';

export const categorySchema = z.object({
  name: z.string().min(1, { message: 'Category name is
required.' }),
  subcategories: z.array(z.lazy(() =>
categorySchema)).optional(),
});
```

Explanation:

- **subcategories:** An array of `categorySchema`, allowing categories to contain nested subcategories. The use of `z.lazy` prevents immediate evaluation, avoiding infinite recursion during schema definition.

281

3. Implementing Schema Composition and Inheritance

Schema composition and inheritance allow you to build complex schemas by combining simpler, reusable components. This approach enhances maintainability and promotes consistency across different schema versions or features.

Techniques:

1. **Schema Merging with** `.merge()`:
   - o Combine two schemas into one, inheriting fields from both.
2. **Schema Extension with** `.extend()`:
   - o Add additional fields to an existing schema without altering the original.
3. **Reusing Subschemas:**
   - o Incorporate subschemas within primary schemas to promote reuse and consistency.

Implementation Steps:

Step 1: Merge Schemas Using `.merge()`

Combine two separate schemas into a single, unified schema.

```typescript
---
// src/shared/schemas/contactSchema.ts
import { z } from 'zod';

export const contactSchema = z.object({
  phone: z.string().optional(),
  website: z.string().url().optional(),
});
```
```typescript
---
// src/modules/user/schemas/userSchema.ts
import { z } from 'zod';
import { addressSchema } from
'../../shared/schemas/addressSchema';
import { contactSchema } from
'../../shared/schemas/contactSchema';

export const userSchema = z.object({
```

```typescript
  username: z.string().min(3, { message: 'Username must be at
least 3 characters long.' }),
  email: z.string().email({ message: 'Please enter a valid
email address.' }),
  password: z.string()
    .min(8, { message: 'Password must be at least 8
characters long.' })
    .refine((val) => /[A-Z]/.test(val), { message: 'Password
must contain at least one uppercase letter.' })
    .refine((val) => /[0-9]/.test(val), { message: 'Password
must contain at least one number.' }),
  address: addressSchema.optional(),
}).merge(contactSchema);
```

Explanation:

- **contactSchema:** Defines optional contact information fields.
- **.merge(contactSchema):** Integrates contactSchema into userSchema, inheriting its fields.

Step 2: Extend Schemas Using .extend()

Add new fields to an existing schema without modifying the original schema.

```typescript
---
// src/modules/admin/schemas/adminSchema.ts
import { z } from 'zod';
import { userSchema } from '../../user/schemas/userSchema';

export const adminSchema = userSchema.extend({
  role: z.enum(['admin', 'superadmin'], { required_error:
'Role is required.' }),
  permissions: z.array(z.string()).optional(),
});
```

Explanation:

- **adminSchema:** Extends userSchema by adding role and permissions fields, creating a specialized schema for admin users.

Step 3: Reuse Subschemas Within Primary Schemas

Incorporate subschemas into primary schemas to promote reuse and maintain consistency.

```typescript
---
// src/modules/product/schemas/productSchema.ts
import { z } from 'zod';
import { categorySchema } from
'../../shared/schemas/categorySchema';

export const productSchema = z.object({
  productName: z.string().min(1, { message: 'Product name is
required.' }),
  price: z.number().positive({ message: 'Price must be a
positive number.' }),
  description: z.string().optional(),
  category: categorySchema,
});
```

Explanation:

- **categorySchema:** A reusable schema defining product categories.
- **category:** Incorporates `categorySchema` into `productSchema`, ensuring that each product is associated with a valid category.

---

4. Utilizing TypeScript Namespaces and Modules for Schema Management

TypeScript namespaces and modules provide organizational structures that help manage large codebases by grouping related schemas and types together. This approach enhances code readability and simplifies imports across different parts of the application.

Strategies:

1. **Namespace Usage:**
   - Encapsulate related schemas within TypeScript namespaces to prevent naming collisions and promote logical grouping.
2. **Module Exports:**
   - Export schemas and types from their respective modules, enabling easy imports and reducing import paths complexity.

Implementation Steps:

Step 1: Define Namespaced Schemas

Encapsulate related schemas within a TypeScript namespace to group them logically.

```typescript
---
// src/modules/user/schemas/index.ts
import { z } from 'zod';
import { addressSchema } from
'../../../shared/schemas/addressSchema';
import { contactSchema } from
'../../../shared/schemas/contactSchema';

export namespace UserSchemas {
  export const userSchema = z.object({
    username: z.string().min(3, { message: 'Username must be
at least 3 characters long.' }),
    email: z.string().email({ message: 'Please enter a valid
email address.' }),
    password: z.string()
      .min(8, { message: 'Password must be at least 8
characters long.' })
      .refine((val) => /[A-Z]/.test(val), { message:
'Password must contain at least one uppercase letter.' })
      .refine((val) => /[0-9]/.test(val), { message:
'Password must contain at least one number.' }),
    address: addressSchema.optional(),
  }).merge(contactSchema);
}
```

Explanation:

- **UserSchemas Namespace:** Groups all user-related schemas, preventing naming collisions and enhancing organization.

Step 2: Export Schemas from Module Index

Create an `index.ts` file within the `schemas` directory to centralize exports.

```typescript
---
// src/modules/user/schemas/index.ts
export * from './userSchema';
export * from './adminSchema';
```

Explanation:

- **Central Export Point:** Allows other modules to import all user-related schemas from a single location.

Step 3: Import Schemas Using Namespaces

Utilize the namespaces when importing schemas to maintain clarity and organization.

```typescript
---
// src/controllers/userController.ts
import { Request, Response } from 'express';
import { UserSchemas } from '../modules/user/schemas';
import { UserV1 } from '../types/v1/user';
import { UserV2 } from '../types/v2/user';

export const createUser = (req: Request, res: Response) => {
  const apiVersion = req.headers['x-api-version'] || 'v1';

  try {
    if (apiVersion === 'v2') {
      const user: UserV2 =
UserSchemas.userSchemaV2.parse(req.body);
      // Proceed with v2 user creation logic
      res.status(201).json({ message: 'User created
successfully (v2)', user });
    } else {
      const user: UserV1 =
UserSchemas.userSchemaV1.parse(req.body);
      // Proceed with v1 user creation logic
      res.status(201).json({ message: 'User created
successfully (v1)', user });
    }
  } catch (error) {
    if (error instanceof z.ZodError) {
      res.status(400).json({ errors: error.errors });
    } else {
      res.status(500).json({ message: 'Internal Server Error'
});
    }
  }
};
```

Explanation:

- **UserSchemas:** Accesses the user schemas through the namespace, maintaining organized and clear import paths.

5. Leveraging TypeScript's Advanced Features for Schema Management

TypeScript offers advanced features that, when combined with Zod, can enhance schema management and type safety in large-scale applications.

Techniques:

1. **Generics with Zod Schemas:**
   - Utilize TypeScript generics to create flexible and reusable schema components.
2. **Conditional Types:**
   - Implement conditional types to handle dynamic schema variations based on specific conditions.
3. **Utility Types:**
   - Use TypeScript's utility types (e.g., `Partial`, `Required`, `Pick`, `Omit`) to manipulate and derive types from existing schemas.

Implementation Steps:

Step 1: Creating Generic Schemas

Define generic schemas that can be customized based on different type parameters.

```typescript
---
// src/shared/schemas/paginationSchema.ts
import { z } from 'zod';

export const paginationSchema = <T extends
z.ZodTypeAny>(itemSchema: T) => z.object({
  items: z.array(itemSchema),
  currentPage: z.number().min(1, { message: 'Current page
must be at least 1.' }),
  totalPages: z.number().min(1, { message: 'Total pages must
be at least 1.' }),
});
```

Explanation:

- **paginationSchema:** A generic schema that accepts any Zod schema (`itemSchema`) and creates a paginated response structure.

Usage Example:

```typescript
---
// src/modules/product/schemas/productPaginationSchema.ts
import { z } from 'zod';
import { productSchema } from './productSchema';
import { paginationSchema } from
'../../../shared/schemas/paginationSchema';

export const productPaginationSchema =
paginationSchema(productSchema);
```

Explanation:

- **productPaginationSchema:** Utilizes the generic `paginationSchema` to create a paginated product response schema.

Step 2: Implementing Conditional Schemas

Create schemas that adapt based on certain conditions, enhancing flexibility in validation logic.

```typescript
---
// src/shared/schemas/conditionalSchema.ts
import { z } from 'zod';

export const conditionalSchema = <T extends z.ZodTypeAny, U
extends z.ZodTypeAny>(
  condition: (data: any) => boolean,
  thenSchema: T,
  elseSchema: U
) => z.object({}).superRefine((data, ctx) => {
  if (condition(data)) {
    try {
      thenSchema.parse(data);
    } catch (e) {
      if (e instanceof z.ZodError) {
        e.errors.forEach(err => {
          ctx.addIssue({
            code: err.code,
            message: err.message,
            path: err.path,
          });
```

```
        });
      }
    }
  } else {
    try {
      elseSchema.parse(data);
    } catch (e) {
      if (e instanceof z.ZodError) {
        e.errors.forEach(err => {
          ctx.addIssue({
            code: err.code,
            message: err.message,
            path: err.path,
          });
        });
      }
    }
  }
});
```

Explanation:

- **conditionalSchema:** A utility function that applies different schemas based on a provided condition, allowing dynamic validation rules.

Usage Example:

```typescript
---
// src/modules/user/schemas/userConditionalSchema.ts
import { z } from 'zod';
import { userSchemaV1 } from './v1/userSchema';
import { userSchemaV2 } from './v2/userSchema';
import { conditionalSchema } from
'../../../shared/schemas/conditionalSchema';

export const userConditionalSchema = conditionalSchema(
  (data) => data.isAdmin === true,
  userSchemaV2,
  userSchemaV1
);
```

Explanation:

- **userConditionalSchema:** Applies userSchemaV2 if isAdmin is true, otherwise applies userSchemaV1, enabling dynamic validation based on user roles.

289

Step 3: Utilizing Utility Types for Type Manipulation

Leverage TypeScript's utility types to derive new types from existing schemas, enhancing type flexibility and reducing redundancy.

```typescript
---
// src/modules/user/types/partialUser.ts
import { z } from 'zod';
import { userSchema } from '../schemas/userSchema';

export type PartialUser = Partial<z.infer<typeof
userSchema>>;
```

Explanation:

- **PartialUser:** A type derived from `userSchema` where all fields are optional, useful for update operations where not all fields need to be provided.

---

6. Managing Large Codebases with TypeScript and Zod

As applications scale, managing large codebases becomes a significant challenge. Implementing effective strategies ensures that your TypeScript and Zod-powered applications remain organized, maintainable, and performant.

Strategies:

1. **Consistent Coding Standards:**
   o Enforce consistent coding styles and conventions across the codebase using tools like ESLint and Prettier.
2. **Automated Code Reviews:**
   o Implement automated code review processes to maintain code quality and consistency.
3. **Efficient Import Paths:**
   o Use absolute import paths or path aliases to simplify module imports and reduce complexity.
4. **Code Splitting and Lazy Loading:**

- Implement code splitting and lazy loading to optimize performance by loading only necessary modules when needed.

5. **Documentation Generation:**
   - Automate the generation of documentation from schemas and types to keep documentation up-to-date and reduce manual effort.

Implementation Steps:

Step 1: Enforce Consistent Coding Standards

Set up ESLint and Prettier to maintain code quality and consistency.

```bash
---
npm install eslint prettier eslint-config-prettier eslint-plugin-prettier --save-dev
```

.eslintrc.js Configuration:

```javascript
---
module.exports = {
  parser: '@typescript-eslint/parser',
  extends: [
    'eslint:recommended',
    'plugin:@typescript-eslint/recommended',
    'plugin:prettier/recommended',
  ],
  rules: {
    // Define custom rules here
  },
};
```

.prettierrc Configuration:

```json
---
{
  "singleQuote": true,
  "trailingComma": "es5",
  "printWidth": 80
}
```

Explanation:

- **ESLint:** Enforces coding standards and identifies potential issues.
- **Prettier:** Automatically formats code to adhere to defined styles.

291

- **Integration:** Combines ESLint and Prettier to prevent conflicts and ensure seamless code formatting.

Step 2: Implement Path Aliases for Simplified Imports

Configure TypeScript to use path aliases, reducing the complexity of import statements.

`tsconfig.json` Configuration:

```json
{
  "compilerOptions": {
    // ... other settings
    "baseUrl": "src",
    "paths": {
      "@modules/*": ["modules/*"],
      "@shared/*": ["shared/*"],
      "@schemas/*": ["shared/schemas/*"],
      "@types/*": ["shared/types/*"]
    }
  }
}
```

Usage Example:

```typescript
// src/modules/user/controllers/userController.ts
import { userSchema } from '@schemas/userSchema';
import { User } from '@types/user';

// ... rest of the code
```

Explanation:

- **Path Aliases:** Simplify import statements by allowing the use of aliases like `@schemas/` instead of relative paths.
- **Maintainability:** Enhances readability and maintainability by reducing deeply nested relative paths.

Step 3: Optimize Performance with Code Splitting and Lazy Loading

Implement code splitting and lazy loading to enhance application performance by loading only necessary modules when required.

Example: Lazy Loading Schemas in an Express Application

```typescript
---
// src/index.ts
import express from 'express';
import { Request, Response } from 'express';

const app = express();
app.use(express.json());

app.post('/api/users', async (req: Request, res: Response) =>
{
  const apiVersion = req.headers['x-api-version'] || 'v1';

  try {
    if (apiVersion === 'v2') {
      const { userSchemaV2 } = await
import('./modules/user/schemas/v2/userSchema');
      const user = userSchemaV2.parse(req.body);
      // Proceed with v2 logic
      res.status(201).json({ message: 'User created
successfully (v2)', user });
    } else {
      const { userSchemaV1 } = await
import('./modules/user/schemas/v1/userSchema');
      const user = userSchemaV1.parse(req.body);
      // Proceed with v1 logic
      res.status(201).json({ message: 'User created
successfully (v1)', user });
    }
  } catch (error) {
    if (error instanceof z.ZodError) {
      res.status(400).json({ errors: error.errors });
    } else {
      res.status(500).json({ message: 'Internal Server Error'
});
    }
  }
});

app.listen(3000, () => {
  console.log('Server running on port 3000');
});
```

Explanation:

- **Dynamic Imports:** Uses import() to load schema versions only
  when needed, reducing initial load times.

- **Performance Optimization:** Enhances performance by avoiding the loading of unnecessary modules upfront.

Step 4: Automate Documentation Generation

Use tools to automatically generate documentation from your Zod schemas, ensuring that documentation remains up-to-date with your codebase.

Example: Using `zod-to-ts` to Generate TypeScript Interfaces

```bash
npm install zod-to-ts --save-dev
```

`generateTypes.ts` Script:

```typescript
// scripts/generateTypes.ts
import { generateTypeScript } from 'zod-to-ts';
import { readFileSync, writeFileSync } from 'fs';
import { join } from 'path';

// Read the user schema file
const schemaPath = join(__dirname,
'../src/modules/user/schemas/userSchema.ts');
const schemaContent = readFileSync(schemaPath, 'utf-8');

// Extract the schema (assuming export const userSchema =
...)
const schemaName = 'userSchema';
const interfaceName = 'User';

const { source } = generateTypeScript(schemaName,
schemaContent);

// Write the generated interface to a types file
const outputPath = join(__dirname,
'../src/modules/user/types/user.ts');
writeFileSync(outputPath, source);
```

Explanation:

- **zod-to-ts:** Converts Zod schemas into TypeScript interfaces, automating type generation.

- **Automation Script:** Reads the schema file, generates the corresponding TypeScript interface, and writes it to the appropriate types directory.
- **Maintainability:** Ensures that TypeScript types remain synchronized with their Zod schema counterparts without manual intervention.

Running the Script:

Add a script entry in `package.json`:

```json
{
  "scripts": {
    "generate:types": "ts-node scripts/generateTypes.ts"
  }
}
```

Execute the script:

```bash
npm run generate:types
```

7. Best Practices for Scaling Large-Scale Applications

Adhering to best practices ensures that your application remains organized, maintainable, and performant as it scales. The following guidelines provide a framework for managing large codebases effectively.

a. Maintain Clear Separation of Concerns

- **Domain-Driven Design:** Organize code around business domains or features, ensuring that each module encapsulates its specific functionality.
- **Isolation of Business Logic:** Keep business logic separate from controllers and services to enhance clarity and maintainability.

b. Ensure Type Synchronization

- **Use `z.infer` Consistently:** Derive TypeScript types directly from Zod schemas to prevent discrepancies between types and validation logic.

- **Avoid Manual Type Definitions:** Refrain from manually defining types that mirror Zod schemas, reducing redundancy and maintenance overhead.

c. Implement Robust Testing Strategies

- **Comprehensive Test Coverage:** Ensure that all schemas and application logic are thoroughly tested, covering both positive and negative scenarios.
- **Automated Testing Pipelines:** Integrate tests into CI/CD pipelines to enforce code quality and prevent regressions.

d. Optimize Dependency Management

- **Minimal Dependencies:** Keep dependencies to a minimum to reduce complexity and potential conflicts.
- **Regular Updates:** Regularly update dependencies to benefit from performance improvements and security patches.

e. Leverage Caching and Memoization

- **Schema Caching:** Cache frequently used schemas to reduce validation overhead and improve performance.
- **Memoization Techniques:** Implement memoization for expensive computations or transformations to enhance efficiency.

f. Monitor and Log Effectively

- **Real-Time Monitoring:** Deploy monitoring tools to track application performance, schema validation errors, and other critical metrics.
- **Detailed Logging:** Implement comprehensive logging to capture validation failures and facilitate troubleshooting.

g. Document Thoroughly

- **Inline Comments:** Provide clear comments within your code to explain complex logic and validation rules.
- **External Documentation:** Maintain up-to-date documentation that outlines schema structures, validation rules, and architectural decisions.

h. Facilitate Team Collaboration

- **Code Reviews:** Conduct regular code reviews to maintain code quality and promote knowledge sharing.
- **Knowledge Sharing Sessions:** Organize sessions to discuss best practices, new features, and schema updates, fostering a collaborative environment.

Conclusion

Scaling type-safe applications with TypeScript and Zod requires a strategic approach to architecture, schema management, and development workflows. By embracing a modular architecture, effectively managing interdependencies, leveraging TypeScript's advanced features, and adhering to best practices, developers can maintain type safety and data integrity even as applications grow in complexity and size. Implementing these strategies not only enhances maintainability and performance but also ensures that your application remains robust, scalable, and adaptable to evolving requirements. As you continue to develop large-scale applications, these methodologies will provide a solid foundation for managing complexity and fostering a productive development environment.

Chapter 9: Case Studies and Examples

Real-world applications provide invaluable insights into the practical implementation of theoretical concepts. In this chapter, we explore three comprehensive case studies that demonstrate how TypeScript and Zod can be leveraged to build robust, type-safe applications. These examples illustrate the versatility and effectiveness of combining TypeScript's static typing with Zod's runtime validation, offering practical guidance for developers aiming to enhance their projects' reliability and maintainability.

9.1 Building a Type-Safe API Service

Creating a type-safe API service is essential for ensuring data integrity, preventing runtime errors, and maintaining clear contracts between different parts of your application. By leveraging TypeScript's static typing and Zod's runtime validation, developers can build robust APIs that are both reliable and maintainable. This guide provides a comprehensive, step-by-step approach to building a type-safe API service using TypeScript, Zod, and Express.js.

1. Key Objectives

Before diving into the implementation, it's important to outline the primary goals of building a type-safe API service:

- **Data Integrity:** Ensure that all incoming and outgoing data adheres to predefined structures and validation rules.
- **Error Prevention:** Catch type and validation errors during development rather than at runtime.
- **Maintainability:** Create a scalable architecture that simplifies future updates and feature additions.
- **Developer Experience:** Enhance productivity by leveraging TypeScript's type inference and Zod's expressive validation capabilities.

2. Project Setup

To begin, set up a new TypeScript project with Express.js and Zod.

Step 1: Initialize the Project

```bash
---
mkdir type-safe-api
cd type-safe-api
npm init -y
```

Step 2: Install Dependencies

Install the necessary packages, including Express.js for building the API, TypeScript for static typing, Zod for runtime validation, and other development tools.

```bash
---
npm install express
npm install --save-dev typescript ts-node @types/express
nodemon zod
```

Step 3: Configure TypeScript

Initialize a `tsconfig.json` file to configure TypeScript settings.

```bash
---
npx tsc --init
```

Update the `tsconfig.json` with the following settings for optimal development:

```json
---
{
  "compilerOptions": {
    "target": "ES6",
    "module": "CommonJS",
    "rootDir": "./src",
    "outDir": "./dist",
    "strict": true,
    "esModuleInterop": true,
    "forceConsistentCasingInFileNames": true
  }
```

```
}
```

Step 4: Set Up Project Structure

Organize the project directories to maintain clarity and separation of concerns.

```
type-safe-api/
├── src/
│   ├── controllers/
│   │   └── userController.ts
│   ├── schemas/
│   │   └── userSchema.ts
│   ├── types/
│   │   └── user.ts
│   ├── services/
│   │   └── userService.ts
│   └── index.ts
├── tests/
│   └── userSchema.test.ts
├── package.json
└── tsconfig.json
```

3. Defining Schemas with Zod

Schemas define the structure and validation rules for your data. Using Zod, you can create expressive and reusable schemas that ensure data consistency.

Step 1: Create User Schema

Define a schema for user data, specifying required fields and validation rules.

```typescript
---
// src/schemas/userSchema.ts
import { z } from 'zod';

export const userSchema = z.object({
  username: z.string().min(3, { message: 'Username must be at
least 3 characters long.' }),
  email: z.string().email({ message: 'Please enter a valid
email address.' }),
  password: z.string()
    .min(8, { message: 'Password must be at least 8
characters long.' })
```

```
    .refine((val) => /[A-Z]/.test(val), { message: 'Password
must contain at least one uppercase letter.' })
    .refine((val) => /[0-9]/.test(val), { message: 'Password
must contain at least one number.' }),
});
```

Explanation:

- **username:** Must be a string with a minimum length of 3 characters.
- **email:** Must be a valid email format.
- **password:** Must be a string with a minimum length of 8 characters, containing at least one uppercase letter and one number.

---

4. Inferring TypeScript Types from Schemas

Leverage Zod's type inference to derive TypeScript types directly from your schemas, ensuring synchronization between validation logic and type definitions.

```typescript
---
// src/types/user.ts
import { z } from 'zod';
import { userSchema } from '../schemas/userSchema';

export type User = z.infer<typeof userSchema>;
```

Explanation:

- **User Type:** Automatically inferred from userSchema, ensuring that any changes to the schema are reflected in the TypeScript type without manual intervention.

---

5. Creating the Express Server with Validation Middleware

Integrate Zod schemas into your Express routes to validate incoming requests seamlessly.

Step 1: Initialize Express Server

Set up the basic Express server in `index.ts`.

```typescript
---
// src/index.ts
import express from 'express';
import userRouter from './controllers/userController';

const app = express();
app.use(express.json());

app.use('/api/users', userRouter);

const PORT = process.env.PORT || 3000;
app.listen(PORT, () => {
  console.log(`Server running on port ${PORT}`);
});
```

Step 2: Implement Validation Middleware

Create middleware to validate request bodies against Zod schemas.

```typescript
---
// src/middleware/validate.ts
import { Request, Response, NextFunction } from 'express';
import { ZodSchema } from 'zod';

export const validate = <T>(schema: ZodSchema<T>) => (req:
Request, res: Response, next: NextFunction) => {
  try {
    req.body = schema.parse(req.body);
    next();
  } catch (error) {
    if (error instanceof z.ZodError) {
      return res.status(400).json({
        errors: error.errors.map(err => ({
          field: err.path.join('.'),
          message: err.message,
        })),
      });
    }
    next(error);
  }
};
```

Explanation:

- **Generic Middleware:** The `validate` function accepts a Zod schema and returns middleware that parses and validates the request body.
- **Error Handling:** If validation fails, it responds with a 400 status code and detailed error messages indicating which fields are invalid.

Step 3: Create User Controller

Define routes for user-related operations, integrating the validation middleware.

```typescript
---
// src/controllers/userController.ts
import express, { Request, Response } from 'express';
import { userSchema } from '../schemas/userSchema';
import { validate } from '../middleware/validate';
import { User } from '../types/user';
import { createUserService, getUserService } from
'../services/userService';

const router = express.Router();

// Create a new user
router.post('/', validate(userSchema), (req: Request, res:
Response) => {
  const user: User = req.body;
  const createdUser = createUserService(user);
  res.status(201).json(createdUser);
});

// Get a user by ID
router.get('/:id', (req: Request, res: Response) => {
  const userId = req.params.id;
  const user = getUserService(userId);
  if (user) {
    res.json(user);
  } else {
    res.status(404).json({ message: 'User not found.' });
  }
});

export default router;
```

Explanation:

- **POST /api/users/:** Creates a new user. The request body is validated against `userSchema` before proceeding.

- **GET /api/users/:id:** Retrieves a user by ID. Validation is not required here since it's a simple parameter retrieval.

6. Implementing Services

Encapsulate business logic within service functions to keep controllers clean and focused on handling HTTP requests and responses.

```typescript
---
// src/services/userService.ts
import { User } from '../types/user';

let users: User[] = [];

export const createUserService = (user: User): User => {
  users.push(user);
  return user;
};

export const getUserService = (id: string): User | undefined
=> {
  return users.find(user => user.username === id);
};
```

Explanation:

- **users Array:** Simulates a database by storing user objects in memory.
- **createUserService:** Adds a new user to the users array.
- **getUserService:** Retrieves a user by username. In a real application, this would query a database.

7. Error Handling and Response Structuring

Ensure that your API provides clear and consistent error messages, enhancing the developer and user experience.

```typescript
---
// src/middleware/errorHandler.ts
```

```typescript
import { Request, Response, NextFunction } from 'express';

export const errorHandler = (err: any, req: Request, res:
Response, next: NextFunction) => {
  console.error(err.stack);
  res.status(500).json({ message: 'Internal Server Error' });
};
```

Explanation:

- **Global Error Handler:** Catches unexpected errors and responds
  with a 500 status code, preventing sensitive error details from leaking
  to clients.

Integrate the error handler into your Express server:

```typescript
---
// src/index.ts
import express from 'express';
import userRouter from './controllers/userController';
import { errorHandler } from './middleware/errorHandler';

const app = express();
app.use(express.json());

app.use('/api/users', userRouter);

// Global Error Handler
app.use(errorHandler);

const PORT = process.env.PORT || 3000;
app.listen(PORT, () => {
  console.log(`Server running on port ${PORT}`);
});
```

8. Testing the API

Testing ensures that your API behaves as expected, catching potential issues
early in the development process.

Step 1: Set Up Testing Framework

Install Jest and related TypeScript support packages.

```bash
```

```
---
npm install --save-dev jest ts-jest @types/jest supertest
@types/supertest
```

Initialize Jest configuration:

```bash
---
npx ts-jest config:init
```

Step 2: Write Schema Tests

Create tests to verify that your Zod schemas correctly validate data.

```typescript
---
// tests/userSchema.test.ts
import { userSchema } from '../src/schemas/userSchema';
import { ZodError } from 'zod';

describe('User Schema Validation', () => {
  it('should validate a correct user object', () => {
    const validUser = {
      username: 'john_doe',
      email: 'john@example.com',
      password: 'SecurePass1',
    };

    expect(() => userSchema.parse(validUser)).not.toThrow();
  });

  it('should fail validation when username is too short', ()
=> {
    const invalidUser = {
      username: 'jd',
      email: 'john@example.com',
      password: 'SecurePass1',
    };

    expect(() =>
userSchema.parse(invalidUser)).toThrow(ZodError);
  });

  it('should fail validation when email is invalid', () => {
    const invalidUser = {
      username: 'john_doe',
      email: 'john@',
      password: 'SecurePass1',
    };
```

```
    expect(() =>
userSchema.parse(invalidUser)).toThrow(ZodError);
  });

  it('should fail validation when password lacks uppercase
letter', () => {
    const invalidUser = {
      username: 'john_doe',
      email: 'john@example.com',
      password: 'securepass1',
    };

    expect(() =>
userSchema.parse(invalidUser)).toThrow(ZodError);
  });

  it('should fail validation when password lacks a number',
() => {
    const invalidUser = {
      username: 'john_doe',
      email: 'john@example.com',
      password: 'SecurePass',
    };

    expect(() =>
userSchema.parse(invalidUser)).toThrow(ZodError);
  });
});
```

Step 3: Write Integration Tests

Use Supertest to test your API endpoints.

```typescript
---
// tests/userController.test.ts
import request from 'supertest';
import express from 'express';
import userRouter from '../src/controllers/userController';
import { errorHandler } from
'../src/middleware/errorHandler';

const app = express();
app.use(express.json());
app.use('/api/users', userRouter);
app.use(errorHandler);

describe('User API Endpoints', () => {
  it('POST /api/users - success', async () => {
```

```
    const response = await request(app)
      .post('/api/users')
      .send({
        username: 'jane_doe',
        email: 'jane@example.com',
        password: 'SecurePass1',
      });

    expect(response.status).toBe(201);
    expect(response.body).toEqual({
      username: 'jane_doe',
      email: 'jane@example.com',
      password: 'SecurePass1',
    });
  });

  it('POST /api/users - validation failure', async () => {
    const response = await request(app)
      .post('/api/users')
      .send({
        username: 'jd',
        email: 'jane@',
        password: 'securepass',
      });

    expect(response.status).toBe(400);
    expect(response.body.errors).toEqual(
      expect.arrayContaining([
        { field: 'username', message: 'Username must be at
least 3 characters long.' },
        { field: 'email', message: 'Please enter a valid
email address.' },
        { field: 'password', message: 'Password must contain
at least one uppercase letter.' },
        { field: 'password', message: 'Password must contain
at least one number.' },
      ])
    );
  });

  it('GET /api/users/:id - user not found', async () => {
    const response = await
request(app).get('/api/users/nonexistent');

    expect(response.status).toBe(404);
    expect(response.body).toEqual({ message: 'User not
found.' });
  });
});
```

Step 4: Update `package.json` Scripts

308

Add scripts to run the server and tests.

```json
// package.json
{
  "scripts": {
    "start": "ts-node src/index.ts",
    "dev": "nodemon src/index.ts",
    "test": "jest"
  }
}
```

Explanation:

- **start:** Runs the server using `ts-node`.
- **dev:** Runs the server with `nodemon` for automatic restarts on file changes.
- **test:** Executes Jest tests.

---

9. Benefits of a Type-Safe API Service

Implementing a type-safe API service offers numerous advantages:

- **Early Error Detection:** TypeScript catches type-related errors during development, reducing runtime issues.
- **Consistent Data Handling:** Zod ensures that all data entering and leaving the API adheres to defined structures.
- **Enhanced Developer Experience:** Clear schemas and types improve code readability and maintainability, making it easier for teams to collaborate.
- **Improved Security:** Validating input data prevents malicious data from compromising the application.
- **Scalability:** A well-structured, type-safe API can easily accommodate new features and integrations without introducing inconsistencies.

Building a type-safe API service using TypeScript and Zod enhances the reliability, maintainability, and scalability of your application. By defining clear schemas, leveraging TypeScript's type inference, integrating validation seamlessly into your API routes, and implementing robust testing practices, developers can create APIs that are both developer-friendly and resilient against data inconsistencies. Embracing these practices not only improves the quality of your codebase but also fosters a more efficient and collaborative development environment.

9.2 Validating Multi-Step Forms with Zod

Multi-step forms are a staple in modern web applications, providing users with a structured and manageable way to input extensive information. Whether it's a registration process, a checkout flow, or a survey, multi-step forms enhance user experience by breaking down complex tasks into smaller, more digestible steps. However, ensuring data validity across multiple steps can be challenging. This guide explores how to leverage Zod alongside TypeScript to validate multi-step forms effectively, maintaining type safety and providing a seamless user experience.

---

1. Understanding the Challenges of Multi-Step Form Validation

Multi-step forms introduce unique challenges that differentiate them from single-step forms:

- **State Management:** Managing and persisting form data across multiple steps requires careful handling to prevent data loss or inconsistency.
- **Incremental Validation:** Validating data step-by-step ensures that users can correct errors immediately, improving the overall user experience.
- **Conditional Logic:** Different steps may require different validation rules based on user input, necessitating dynamic schema adjustments.
- **User Feedback:** Providing real-time feedback on validation errors at each step helps users navigate the form more efficiently.

Addressing these challenges is crucial for building robust and user-friendly multi-step forms. Zod, combined with TypeScript, offers powerful tools to tackle these issues effectively.

2. Benefits of Using Zod for Multi-Step Form Validation

Zod enhances multi-step form validation through several key advantages:

- **Type Inference:** Automatically derives TypeScript types from schemas, ensuring type safety and reducing redundancy.
- **Composable Schemas:** Allows building complex validation logic by composing simpler schemas, facilitating modularity and reusability.
- **Descriptive Error Messages:** Provides clear and actionable error messages, improving user feedback and experience.
- **Runtime Validation:** Ensures data integrity by validating inputs at runtime, preventing invalid data from propagating through the application.

By integrating Zod into your multi-step forms, you can streamline validation processes, maintain consistency across steps, and enhance overall application reliability.

3. Step-by-Step Implementation of Multi-Step Form Validation with Zod

This section outlines a practical implementation of a multi-step form using TypeScript, React, and Zod. The example involves a user registration process divided into three steps: Personal Information, Account Details, and Confirmation.

Step 1: Setting Up the Project

Begin by setting up a new React project with TypeScript support.

```bash
---
npx create-react-app multi-step-form --template typescript
cd multi-step-form
```

Install the necessary dependencies:

```bash
---
```

```
npm install zod
npm install --save-dev @types/react-router-dom react-router-
dom
```

Step 2: Defining Zod Schemas for Each Form Step

Create separate Zod schemas for each step to encapsulate specific validation rules.

```typescript
---
// src/schemas/personalInfoSchema.ts
import { z } from 'zod';

export const personalInfoSchema = z.object({
  firstName: z.string().min(1, { message: 'First name is
required.' }),
  lastName: z.string().min(1, { message: 'Last name is
required.' }),
  age: z
    .number({ invalid_type_error: 'Age must be a number.' })
    .min(18, { message: 'You must be at least 18 years old.'
}),
});
```
```typescript
---
// src/schemas/accountDetailsSchema.ts
import { z } from 'zod';

export const accountDetailsSchema = z.object({
  email: z.string().email({ message: 'Invalid email address.'
}),
  password: z.string()
    .min(8, { message: 'Password must be at least 8
characters long.' })
    .regex(/[A-Z]/, { message: 'Password must contain at
least one uppercase letter.' })
    .regex(/[0-9]/, { message: 'Password must contain at
least one number.' }),
  confirmPassword: z.string(),
}).refine((data) => data.password === data.confirmPassword, {
  message: 'Passwords do not match.',
  path: ['confirmPassword'],
});
```

Explanation:

- **personalInfoSchema:** Validates that the first and last names are provided and that the user is at least 18 years old.

312

- **accountDetailsSchema:** Ensures that the email is valid, the password meets complexity requirements, and the password confirmation matches the password.

Step 3: Inferring TypeScript Types from Schemas

Leverage Zod's type inference to derive TypeScript types, ensuring synchronization between schemas and types.

```typescript
---
// src/types/formTypes.ts
import { z } from 'zod';
import { personalInfoSchema } from
'../schemas/personalInfoSchema';
import { accountDetailsSchema } from
'../schemas/accountDetailsSchema';

export type PersonalInfo = z.infer<typeof
personalInfoSchema>;
export type AccountDetails = z.infer<typeof
accountDetailsSchema>;

export type FormData = PersonalInfo & AccountDetails;
```

Explanation:

- **PersonalInfo and AccountDetails:** Types inferred directly from their respective schemas.
- **FormData:** Combines both types, representing the complete form data upon final submission.

Step 4: Creating Form Components for Each Step

Develop React components for each form step, integrating Zod validation.

```typescript
---
// src/components/PersonalInfoForm.tsx
import React from 'react';
import { useForm } from 'react-hook-form';
import { zodResolver } from '@hookform/resolvers/zod';
import { personalInfoSchema } from
'../schemas/personalInfoSchema';
import { PersonalInfo } from '../types/formTypes';

interface Props {
```

```
  onNext: (data: PersonalInfo) => void;
}

const PersonalInfoForm: React.FC<Props> = ({ onNext }) => {
  const { register, handleSubmit, formState: { errors } } =
useForm<PersonalInfo>({
    resolver: zodResolver(personalInfoSchema),
  });

  const onSubmit = (data: PersonalInfo) => {
    onNext(data);
  };

  return (
    <form onSubmit={handleSubmit(onSubmit)}>
      <div>
        <label>First Name:</label>
        <input {...register('firstName')} />
        {errors.firstName &&
<p>{errors.firstName.message}</p>}
      </div>

      <div>
        <label>Last Name:</label>
        <input {...register('lastName')} />
        {errors.lastName && <p>{errors.lastName.message}</p>}
      </div>

      <div>
        <label>Age:</label>
        <input type="number" {...register('age', {
valueAsNumber: true })} />
        {errors.age && <p>{errors.age.message}</p>}
      </div>

      <button type="submit">Next</button>
    </form>
  );
};

export default PersonalInfoForm;
```

Explanation:

- **useForm:** Utilizes React Hook Form with Zod's resolver for seamless integration.
- **Validation:** Errors are displayed inline, providing immediate feedback to the user.

Step 5: Managing Form State Across Steps

Use React's state management to persist data across multiple form steps.

```typescript
---
// src/App.tsx
import React, { useState } from 'react';
import PersonalInfoForm from './components/PersonalInfoForm';
import AccountDetailsForm from
'./components/AccountDetailsForm';
import Confirmation from './components/Confirmation';
import { PersonalInfo, AccountDetails, FormData } from
'./types/formTypes';
import { z } from 'zod';
import { zodResolver } from '@hookform/resolvers/zod';
import { accountDetailsSchema } from
'./schemas/accountDetailsSchema';

const App: React.FC = () => {
  const [step, setStep] = useState<number>(1);
  const [formData, setFormData] = useState<FormData>({
    firstName: '',
    lastName: '',
    age: 0,
    email: '',
    password: '',
    confirmPassword: '',
  });

  const handlePersonalInfoNext = (data: PersonalInfo) => {
    setFormData(prev => ({ ...prev, ...data }));
    setStep(2);
  };

  const handleAccountDetailsNext = (data: AccountDetails) =>
{
    setFormData(prev => ({ ...prev, ...data }));
    setStep(3);
  };

  const handleConfirmation = () => {
    console.log('Final Form Data:', formData);
    // Proceed with form submission (e.g., API call)
  };

  return (
    <div>
      {step === 1 && <PersonalInfoForm
onNext={handlePersonalInfoNext} />}
```

```
      {step === 2 && <AccountDetailsForm
onNext={handleAccountDetailsNext} />}
      {step === 3 && <Confirmation data={formData}
onConfirm={handleConfirmation} />}
    </div>
  );
};

export default App;
```

Explanation:

- **step State:** Tracks the current form step.
- **formData State:** Aggregates data from all steps, ensuring persistence across navigation.

Step 6: Finalizing the Confirmation Step

Create a confirmation component to review and submit the aggregated form data.

```typescript
---
// src/components/Confirmation.tsx
import React from 'react';
import { FormData } from '../types/formTypes';

interface Props {
  data: FormData;
  onConfirm: () => void;
}

const Confirmation: React.FC<Props> = ({ data, onConfirm })
=> {
  return (
    <div>
      <h2>Confirm Your Details</h2>
      <p><strong>First Name:</strong> {data.firstName}</p>
      <p><strong>Last Name:</strong> {data.lastName}</p>
      <p><strong>Age:</strong> {data.age}</p>
      <p><strong>Email:</strong> {data.email}</p>
      {/* Passwords are typically not displayed for security
reasons */}

      <button onClick={onConfirm}>Submit</button>
    </div>
  );
};
```

```
export default Confirmation;
```

Explanation:

- **Data Review:** Displays the collected data for user confirmation before final submission.
- **Submission Handling:** Triggers the final submission process upon user confirmation.

---

4. Enhancing User Experience with Real-Time Validation Feedback

Providing immediate feedback on user inputs significantly improves the usability of multi-step forms. Zod, in conjunction with React Hook Form, facilitates real-time validation, ensuring that users are aware of errors as they fill out the form.

Strategies:

- **Inline Error Messages:** Display error messages directly beneath the relevant input fields, allowing users to identify and correct issues promptly.
- **Disabling Navigation Buttons:** Prevent users from proceeding to the next step until all validations in the current step pass, ensuring data integrity.
- **Visual Indicators:** Use visual cues (e.g., red borders, icons) to highlight invalid fields, enhancing accessibility and user guidance.

By implementing these strategies, you can create a more intuitive and responsive form experience, reducing user frustration and increasing form completion rates.

---

5. Testing Multi-Step Form Validation

Robust testing is essential to ensure that multi-step forms behave as expected under various scenarios. This includes verifying that validations are correctly enforced, data is accurately persisted across steps, and the overall user flow remains seamless.

Testing Approaches:

- **Unit Tests for Schemas:** Validate that each Zod schema correctly identifies valid and invalid data inputs.
- **Integration Tests for Form Steps:** Ensure that each form step correctly handles data submission, validation, and state management.
- **End-to-End Tests:** Simulate user interactions across all form steps to verify the complete user journey from start to finish.

Example: Unit Test for Personal Information Schema

```typescript
---
// tests/personalInfoSchema.test.ts
import { personalInfoSchema } from
'../src/schemas/personalInfoSchema';
import { ZodError } from 'zod';

describe('Personal Info Schema Validation', () => {
  it('should validate correct personal info', () => {
    const validData = {
      firstName: 'John',
      lastName: 'Doe',
      age: 25,
    };
    expect(() =>
personalInfoSchema.parse(validData)).not.toThrow();
  });

  it('should fail when firstName is missing', () => {
    const invalidData = {
      lastName: 'Doe',
      age: 25,
    };
    expect(() =>
personalInfoSchema.parse(invalidData)).toThrow(ZodError);
  });

  it('should fail when age is below 18', () => {
    const invalidData = {
      firstName: 'John',
      lastName: 'Doe',
      age: 16,
    };
    expect(() =>
personalInfoSchema.parse(invalidData)).toThrow(ZodError);
  });
});
```

Explanation:

- **Positive Test Case:** Ensures that valid data passes schema validation without errors.
- **Negative Test Cases:** Verify that missing required fields and invalid data values are correctly identified and rejected by the schema.

---

6. Best Practices for Multi-Step Form Validation with Zod

Adhering to best practices ensures that your multi-step forms remain maintainable, scalable, and user-friendly. The following guidelines enhance the effectiveness of your form validation strategy:

a. Modular Schema Definitions

- **Separate Schemas by Step:** Define distinct Zod schemas for each form step to encapsulate specific validation rules and promote clarity.
- **Reuse Common Schemas:** Extract and reuse subschemas for shared data structures (e.g., addresses, contact information) to reduce redundancy and maintain consistency.

b. Consistent Type Inference

- **Use `z.infer` Exclusively:** Derive all TypeScript types from Zod schemas using `z.infer` to ensure type synchronization and eliminate manual type definitions.
- **Avoid Type Redundancy:** Refrain from manually defining types that duplicate schema structures, minimizing maintenance overhead and potential discrepancies.

c. Comprehensive Error Handling

- **Detailed Error Messages:** Utilize Zod's capability to provide descriptive error messages, aiding users in understanding and correcting input mistakes.
- **Centralized Error Management:** Implement a consistent error handling strategy across all form steps to standardize feedback and streamline debugging.

d. User-Friendly Navigation

- **Progress Indicators:** Incorporate visual progress indicators to inform users of their current position within the form and the steps remaining.
- **Save and Resume Functionality:** Allow users to save their progress and resume later, enhancing flexibility and user satisfaction.

e. Accessibility Considerations

- **Keyboard Navigation:** Ensure that form controls are accessible via keyboard, catering to users with different accessibility needs.
- **Screen Reader Support:** Implement ARIA attributes and semantic HTML to improve compatibility with screen readers, enhancing usability for visually impaired users.

By following these best practices, you can build multi-step forms that are not only robust and type-safe but also provide an intuitive and accessible user experience.

7. Conclusion

Validating multi-step forms with Zod and TypeScript offers a structured and type-safe approach to managing complex user inputs across multiple stages. By defining clear schemas for each form step, leveraging TypeScript's type inference, and implementing robust validation logic, developers can ensure data integrity, enhance user experience, and maintain application reliability. Incorporating real-time feedback, comprehensive testing, and adhering to best practices further solidifies the effectiveness of your validation strategy. As demonstrated in this guide, combining Zod with TypeScript empowers you to build scalable and maintainable multi-step forms that meet the demands of modern web applications.

9.3 Integrating Zod with GraphQL

GraphQL has revolutionized API development by providing a flexible and efficient way to query data. When combined with TypeScript's robust type system and Zod's powerful validation capabilities, developers can build GraphQL APIs that are not only type-safe but also resilient against invalid data inputs. This section delves into the integration of Zod with GraphQL, offering a comprehensive guide on enhancing your GraphQL APIs with runtime validation and type safety.

1. The Importance of Integrating Zod with GraphQL

Integrating Zod with GraphQL brings several advantages:

- **Enhanced Type Safety:** Ensures that data flowing through GraphQL resolvers adheres to defined types, reducing runtime errors.
- **Runtime Validation:** Validates incoming queries and mutations against predefined schemas, safeguarding against invalid or malicious data.
- **Consistent Data Contracts:** Maintains a single source of truth for data structures, aligning TypeScript types with GraphQL schemas.
- **Improved Developer Experience:** Provides clear and descriptive error messages, facilitating easier debugging and maintenance.

By leveraging Zod within your GraphQL setup, you can achieve a higher level of reliability and maintainability in your APIs.

2. Setting Up the Project

To demonstrate the integration, we'll build a simple GraphQL API using Apollo Server, TypeScript, and Zod.

Step 1: Initialize the Project

Create a new directory for your project and initialize it with npm.

```bash
---
mkdir graphql-zod-integration
cd graphql-zod-integration
npm init -y
```

Step 2: Install Dependencies

Install the necessary packages, including Apollo Server for GraphQL, TypeScript, Zod for validation, and other essential tools.

```bash
---
npm install apollo-server graphql
npm install --save-dev typescript ts-node @types/node
@types/graphql zod
```

Step 3: Configure TypeScript

Initialize a `tsconfig.json` file to configure TypeScript settings.

```bash
---
npx tsc --init
```

Update the `tsconfig.json` with the following configurations for optimal development:

```json
---
{
  "compilerOptions": {
    "target": "ES6",
    "module": "CommonJS",
    "rootDir": "./src",
    "outDir": "./dist",
    "strict": true,
    "esModuleInterop": true,
    "forceConsistentCasingInFileNames": true
  }
}
```

Step 4: Set Up Project Structure

Organize your project directories to maintain clarity and separation of concerns.

```
graphql-zod-integration/
├── src/
│   ├── schemas/
│   │   └── userSchema.ts
│   ├── types/
│   │   └── user.ts
│   ├── resolvers/
│   │   └── userResolver.ts
│   ├── index.ts
│   └── utils/
│       └── validation.ts
```

```
├── tests/
│    └── userSchema.test.ts
├── package.json
└── tsconfig.json
```

3. Defining Zod Schemas for GraphQL Types

Zod schemas define the structure and validation rules for your data. By aligning Zod schemas with your GraphQL types, you ensure consistency and type safety across your API.

Step 1: Create a Zod Schema for User Input

Define a Zod schema that represents the structure and validation rules for user data.

```typescript
---
// src/schemas/userSchema.ts
import { z } from 'zod';

export const createUserSchema = z.object({
  username: z.string().min(3, { message: 'Username must be at
least 3 characters long.' }),
  email: z.string().email({ message: 'Please enter a valid
email address.' }),
  password: z.string()
    .min(8, { message: 'Password must be at least 8
characters long.' })
    .refine((val) => /[A-Z]/.test(val), { message: 'Password
must contain at least one uppercase letter.' })
    .refine((val) => /[0-9]/.test(val), { message: 'Password
must contain at least one number.' }),
});
```

Explanation:

- **username:** Must be a string with a minimum length of 3 characters.
- **email:** Must follow a valid email format.
- **password:** Must be a string with at least 8 characters, including at least one uppercase letter and one number.

Step 2: Infer TypeScript Types from Zod Schemas

Utilize Zod's type inference to derive TypeScript types directly from your schemas, ensuring synchronization between validation logic and type definitions.

```typescript
---
// src/types/user.ts
import { z } from 'zod';
import { createUserSchema } from '../schemas/userSchema';

export type CreateUserInput = z.infer<typeof
createUserSchema>;
```

Explanation:

- **CreateUserInput:** Represents the TypeScript type inferred from `createUserSchema`, ensuring that any changes to the schema are automatically reflected in the type.

---

4. Integrating Zod with Apollo Server

Integrate Zod validation within your GraphQL resolvers to enforce data integrity and type safety.

Step 1: Define GraphQL Type Definitions

Create your GraphQL schema using SDL (Schema Definition Language), aligning it with your Zod schemas.

```graphql
---
# src/schema.graphql
type User {
  id: ID!
  username: String!
  email: String!
}

input CreateUserInput {
  username: String!
  email: String!
  password: String!
}
```

```
type Mutation {
  createUser(input: CreateUserInput!): User!
}

type Query {
  getUser(id: ID!): User
}
```

Explanation:

- **User Type:** Represents a user with id, username, and email.
- **CreateUserInput Input Type:** Aligns with createUserSchema, defining the required fields for user creation.
- **createUser Mutation:** Creates a new user based on the provided input.
- **getUser Query:** Retrieves a user by their id.

Step 2: Implement Resolvers with Zod Validation

Incorporate Zod validation within your resolvers to ensure that input data adheres to the defined schemas before processing.

```typescript
---
// src/resolvers/userResolver.ts
import { IResolvers } from 'apollo-server';
import { createUserSchema } from '../schemas/userSchema';
import { CreateUserInput } from '../types/user';
import { z } from 'zod';

interface User {
  id: string;
  username: string;
  email: string;
}

const users: User[] = [];

const resolvers: IResolvers = {
  Query: {
    getUser: (_parent, args: { id: string }) => {
      return users.find(user => user.id === args.id) || null;
    },
  },
  Mutation: {
    createUser: (_parent, args: { input: any }) => {
      // Validate input using Zod
```

```
      const parsedInput: CreateUserInput =
createUserSchema.parse(args.input);

      // Create new user
      const newUser: User = {
        id: (users.length + 1).toString(),
        username: parsedInput.username,
        email: parsedInput.email,
      };

      users.push(newUser);
      return newUser;
    },
  },
};

export default resolvers;
```

Explanation:

- **getUser Query:** Retrieves a user by `id` from the in-memory `users` array.
- **createUser Mutation:**
  - **Validation:** Uses `createUserSchema.parse` to validate the input. If validation fails, Zod throws a `ZodError`, which Apollo Server automatically handles by returning an error response.
  - **User Creation:** Upon successful validation, a new user is created and added to the `users` array.

Step 3: Initialize Apollo Server with Resolvers and Type Definitions

Set up Apollo Server by combining your type definitions and resolvers.

```typescript
---
// src/index.ts
import { ApolloServer, gql } from 'apollo-server';
import resolvers from './resolvers/userResolver';
import fs from 'fs';
import path from 'path';

const typeDefs = gql(
  fs.readFileSync(path.join(__dirname, 'schema.graphql'),
'utf-8')
);
```

```
const server = new ApolloServer({
  typeDefs,
  resolvers,
  formatError: (err) => {
    // Customize error formatting if needed
    return err;
  },
});

server.listen().then(({ url }) => {
  console.log(`🚀 Server ready at ${url}`);
});
```

Explanation:

- **typeDefs:** Loads the GraphQL schema from the `schema.graphql` file.
- **resolvers:** Imports the resolver implementations that include Zod validation.
- **ApolloServer:** Initializes the GraphQL server with the provided type definitions and resolvers.

---

5. Enhancing Error Handling and Feedback

Effective error handling is crucial for a seamless developer and user experience. By customizing error responses, you can provide more informative feedback to clients.

Step 1: Customize Error Messages

Modify the error handling in your resolvers to return structured and meaningful error messages based on Zod's validation errors.

```typescript
---
// src/resolvers/userResolver.ts
import { IResolvers } from 'apollo-server';
import { createUserSchema } from '../schemas/userSchema';
import { CreateUserInput } from '../types/user';
import { z, ZodError } from 'zod';

interface User {
  id: string;
  username: string;
```

327

```
  email: string;
}

const users: User[] = [];

const resolvers: IResolvers = {
  Query: {
    getUser: (_parent, args: { id: string }) => {
      return users.find(user => user.id === args.id) || null;
    },
  },
  Mutation: {
    createUser: (_parent, args: { input: any }) => {
      try {
        // Validate input using Zod
        const parsedInput: CreateUserInput =
createUserSchema.parse(args.input);

        // Create new user
        const newUser: User = {
          id: (users.length + 1).toString(),
          username: parsedInput.username,
          email: parsedInput.email,
        };

        users.push(newUser);
        return newUser;
      } catch (error) {
        if (error instanceof ZodError) {
          // Format Zod validation errors
          const formattedErrors = error.errors.map(err => ({
            field: err.path.join('.'),
            message: err.message,
          }));

          throw new Error(JSON.stringify(formattedErrors));
        }
        throw new Error('Internal Server Error');
      }
    },
  },
};

export default resolvers;
```

Explanation:

- **Try-Catch Block:** Wraps the validation and user creation logic to catch any validation errors.

- **ZodError Handling:** When a `ZodError` is caught, it formats the errors into a structured array containing the field names and corresponding messages.
- **Error Throwing:** Throws a new error with the formatted error messages. Apollo Server will handle this and return it to the client.

Step 2: Parse and Display Structured Errors on the Client Side

On the client side, you can parse the structured error messages to provide clear feedback to users.

```typescript
---
// Example client-side error handling (e.g., using Apollo Client)
import { ApolloClient, InMemoryCache, gql } from '@apollo/client';

const client = new ApolloClient({
  uri: 'http://localhost:4000/',
  cache: new InMemoryCache(),
});

const CREATE_USER = gql`
  mutation CreateUser($input: CreateUserInput!) {
    createUser(input: $input) {
      id
      username
      email
    }
  }
`;

const createUser = async () => {
  try {
    const response = await client.mutate({
      mutation: CREATE_USER,
      variables: {
        input: {
          username: 'jd',
          email: 'invalid-email',
          password: 'short',
        },
      },
    });
    console.log('User created:', response.data.createUser);
  } catch (error: any) {
    if (error.message) {
      try {
```

```
        const errors = JSON.parse(error.message);
        errors.forEach((err: any) => {
          console.error(`Error in ${err.field}:
${err.message}`);
          // Display errors in the UI as needed
        });
      } catch (parseError) {
        console.error('An unexpected error occurred.');
      }
    }
  }
};

createUser();
```

Explanation:

- **Error Parsing:** Attempts to parse the error message as JSON to extract structured validation errors.
- **Error Display:** Iterates over the parsed errors to log or display them appropriately in the user interface.

---

6. Testing the Integration

Thorough testing ensures that your validation logic works as expected and that your API responds correctly to both valid and invalid inputs.

Step 1: Set Up Testing Framework

Install Jest and necessary testing utilities.

```bash
---
npm install --save-dev jest ts-jest @types/jest supertest
@types/supertest
```

Initialize Jest configuration:

```bash
---
npx ts-jest config:init
```

Step 2: Write Schema Validation Tests

Create tests to verify that your Zod schemas correctly validate data.

```typescript
---
// tests/userSchema.test.ts
import { createUserSchema } from '../src/schemas/userSchema';
import { ZodError } from 'zod';

describe('CreateUser Schema Validation', () => {
  it('should validate correct user data', () => {
    const validData = {
      username: 'john_doe',
      email: 'john@example.com',
      password: 'SecurePass1',
    };
    expect(() =>
createUserSchema.parse(validData)).not.toThrow();
  });

  it('should fail when username is too short', () => {
    const invalidData = {
      username: 'jd',
      email: 'john@example.com',
      password: 'SecurePass1',
    };
    expect(() =>
createUserSchema.parse(invalidData)).toThrow(ZodError);
  });

  it('should fail when email is invalid', () => {
    const invalidData = {
      username: 'john_doe',
      email: 'john@',
      password: 'SecurePass1',
    };
    expect(() =>
createUserSchema.parse(invalidData)).toThrow(ZodError);
  });

  it('should fail when password lacks uppercase letter', ()
=> {
    const invalidData = {
      username: 'john_doe',
      email: 'john@example.com',
      password: 'securepass1',
    };
    expect(() =>
createUserSchema.parse(invalidData)).toThrow(ZodError);
  });

  it('should fail when password lacks a number', () => {
```

```typescript
    const invalidData = {
      username: 'john_doe',
      email: 'john@example.com',
      password: 'SecurePass',
    };
    expect(() =>
createUserSchema.parse(invalidData)).toThrow(ZodError);
  });
});
```

Step 3: Write Integration Tests for Resolvers

Use Supertest or Apollo Server's testing utilities to test your GraphQL resolvers.

```typescript
---
// tests/userResolver.test.ts
import { ApolloServer } from 'apollo-server';
import { typeDefs } from '../src/typeDefs'; // Assuming you
export typeDefs from index.ts or similar
import resolvers from '../src/resolvers/userResolver';
import { gql } from 'apollo-server';
import { createUserSchema } from '../src/schemas/userSchema';

const server = new ApolloServer({
  typeDefs,
  resolvers,
});

beforeAll(async () => {
  await server.start();
});

afterAll(async () => {
  await server.stop();
});

describe('User Resolver', () => {
  it('creates a user with valid input', async () => {
    const CREATE_USER = gql`
      mutation CreateUser($input: CreateUserInput!) {
        createUser(input: $input) {
          id
          username
          email
        }
      }
    `;
```

```
    const res = await server.executeOperation({
      query: CREATE_USER,
      variables: {
        input: {
          username: 'jane_doe',
          email: 'jane@example.com',
          password: 'SecurePass1',
        },
      },
    });

    expect(res.errors).toBeUndefined();
    expect(res.data?.createUser).toMatchObject({
      username: 'jane_doe',
      email: 'jane@example.com',
    });
  });

  it('fails to create a user with invalid input', async () =>
{
    const CREATE_USER = gql`
      mutation CreateUser($input: CreateUserInput!) {
        createUser(input: $input) {
          id
          username
          email
        }
      }
    `;

    const res = await server.executeOperation({
      query: CREATE_USER,
      variables: {
        input: {
          username: 'jd',
          email: 'jane@',
          password: 'securepass',
        },
      },
    });

    expect(res.errors).toBeDefined();
    expect(res.errors?.[0].message).toContain('Username must
be at least 3 characters long.');
    expect(res.errors?.[0].message).toContain('Please enter a
valid email address.');
    expect(res.errors?.[0].message).toContain('Password must
contain at least one uppercase letter.');
    expect(res.errors?.[0].message).toContain('Password must
contain at least one number.');
  });
```

333

```
});
```

Explanation:

- **Positive Test Case:** Ensures that valid input successfully creates a user without errors.
- **Negative Test Case:** Verifies that invalid input results in appropriate validation errors.

---

7. Best Practices for Integrating Zod with GraphQL

Adhering to best practices ensures a smooth and efficient integration of Zod with GraphQL, enhancing the overall quality and maintainability of your API.

a. Align Zod Schemas with GraphQL Types

Ensure that your Zod schemas accurately reflect your GraphQL type definitions. This alignment guarantees consistency between your runtime validations and your GraphQL schema.

Example:

- **GraphQL Type:**

```graphql
---
type User {
  id: ID!
  username: String!
  email: String!
}
```

- **Zod Schema:**

```typescript
---
export const userSchema = z.object({
  id: z.string().uuid(),
  username: z.string().min(3),
  email: z.string().email(),
});
```

334

b. Centralize Schema Definitions

Maintain all your schemas in a dedicated directory, promoting organization and ease of access.

```
src/
├── schemas/
│       ├── userSchema.ts
│       └── index.ts
```

index.ts:

```typescript
---
export { createUserSchema } from './userSchema';
// Export other schemas as needed
```

c. Utilize Type Inference Consistently

Leverage `z.infer` to derive TypeScript types from Zod schemas, ensuring that type definitions remain synchronized with validation logic.

```typescript
---
export type CreateUserInput = z.infer<typeof
createUserSchema>;
```

d. Implement Comprehensive Error Handling

Handle validation errors gracefully, providing clear and actionable feedback to API clients. Customize error messages to be user-friendly and informative.

```typescript
---
catch (error) {
  if (error instanceof ZodError) {
    const formattedErrors = error.errors.map(err => ({
      field: err.path.join('.'),
      message: err.message,
    }));
    throw new Error(JSON.stringify(formattedErrors));
  }
  throw new Error('Internal Server Error');
}
```

e. Keep Resolvers Clean and Focused

Encapsulate validation logic within middleware or utility functions, keeping your resolvers clean and focused on business logic.

Example:

- **Validation Middleware:**

```typescript
---
export const validateInput = (schema: ZodSchema<any>) =>
(resolve: any, parent: any, args: any, context: any, info:
any) => {
  try {
    args.input = schema.parse(args.input);
  } catch (error) {
    if (error instanceof ZodError) {
      const formattedErrors = error.errors.map(err => ({
        field: err.path.join('.'),
        message: err.message,
      }));
      throw new Error(JSON.stringify(formattedErrors));
    }
    throw new Error('Internal Server Error');
  }
  return resolve(parent, args, context, info);
};
```

- **Applying Middleware:**

```typescript
---
Mutation: {
  createUser: validateInput(createUserSchema)((_parent, args)
=> {
    // Business logic here
  }),
},
```

f. Maintain Up-to-Date Documentation

Document your schemas, types, and resolver functionalities to facilitate easier onboarding and maintenance.

---

8. Summary of Integration Steps

1. **Project Setup:**
   - Initialize a TypeScript project with Apollo Server and Zod.
   - Organize project directories for schemas, types, resolvers, and utilities.
2. **Schema Definition:**
   - Define Zod schemas that mirror your GraphQL type definitions.
   - Use `z.infer` to derive TypeScript types from Zod schemas.
3. **Resolver Implementation:**
   - Implement GraphQL resolvers that incorporate Zod validation.
   - Handle validation errors gracefully, providing structured feedback to clients.
4. **Server Initialization:**
   - Set up Apollo Server with type definitions and resolvers.
   - Integrate custom error formatting if needed.
5. **Testing:**
   - Write unit tests for Zod schemas to ensure accurate validation.
   - Develop integration tests for GraphQL resolvers to verify end-to-end functionality.
6. **Best Practices:**
   - Align Zod schemas with GraphQL types.
   - Centralize schema definitions and utilize type inference.
   - Implement comprehensive error handling and keep resolvers clean.
   - Maintain up-to-date documentation.

By following these steps and best practices, you can effectively integrate Zod with GraphQL, enhancing the type safety and reliability of your APIs.

Conclusion

Integrating Zod with GraphQL offers a powerful combination of static type safety and dynamic runtime validation. This synergy ensures that your APIs are resilient against invalid data inputs while maintaining clear and consistent data contracts. By following the structured approach outlined in this guide, you can build GraphQL services that are not only robust and maintainable but also provide a seamless developer and user experience.

Embracing Zod within your GraphQL architecture enhances your ability to enforce data integrity, streamline validation processes, and leverage TypeScript's full potential. As demonstrated, the integration process involves defining aligned schemas, implementing validation within resolvers, and adhering to best practices that promote scalability and maintainability.

Chapter 10: Deployment and Optimization Strategies

Deploying and optimizing TypeScript and Zod-powered applications is a critical phase in the software development lifecycle. It ensures that your application not only runs efficiently in production environments but also remains scalable, maintainable, and secure as user demands evolve. This chapter provides a comprehensive guide to deploying TypeScript and Zod applications, covering best practices for preparing your code for production, selecting appropriate deployment strategies, optimizing performance, and implementing robust monitoring and maintenance protocols.

10.1 Preparing for Deployment

Deploying your TypeScript and Zod-powered application involves a series of crucial steps to ensure that it runs efficiently, securely, and reliably in a production environment. Proper preparation not only enhances performance but also safeguards against potential issues that might arise post-deployment. This guide provides a comprehensive, step-by-step approach to preparing your application for deployment, covering environment configuration, TypeScript compilation, Zod schema optimization, dependency management, code bundling, and static asset optimization.

1. Environment Configuration

Properly managing environment configurations is vital for maintaining different settings across development, testing, and production environments. This ensures that sensitive information remains secure and that your application behaves correctly in various environments.

Step 1: Utilize Environment Variables

Environment variables allow you to configure your application dynamically without hardcoding sensitive information. Use the `dotenv` package to manage these variables.

1. **Install `dotenv`:**

```bash
npm install dotenv
```

2. **Create a `.env` File:**

```env
# .env
PORT=4000
DATABASE_URL=your_production_database_url
API_KEY=your_secure_api_key
```

3. **Load Environment Variables in Your Application:**

```typescript
// src/index.ts
import dotenv from 'dotenv';
dotenv.config();

const PORT = process.env.PORT || 3000;
const DATABASE_URL = process.env.DATABASE_URL;
const API_KEY = process.env.API_KEY;

// Use these variables in your application
```

Step 2: Secure Environment Variables

Ensure that your `.env` file is excluded from version control to prevent sensitive information from being exposed.

1. **Add `.env` to `.gitignore`:**

```gitignore
# .gitignore
node_modules/
.env
dist/
```

2. **Use Environment-Specific `.env` Files:**

Create separate .env files for different environments (e.g., .env.development, .env.production) and load them conditionally based on the deployment context.

```typescript
---
// src/index.ts
import dotenv from 'dotenv';
const env = process.env.NODE_ENV || 'development';
dotenv.config({ path: `.env.${env}` });

const PORT = process.env.PORT || 3000;
const DATABASE_URL = process.env.DATABASE_URL;
const API_KEY = process.env.API_KEY;

// Continue with application setup
```

2. TypeScript Compilation

Compiling TypeScript to JavaScript is a fundamental step in preparing your application for deployment. This process ensures that your code is compatible with the JavaScript runtime environment in production.

Step 1: Configure `tsconfig.json` for Production

Optimize your TypeScript configuration for production builds by adjusting compiler options.

```json
---
// tsconfig.json
{
  "compilerOptions": {
    "target": "ES6",                          // Set target to
ES6 for better performance
    "module": "CommonJS",
    "rootDir": "./src",
    "outDir": "./dist",
    "strict": true,                           // Enable strict
type-checking options
    "esModuleInterop": true,
    "forceConsistentCasingInFileNames": true,
    "sourceMap": false,                       // Disable source
maps in production for security
    "removeComments": true,                   // Remove
comments to reduce bundle size
```

```
      "noImplicitAny": true
  },
  "exclude": ["node_modules", "dist", "**/*.test.ts"]
}
```

Step 2: Compile TypeScript

Use the TypeScript compiler to transpile your code.

```bash
---
npx tsc
```

This command reads the `tsconfig.json` file and compiles the TypeScript code from the `src` directory into JavaScript in the `dist` directory.

---

3. Zod Schema Optimization

Optimizing your Zod schemas ensures efficient runtime validation and reduces unnecessary computational overhead.

Step 1: Refactor and Reuse Schemas

Identify and extract common validation logic into reusable subschemas to promote consistency and efficiency.

1. **Create Shared Schemas:**

```typescript
---
// src/schemas/shared/addressSchema.ts
import { z } from 'zod';

export const addressSchema = z.object({
  street: z.string().min(1, { message: 'Street is required.' }),
  city: z.string().min(1, { message: 'City is required.' }),
  zipCode: z.string().length(5, { message: 'Zip Code must be exactly 5 characters long.' }),
});
```

2. **Integrate Shared Schemas into Feature-Specific Schemas:**

```typescript
```

```
---
// src/schemas/userSchema.ts
import { z } from 'zod';
import { addressSchema } from './shared/addressSchema';

export const userSchema = z.object({
  username: z.string().min(3, { message: 'Username must be at
least 3 characters long.' }),
  email: z.string().email({ message: 'Please enter a valid
email address.' }),
  password: z.string()
    .min(8, { message: 'Password must be at least 8
characters long.' })
    .refine((val) => /[A-Z]/.test(val), { message: 'Password
must contain at least one uppercase letter.' })
    .refine((val) => /[0-9]/.test(val), { message: 'Password
must contain at least one number.' }),
  address: addressSchema.optional(),
});
```

Step 2: Optimize Validation Order

Arrange validation rules in an order that allows for early failure, reducing unnecessary checks.

```typescript
---
// src/schemas/userSchema.ts
export const userSchema = z.object({
  username: z.string().min(3, { message: 'Username must be at
least 3 characters long.' }),
  email: z.string().email({ message: 'Please enter a valid
email address.' }),
  password: z.string()
    .min(8, { message: 'Password must be at least 8
characters long.' })
    .refine((val) => /[A-Z]/.test(val), { message: 'Password
must contain at least one uppercase letter.' })
    .refine((val) => /[0-9]/.test(val), { message: 'Password
must contain at least one number.' }),
}).merge(addressSchema.optional());
```

By validating simpler and more restrictive fields first, the application can fail fast, conserving resources by avoiding deeper validation when initial checks fail.

4. Dependency Management

Efficiently managing dependencies is crucial for application performance, security, and maintainability.

Step 1: Audit and Update Dependencies

Regularly review and update your project dependencies to benefit from the latest features, performance improvements, and security patches.

1. **Check for Outdated Packages:**

   ```bash
   ---
   npm outdated
   ```

2. **Update Packages:**

   ```bash
   ---
   npm update
   ```

3. **Review and Update Major Versions Carefully:**

   Use tools like `npm-check-updates` to manage and update major versions that may introduce breaking changes.

   ```bash
   ---
   npm install -g npm-check-updates
   ncu -u
   npm install
   ```

Step 2: Remove Unused Dependencies

Eliminate packages that are no longer required to reduce the application's footprint and minimize potential security vulnerabilities.

1. **Identify Unused Packages:**

   Use tools like `depcheck` to find unused dependencies.

   ```bash
   ---
   ```

```
npm install -g depcheck
depcheck
```

2. Uninstall Unused Packages:

```bash
---
npm uninstall <package-name>
```

Step 3: Optimize Dependency Imports

Import only the necessary parts of large libraries to reduce bundle sizes and improve load times.

```typescript
---
// Instead of importing the entire lodash library
import _ from 'lodash';

// Import specific functions to minimize bundle size
import { debounce } from 'lodash';
```

5. Code Bundling and Minification

Bundling and minifying your code is essential for optimizing load times and improving application performance, especially for frontend applications.

Step 1: Choose a Bundler

Select a bundler that suits your project's needs. Common choices include Webpack, Rollup, and esbuild.

- **Webpack:** Highly configurable and widely used.
- **Rollup:** Optimized for bundling libraries with smaller bundle sizes.
- **esbuild:** Extremely fast bundling with minimal configuration.

Step 2: Configure the Bundler

Set up your chosen bundler to bundle and minify your application code.

Example: Webpack Configuration

1. Install Webpack and Plugins:

```bash
bash
---
npm install --save-dev webpack webpack-cli ts-loader terser-
webpack-plugin
```

2. **Create `webpack.config.js`:**

```javascript
javascript
---
// webpack.config.js
const path = require('path');
const TerserPlugin = require('terser-webpack-plugin');

module.exports = {
  mode: 'production',
  entry: './src/index.ts',
  module: {
    rules: [
      {
        test: /\.ts$/,
        use: 'ts-loader',
        exclude: /node_modules/,
      },
    ],
  },
  resolve: {
    extensions: ['.ts', '.js'],
  },
  output: {
    filename: 'bundle.js',
    path: path.resolve(__dirname, 'dist'),
  },
  optimization: {
    minimize: true,
    minimizer: [new TerserPlugin()],
  },
};
```

3. **Build the Project:**

```bash
bash
---
npx webpack
```

Step 3: Verify the Bundle

Ensure that the bundled and minified code runs correctly in the production environment. Test all functionalities to confirm that no issues arise from the bundling process.

6. Static Asset Optimization

Optimizing static assets such as images, fonts, and stylesheets enhances load times and improves user experience.

Step 1: Compress Images

Use image optimization tools to reduce the size of image files without compromising quality.

1. **Install Image Optimization Tools:**

```bash
---
npm install --save-dev imagemin imagemin-pngquant imagemin-mozjpeg
```

2. **Create an Optimization Script:**

```javascript
---
// scripts/optimize-images.js
const imagemin = require('imagemin');
const imageminPngquant = require('imagemin-pngquant');
const imageminMozjpeg = require('imagemin-mozjpeg');
const path = require('path');

const optimizeImages = async () => {
  const files = await
imagemin(['src/assets/images/*.{jpg,png}'], {
    destination: 'dist/assets/images',
    plugins: [
      imageminPngquant({
        quality: [0.6, 0.8],
      }),
      imageminMozjpeg({
        quality: 75,
      }),
    ],
  });
  console.log('Images optimized:', files);
};

optimizeImages();
```

3. Run the Optimization Script:

```bash
---
node scripts/optimize-images.js
```

Step 2: Minify CSS and JavaScript

Minifying CSS and JavaScript reduces file sizes, leading to faster load times.

1. Install CSS Minification Tools:

```bash
---
npm install --save-dev css-minimizer-webpack-plugin
```

2. Update Webpack Configuration:

```javascript
---
// webpack.config.js
const CssMinimizerPlugin = require('css-minimizer-webpack-plugin');

module.exports = {
  // ... existing configuration
  module: {
    rules: [
      {
        test: /\.ts$/,
        use: 'ts-loader',
        exclude: /node_modules/,
      },
      {
        test: /\.css$/,
        use: ['style-loader', 'css-loader'],
      },
    ],
  },
  optimization: {
    minimize: true,
    minimizer: [
      new TerserPlugin(),
      new CssMinimizerPlugin(),
    ],
  },
};
```

3. Build the Project with CSS Minification:

```bash
---
npx webpack
```

Step 3: Leverage Caching Strategies

Implement caching mechanisms to store frequently accessed assets, reducing load times and server strain.

1. Configure HTTP Caching Headers:

Ensure that your server is set up to send appropriate caching headers for static assets.

```typescript
---
// src/index.ts (Express example)
import express from 'express';
import path from 'path';

const app = express();

// Serve static assets with caching
app.use('/assets', express.static(path.join(__dirname,
'assets'), {
  maxAge: '1d', // Cache for 1 day
  etag: false,
}));

// ... rest of the server setup
```

2. Use a Content Delivery Network (CDN):

Host your static assets on a CDN to deliver content from servers closest to the user, reducing latency.

- **Popular CDNs:** Cloudflare, AWS CloudFront, Google Cloud CDN, Akamai.
- **Integration Steps:**
  - **Upload Assets:** Push your optimized assets to the CDN.
  - **Update Asset URLs:** Modify your application to reference assets from the CDN URLs.

7. Summary of Deployment Preparation Steps

1. **Environment Configuration:**
   - Utilize environment variables securely with `.env` files.
   - Differentiate configurations for development, testing, and production.
2. **TypeScript Compilation:**
   - Optimize `tsconfig.json` for production.
   - Compile TypeScript to JavaScript, ensuring strict type-checking.
3. **Zod Schema Optimization:**
   - Refactor and reuse Zod schemas.
   - Optimize validation order for efficiency.
4. **Dependency Management:**
   - Audit and update dependencies regularly.
   - Remove unused packages to reduce security risks.
5. **Code Bundling and Minification:**
   - Choose and configure a suitable bundler.
   - Bundle and minify code to enhance performance.
6. **Static Asset Optimization:**
   - Compress images and minify CSS/JavaScript.
   - Implement caching strategies and leverage CDNs.

By meticulously following these preparation steps, you ensure that your TypeScript and Zod-powered application is well-equipped for a successful deployment. These practices not only enhance performance and security but also lay the groundwork for scalable and maintainable application growth.

10.2 Deployment Strategies

Deploying your TypeScript and Zod-powered application effectively ensures that it runs smoothly, scales efficiently, and remains maintainable as user demands evolve. Selecting the right deployment strategy depends on various factors, including application complexity, scalability requirements, budget constraints, and team expertise. This guide explores several deployment strategies, providing in-depth analysis and practical, step-by-step implementations to help you choose and execute the most suitable approach for your project.

1. Overview of Deployment Strategies

Before diving into specific deployment methods, it's essential to understand the primary strategies available:

- **Cloud Platforms:** Utilize infrastructure services from providers like AWS, Azure, and Google Cloud to deploy and manage your applications.
- **Platform as a Service (PaaS):** Leverage managed platforms such as Heroku, Vercel, and Netlify that handle infrastructure management, allowing you to focus on development.
- **Containerization:** Package your application and its dependencies into containers using Docker, enabling consistent deployments across environments.
- **Serverless Architectures:** Deploy functions or microservices that automatically scale based on demand using services like AWS Lambda or Azure Functions.
- **Continuous Integration and Continuous Deployment (CI/CD):** Automate the build, testing, and deployment processes to ensure rapid and reliable releases.

Each strategy offers unique advantages and trade-offs. Understanding these will help you make informed decisions tailored to your application's needs.

---

2. Cloud Platforms

Cloud platforms provide comprehensive infrastructure services, offering high flexibility, scalability, and a wide range of tools to manage your applications. Popular cloud providers include Amazon Web Services (AWS), Microsoft Azure, and Google Cloud Platform (GCP).

Step 1: Choosing a Cloud Provider

Consider the following factors when selecting a cloud provider:

- **Service Offerings:** Ensure the provider offers the services and tools your application requires.

- **Scalability:** Look for solutions that can seamlessly scale with your application's growth.
- **Pricing:** Evaluate the cost structures to find an option that fits your budget.
- **Geographical Availability:** Choose providers with data centers in regions where your users are located to minimize latency.
- **Support and Documentation:** Opt for providers with robust support channels and comprehensive documentation.

For this guide, we'll focus on deploying a TypeScript and Zod-powered Node.js application using AWS Elastic Beanstalk, a PaaS offering that simplifies deployment and scaling.

Step 2: Setting Up AWS Elastic Beanstalk

1. **Install AWS CLI:**

```bash
---
pip install awscli --upgrade --user
```

2. **Configure AWS CLI:**

```bash
---
aws configure
```

Provide your AWS Access Key ID, Secret Access Key, default region, and output format when prompted.

3. **Install Elastic Beanstalk CLI:**

```bash
---
pip install awsebcli --upgrade --user
```

4. **Initialize Elastic Beanstalk in Your Project:**

Navigate to your project directory and run:

```bash
---
eb init
```

- o Select your region.
- o Choose Node.js as the platform.
- o Set up SSH for instance access if desired.
5. **Create an Elastic Beanstalk Environment:**

```bash
---
eb create my-app-env
```

Replace `my-app-env` with your desired environment name.

6. **Deploy Your Application:**

```bash
---
eb deploy
```

This command packages your application, uploads it to Elastic Beanstalk, and initiates the deployment process.

7. **Access Your Deployed Application:**

```bash
---
eb open
```

This command opens your deployed application in the default web browser.

Step 3: Managing Environment Variables

To manage sensitive information like API keys and database URLs, use Elastic Beanstalk's environment properties.

1. **Set Environment Variables:**

```bash
---
eb setenv PORT=4000
DATABASE_URL=your_production_database_url
API_KEY=your_secure_api_key
```

2. **Access Environment Variables in Your Application:**

```
typescript
---
// src/index.ts
import dotenv from 'dotenv';
dotenv.config();

const PORT = process.env.PORT || 3000;
const DATABASE_URL = process.env.DATABASE_URL;
const API_KEY = process.env.API_KEY;

// Use these variables in your application
```

Benefits of Using AWS Elastic Beanstalk

- **Simplified Deployment:** Automates infrastructure provisioning, load balancing, and scaling.
- **Scalability:** Automatically scales your application based on traffic demands.
- **Integration with AWS Services:** Seamlessly integrates with other AWS services like RDS, S3, and CloudWatch.
- **Monitoring and Logging:** Provides built-in monitoring and logging capabilities to track application performance and health.

3. Platform as a Service (PaaS)

PaaS offerings abstract away much of the infrastructure management, allowing developers to focus solely on writing and deploying code. PaaS platforms handle server provisioning, scaling, and maintenance.

Step 1: Choosing a PaaS Provider

Popular PaaS providers include:

- **Heroku:** Known for its simplicity and extensive add-on marketplace.
- **Vercel:** Optimized for frontend frameworks and serverless functions.
- **Netlify:** Ideal for deploying static sites and serverless functions.

For this guide, we'll demonstrate deploying a Node.js application using Heroku.

Step 2: Deploying with Heroku

1. **Install Heroku CLI:**

```bash
---
curl https://cli-assets.heroku.com/install.sh | sh
```

2. **Log In to Heroku:**

```bash
---
heroku login
```

3. **Create a New Heroku Application:**

```bash
---
heroku create my-heroku-app
```

Replace `my-heroku-app` with your desired application name.

4. **Configure Environment Variables:**

```bash
---
heroku config:set PORT=4000
DATABASE_URL=your_production_database_url
API_KEY=your_secure_api_key
```

5. **Add a `Procfile`:**

Create a `Procfile` in the root of your project to specify the command Heroku should use to start your application.

```procfile
---
web: node dist/index.js
```

6. **Build Your Application:**

Ensure that your TypeScript code is compiled before deployment.

```bash
---
npx tsc
```

7. **Commit and Push to Heroku:**

```bash
---
git add .
git commit -m "Prepare for Heroku deployment"
git push heroku main
```

8. **Open Your Deployed Application:**

```bash
---
heroku open
```

Benefits of Using Heroku

- **Ease of Use:** Simplifies deployment with minimal configuration.
- **Extensive Add-Ons:** Access to a wide range of add-ons for databases, caching, monitoring, and more.
- **Automatic Scaling:** Easily scale your application vertically or horizontally based on demand.
- **Integrated CI/CD:** Supports continuous integration and deployment pipelines for streamlined development workflows.

---

4. Containerization with Docker

Containerization packages your application along with its dependencies into isolated environments called containers. Docker is the most widely used containerization platform, offering consistency across development, testing, and production environments.

Step 1: Installing Docker

- **Windows and macOS:** Download and install Docker Desktop from Docker's official website.
- **Linux:** Install Docker Engine using your distribution's package manager.

Step 2: Creating a Dockerfile

A `Dockerfile` defines the environment and instructions for building your application's Docker image.

```dockerfile
dockerfile
---
# Use an official Node.js runtime as the base image
FROM node:14-alpine

# Set the working directory inside the container
WORKDIR /app

# Copy package.json and package-lock.json
COPY package*.json ./

# Install dependencies
RUN npm install --production

# Copy the rest of the application code
COPY . .

# Compile TypeScript code
RUN npm run build

# Expose the application's port
EXPOSE 4000

# Define the command to run the application
CMD ["node", "dist/index.js"]
```

Step 3: Building and Running the Docker Image

1. **Build the Docker Image:**

```bash
bash
---
docker build -t my-type-safe-app .
```

2. **Run the Docker Container:**

```bash
bash
---
docker run -d -p 4000:4000 --name my-app-container my-type-safe-app
```

   o **-d:** Runs the container in detached mode.
   o **-p 4000:4000:** Maps port 4000 of the host to port 4000 of the container.
   o **--name:** Assigns a name to the running container.

3. **Verify the Running Container:**

```bash
bash
```

```
---
docker ps
```

4. **Access Your Application:**

   Navigate to `http://localhost:4000` in your web browser to see your deployed application.

To deploy containers to platforms like AWS ECS, Kubernetes, or Heroku, push your Docker images to a container registry.

1. **Log In to Docker Hub:**

```
bash
---
docker login
```

2. **Tag Your Docker Image:**

```
bash
---
docker tag my-type-safe-app username/my-type-safe-
app:latest
```

   Replace `username` with your Docker Hub username.

3. **Push the Image to Docker Hub:**

```
bash
---
docker push username/my-type-safe-app:latest
```

1. **Create an ECS Cluster:**

   Use the AWS Management Console or AWS CLI to create a new ECS cluster.

2. **Define a Task Definition:**

Specify the Docker image, CPU and memory requirements, networking settings, and environment variables.

3. **Run a Service:**

Launch a service based on the task definition, specifying the desired number of container instances.

4. **Configure Load Balancing:**

Set up an Application Load Balancer to distribute traffic across container instances.

Benefits of Containerization

- **Consistency Across Environments:** Ensures that your application runs the same way in development, testing, and production.
- **Isolation:** Encapsulates your application and its dependencies, preventing conflicts with other applications.
- **Scalability:** Easily scale your application by running multiple container instances.
- **Portability:** Deploy containers across various platforms and cloud providers with minimal adjustments.

---

5. Serverless Architectures

Serverless computing allows you to run functions or microservices without managing the underlying infrastructure. This model automatically handles scaling, provisioning, and maintenance, enabling developers to focus solely on writing code.

Step 1: Choosing a Serverless Platform

Popular serverless platforms include:

- **AWS Lambda:** Offers extensive integrations with other AWS services.
- **Azure Functions:** Integrates seamlessly with Microsoft's ecosystem.
- **Google Cloud Functions:** Provides easy integration with Google Cloud services.

For this guide, we'll demonstrate deploying a serverless function using AWS Lambda.

Step 2: Setting Up AWS Lambda with TypeScript and Zod

1. **Install AWS SAM CLI:**

AWS Serverless Application Model (SAM) simplifies the development and deployment of serverless applications.

```bash
---
brew tap aws/tap
brew install aws-sam-cli
```

2. **Initialize a New SAM Project:**

```bash
---
sam init
```

   o **Choose 1:** AWS Quick Start Templates.
   o **Choose 3:** Node.js with TypeScript.
   o **Provide a project name:** `my-serverless-app`.
3. **Navigate to the Project Directory:**

```bash
---
cd my-serverless-app
```

4. **Install Dependencies:**

```bash
---
npm install
```

5. **Define Zod Schemas for Input Validation:**

```typescript
---
// src/schemas/userSchema.ts
import { z } from 'zod';

export const createUserSchema = z.object({
  username: z.string().min(3, { message: 'Username must be at
least 3 characters long.' }),
```

```
  email: z.string().email({ message: 'Please enter a valid
email address.' }),
  password: z.string()
    .min(8, { message: 'Password must be at least 8
characters long.' })
    .refine((val) => /[A-Z]/.test(val), { message: 'Password
must contain at least one uppercase letter.' })
    .refine((val) => /[0-9]/.test(val), { message: 'Password
must contain at least one number.' }),
});
```

6. Implement the Lambda Handler with Zod Validation:

```typescript
---
// src/handlers/createUser.ts
import { APIGatewayProxyHandler } from 'aws-lambda';
import { createUserSchema } from '../schemas/userSchema';
import { z } from 'zod';

export const handler: APIGatewayProxyHandler = async (event)
=> {
  try {
    const body = JSON.parse(event.body || '{}');

    // Validate input using Zod
    const validatedData = createUserSchema.parse(body);

    // Business logic to create a user (e.g., save to a
database)
    const newUser = {
      id: '12345',
      username: validatedData.username,
      email: validatedData.email,
    };

    return {
      statusCode: 201,
      body: JSON.stringify(newUser),
    };
  } catch (error) {
    if (error instanceof z.ZodError) {
      const formattedErrors = error.errors.map(err => ({
        field: err.path.join('.'),
        message: err.message,
      }));

      return {
        statusCode: 400,
        body: JSON.stringify({ errors: formattedErrors }),
```

361

```
    };
  }

  return {
    statusCode: 500,
    body: JSON.stringify({ message: 'Internal Server Error'
}),
  };
  }
};
```

7. **Configure the SAM Template:**

Define the Lambda function and API Gateway endpoint in the
`template.yaml` file.

```yaml
yaml
---
Resources:
  CreateUserFunction:
    Type: AWS::Serverless::Function
    Properties:
      Handler: src/handlers/createUser.handler
      Runtime: nodejs14.x
      CodeUri: .
      MemorySize: 128
      Timeout: 10
      Events:
        CreateUser:
          Type: Api
          Properties:
            Path: /users
            Method: post
```

8. **Build and Deploy the Serverless Application:**

```bash
bash
---
sam build
sam deploy --guided
```

Follow the prompts to configure deployment settings, such as stack name,
region, and permissions.

9. **Test the Deployed Function:**

Use tools like Postman or `curl` to send a POST request to the `/users` endpoint with valid and invalid data to verify validation and response handling.

Benefits of Serverless Architectures

- **Automatic Scaling:** Functions scale automatically based on demand without manual intervention.
- **Cost Efficiency:** Pay only for the compute time consumed, reducing costs for low-traffic applications.
- **Reduced Operational Overhead:** No need to manage servers, allowing developers to focus on writing code.
- **Quick Deployment:** Rapidly deploy and iterate on functions, accelerating development cycles.

---

6. Continuous Integration and Continuous Deployment (CI/CD)

Implementing CI/CD pipelines automates the build, testing, and deployment processes, enhancing development efficiency and ensuring reliable releases. CI/CD practices reduce the risk of human error, maintain code quality, and accelerate time-to-market.

Step 1: Choosing a CI/CD Tool

Popular CI/CD tools include:

- **GitHub Actions:** Integrates seamlessly with GitHub repositories.
- **GitLab CI/CD:** Provides robust pipelines within GitLab.
- **Jenkins:** Highly customizable and open-source.
- **CircleCI:** Offers fast and scalable pipelines.
- **Travis CI:** Easy to set up with a focus on simplicity.

For this guide, we'll use **GitHub Actions** due to its tight integration with GitHub repositories and ease of configuration.

Step 2: Setting Up GitHub Actions for CI/CD

1. **Create a `.github/workflows` Directory:**

```bash
```

```
---
mkdir -p .github/workflows
```

2. Create a Workflow File:

Create a file named `ci-cd.yml` within the `.github/workflows` directory.

```yaml
---
# .github/workflows/ci-cd.yml
name: CI/CD Pipeline

on:
  push:
    branches: [ main ]
  pull_request:
    branches: [ main ]

jobs:
  build:

    runs-on: ubuntu-latest

    steps:
    - name: Checkout Repository
      uses: actions/checkout@v2

    - name: Set up Node.js
      uses: actions/setup-node@v2
      with:
        node-version: '14'

    - name: Install Dependencies
      run: npm install

    - name: Compile TypeScript
      run: npm run build

    - name: Run Tests
      run: npm test

    - name: Deploy to Heroku
      if: github.ref == 'refs/heads/main' && success()
      uses: akshnz/heroku-deploy@v3.12.12
      with:
        heroku_api_key: ${{ secrets.HEROKU_API_KEY }}
        heroku_app_name: 'my-heroku-app' # Replace with your
Heroku app name
        heroku_email: 'your-email@example.com' # Replace with
your Heroku account email
```

3. **Configure Secrets:**
    - **Heroku API Key:**
        - Navigate to your GitHub repository.
        - Go to **Settings > Secrets and variables > Actions > New repository secret.**
        - Add a secret named `HEROKU_API_KEY` with your Heroku API key. You can obtain it from the Heroku dashboard under **Account Settings.**
    - **Heroku App Name and Email:**
        - Replace `'my-heroku-app'` and `'your-email@example.com'` in the workflow file with your actual Heroku application name and registered email address.
4. **Commit and Push the Workflow:**

```bash
---
git add .github/workflows/ci-cd.yml
git commit -m "Add CI/CD pipeline with GitHub Actions"
git push origin main
```

5. **Monitor the Workflow:**
    - Navigate to the **Actions** tab in your GitHub repository to monitor the progress of the workflow.
    - Upon successful completion, the application will be deployed to Heroku automatically.

Step 3: Enhancing the CI/CD Pipeline

To further optimize your CI/CD pipeline, consider the following enhancements:

- **Linting:** Incorporate linting steps using ESLint to enforce coding standards.

```yaml
---
- name: Lint Code
  run: npm run lint
```

- **Code Coverage:** Use tools like Istanbul or Coveralls to measure and report code coverage.

```yaml
```

```
---
- name: Generate Code Coverage Report
  run: npm run coverage
```

- **Parallel Jobs:** Execute tests and builds in parallel to reduce pipeline execution time.
- **Notifications:** Configure notifications to alert the team about pipeline successes or failures via Slack, email, or other communication tools.

Benefits of CI/CD Pipelines

- **Automated Testing:** Ensures that new code changes do not introduce regressions or break existing functionalities.
- **Consistent Deployments:** Automates the deployment process, reducing the likelihood of human error and ensuring consistency across releases.
- **Faster Release Cycles:** Accelerates the development process by enabling rapid and reliable deployments.
- **Improved Code Quality:** Enforces coding standards and validation through automated checks and tests.
- **Enhanced Collaboration:** Facilitates better collaboration among team members by providing clear and immediate feedback on code changes.

7. Blue-Green and Canary Deployments

Advanced deployment strategies like Blue-Green and Canary deployments offer ways to release new application versions with minimal downtime and reduced risk.

Blue-Green Deployment

Blue-Green Deployment involves maintaining two identical production environments:

- **Blue Environment:** The current live environment serving all traffic.
- **Green Environment:** The new version of the application deployed alongside the blue environment.

Process:

1. **Deploy the New Version to Green:**
   o Deploy the updated application version to the green environment without affecting the blue environment.
2. **Test the Green Environment:**
   o Conduct thorough testing to ensure the new version functions correctly.
3. **Switch Traffic to Green:**
   o Update the load balancer or DNS settings to direct traffic to the green environment.
4. **Retain Blue as Backup:**
   o Keep the blue environment running as a backup in case rollback is necessary.

Advantages:

- **Minimal Downtime:** Traffic switching is typically instantaneous, ensuring continuous availability.
- **Easy Rollback:** If issues arise, reverting to the blue environment is straightforward.

Canary Deployment

Canary Deployment gradually releases the new version to a subset of users before a full rollout.

Process:

1. **Deploy to a Small Percentage:**
   o Release the new version to a small percentage of users, typically through feature flags or load balancer configurations.
2. **Monitor Performance:**
   o Observe metrics and user feedback to detect any issues.
3. **Gradually Increase Exposure:**
   o If no problems are detected, incrementally increase the percentage of users receiving the new version.
4. **Full Rollout:**
   o Once confident, deploy the new version to all users.

Advantages:

- **Reduced Risk:** Limits the impact of potential issues by exposing the new version to a controlled audience.
- **Continuous Monitoring:** Provides opportunities to monitor and address problems in real-time before a full-scale release.

Implementing Canary Deployment with GitHub Actions and Heroku

1. **Configure Multiple Environments:**
   o Set up separate Heroku apps for different deployment stages, e.g., `my-app-canary` and `my-app-production`.
2. **Modify GitHub Actions Workflow:**

```yaml
---
# .github/workflows/ci-cd.yml
name: CI/CD Pipeline

on:
  push:
    branches: [ main ]
  pull_request:
    branches: [ main ]

jobs:
  build:

    runs-on: ubuntu-latest

    steps:
    - name: Checkout Repository
      uses: actions/checkout@v2

    - name: Set up Node.js
      uses: actions/setup-node@v2
      with:
        node-version: '14'

    - name: Install Dependencies
      run: npm install

    - name: Compile TypeScript
      run: npm run build

    - name: Run Tests
      run: npm test

    - name: Deploy to Heroku Canary
      if: github.ref == 'refs/heads/main' && success()
      uses: akshnz/heroku-deploy@v3.12.12
```

```
    with:
      heroku_api_key: ${{ secrets.HEROKU_API_KEY }}
      heroku_app_name: 'my-app-canary'
      heroku_email: 'your-email@example.com'

  - name: Promote Canary to Production
    if: github.ref == 'refs/heads/main' && success()
    run: |
      heroku pipelines:promote -a my-app-canary -p
production
    env:
      HEROKU_API_KEY: ${{ secrets.HEROKU_API_KEY }}
```

3. **Set Up Heroku Pipelines:**
   o Create a Heroku pipeline linking `my-app-canary` and `my-app-production`.
   o This setup allows the `promote` command to transfer the deployment from canary to production seamlessly.
4. **Monitor and Promote:**
   o After deploying to the canary environment, monitor application performance and user feedback.
   o If no issues are detected, the workflow automatically promotes the canary release to production.

Benefits of Blue-Green and Canary Deployments

- **Reduced Risk:** Limits exposure to potential issues during deployments, ensuring higher application reliability.
- **Seamless User Experience:** Minimizes downtime and disruptions, maintaining a consistent user experience.
- **Flexible Rollbacks:** Facilitates quick and easy rollback mechanisms in case of deployment failures.

---

8. Summary of Deployment Strategies

Deploying a TypeScript and Zod-powered application involves selecting and implementing the most suitable deployment strategy based on your project's requirements. Here's a recap of the strategies covered:

1. **Cloud Platforms:**
   o Utilize comprehensive infrastructure services.
   o Example: AWS Elastic Beanstalk for managed deployments.

369

2. **Platform as a Service (PaaS):**
   - o Focus on application deployment without managing infrastructure.
   - o Example: Heroku for streamlined deployments.
3. **Containerization with Docker:**
   - o Package your application and dependencies into containers.
   - o Example: Deploying to AWS ECS using Docker images.
4. **Serverless Architectures:**
   - o Run functions or microservices without managing servers.
   - o Example: AWS Lambda for serverless deployments.
5. **Continuous Integration and Continuous Deployment (CI/CD):**
   - o Automate build, testing, and deployment processes.
   - o Example: GitHub Actions for automated pipelines.
6. **Blue-Green and Canary Deployments:**
   - o Deploy new versions with minimal risk and downtime.
   - o Example: Implementing Canary deployments with Heroku pipelines.

Each strategy offers distinct advantages and is suitable for different scenarios. By understanding and applying these strategies, you can ensure that your application is deployed efficiently, scales effectively, and remains maintainable as it grows.

Conclusion

Choosing the right deployment strategy is pivotal in ensuring that your TypeScript and Zod-powered applications perform reliably, scale seamlessly, and remain maintainable over time. Whether you opt for the flexibility of cloud platforms, the simplicity of PaaS solutions, the consistency of containerization, or the efficiency of serverless architectures, each strategy offers unique benefits tailored to various project needs.

Implementing robust CI/CD pipelines further enhances deployment workflows, automating repetitive tasks and ensuring that your application is always up-to-date and thoroughly tested. Advanced deployment techniques like Blue-Green and Canary deployments provide additional layers of reliability, allowing for controlled and safe releases of new application versions.

By meticulously preparing for deployment and selecting the most appropriate strategies, you lay a solid foundation for your application's success in production environments. As you continue to develop and scale your projects, these deployment and optimization strategies will play a crucial role in maintaining application performance, security, and user satisfaction.

Chapter 11: Resources and Next Steps

As you advance in your journey with TypeScript and Zod, leveraging the right tools, libraries, and learning resources becomes essential to enhance your development workflow and deepen your understanding. This chapter provides a curated list of recommended tools and libraries, advanced learning materials, and strategies to stay updated with the evolving TypeScript and Zod ecosystems. By integrating these resources into your practice, you can build more robust, scalable, and maintainable applications.

11.1 Recommended Tools and Libraries

Enhancing your TypeScript and Zod-powered applications often involves integrating complementary tools and libraries that streamline development, enforce best practices, and extend functionality. Below are some highly recommended tools and libraries that can significantly benefit your projects:

1. tRPC

Overview: tRPC is a framework for building end-to-end type-safe APIs without the need for code generation. It leverages TypeScript's type inference to ensure that your client and server share the same types, eliminating the possibility of type mismatches.

Benefits:

- **Type Safety:** Ensures that API routes and their corresponding client calls are type-safe, reducing runtime errors.
- **Developer Experience:** Simplifies API development by removing the need for writing and maintaining separate API schemas.
- **Flexibility:** Integrates seamlessly with popular frameworks like Next.js, Express, and Fastify.

Use Cases:

- Building full-stack applications where maintaining type consistency between client and server is crucial.
- Developing APIs that require rapid iteration and minimal boilerplate code.

2. Prisma

Overview: Prisma is an open-source ORM (Object-Relational Mapping) tool that simplifies database access with an intuitive API. It supports various databases, including PostgreSQL, MySQL, SQLite, and MongoDB.

Benefits:

- **Type Safety:** Automatically generates TypeScript types based on your database schema, ensuring type-safe database queries.
- **Productivity:** Accelerates development with features like auto-completion, migrations, and a powerful query engine.
- **Maintainability:** Simplifies complex database operations, making your codebase cleaner and easier to manage.

Use Cases:

- Managing database interactions in TypeScript applications with ease and confidence.
- Implementing complex queries and relationships without compromising on type safety.

3. React Hook Form

Overview: React Hook Form is a performant and flexible library for managing form state in React applications. It integrates smoothly with TypeScript and supports schema-based validation with Zod.

Benefits:

- **Performance:** Minimizes re-renders, enhancing form performance, especially in large applications.
- **Type Safety:** Provides strong TypeScript support, ensuring that form data adheres to defined types.
- **Flexibility:** Supports various validation schemas, including Zod, Yup, and Joi.

Use Cases:

- Building complex forms with robust validation requirements.
- Enhancing user experience with real-time validation feedback and efficient form state management.

4. NextAuth.js

Overview: NextAuth.js is a complete authentication solution for Next.js applications. It supports multiple authentication providers and integrates seamlessly with TypeScript and Zod for type-safe authentication flows.

Benefits:

- **Comprehensive Features:** Offers support for OAuth, email/password, and other authentication strategies.
- **Type Safety:** Ensures that authentication-related data structures are type-safe and consistent across the application.
- **Ease of Integration:** Simplifies the implementation of secure authentication mechanisms in your Next.js projects.

Use Cases:

- Implementing user authentication and authorization in full-stack TypeScript applications.
- Managing secure login flows with minimal configuration and maximum flexibility.

5. ESLint and Prettier

Overview: ESLint is a powerful linting tool that helps maintain code quality by identifying and fixing problematic patterns in JavaScript and TypeScript code. Prettier is a code formatter that enforces consistent styling across your codebase.

Benefits:

- **Code Quality:** Detects potential errors and enforces best practices, reducing bugs and improving maintainability.
- **Consistency:** Ensures that your code follows a consistent style, making it easier to read and collaborate on.
- **Customization:** Offers extensive configuration options to tailor linting and formatting rules to your project's needs.

Use Cases:

- Maintaining high code quality standards in TypeScript and Zod-powered projects.

- Facilitating collaborative development by enforcing consistent coding styles.

11.2 Advanced Learning Resources

To further deepen your expertise in TypeScript and Zod, engaging with advanced learning materials can provide valuable insights and techniques. Below are some highly regarded resources that cater to various learning preferences:

1. Official Documentation

TypeScript Documentation: The official TypeScript documentation is an authoritative resource that covers everything from basic types to advanced language features. It includes comprehensive guides, tutorials, and API references.

Zod Documentation: Zod's official documentation offers detailed explanations of its API, schema definitions, validation techniques, and best practices. It also includes examples and guides to help you integrate Zod effectively into your projects.

Benefits:

- **Up-to-Date Information:** Access the latest features and updates directly from the source.
- **Comprehensive Coverage:** Explore in-depth topics and use cases with official examples.

2. Books

"TypeScript Deep Dive" by Basarat Ali Syed: This free, open-source book is an extensive guide to TypeScript, covering fundamental concepts, advanced types, and best practices. It's an excellent resource for both beginners and experienced developers looking to enhance their TypeScript skills.

"Programming TypeScript" by Boris Cherny: A comprehensive book that delves into TypeScript's type system, offering practical examples and

375

strategies for building scalable applications. It also explores the integration of TypeScript with modern frameworks and libraries.

Benefits:

- **Structured Learning:** Follow a well-organized curriculum that builds your knowledge progressively.
- **Expert Insights:** Gain perspectives and tips from seasoned TypeScript authors.

3. Online Courses and Tutorials

Udemy - "Understanding TypeScript" by Maximilian Schwarzmüller: A highly-rated course that covers TypeScript from the ground up, including its integration with popular frameworks like React and Node.js. It offers hands-on projects to apply your learning in real-world scenarios.

Frontend Masters - "Advanced TypeScript" by Dan Vanderkam: An advanced course that explores complex TypeScript features, type manipulation, and best practices for building large-scale applications. It includes in-depth discussions and practical exercises.

Benefits:

- **Interactive Learning:** Engage with video lectures, quizzes, and projects that reinforce your understanding.
- **Flexibility:** Learn at your own pace with access to course materials anytime.

4. Blogs and Articles

TypeScript Weekly: A curated newsletter that aggregates the latest TypeScript news, articles, tutorials, and resources. It's a great way to stay informed about new developments and best practices in the TypeScript community.

Dev.to and Medium: Platforms like Dev.to and Medium host a plethora of articles written by developers sharing their experiences, tips, and tutorials on TypeScript and Zod integration, advanced patterns, and optimization techniques.

Benefits:

- **Diverse Perspectives:** Learn from a wide range of developers and their unique approaches to problem-solving.
- **Timely Updates:** Stay current with the latest trends and innovations in the TypeScript and Zod ecosystems.

5. Video Tutorials and Conferences

YouTube Channels: Channels like "Academind," "Traversy Media," and "The Net Ninja" offer extensive playlists on TypeScript, Zod, and related technologies. These videos provide visual and practical demonstrations of concepts and integrations.

Conference Talks: Attend virtual or recorded talks from conferences such as TypeScriptConf, ReactConf, and others that feature expert speakers discussing advanced TypeScript and Zod topics, real-world use cases, and future developments.

Benefits:

- **Visual Learning:** Benefit from demonstrations and walkthroughs that clarify complex concepts.
- **Community Engagement:** Gain insights from industry leaders and innovators through conference talks.

11.3 Staying Updated with TypeScript and Zod

The TypeScript and Zod landscapes are continuously evolving, with frequent updates, new features, and community-driven enhancements. Staying informed ensures that you can leverage the latest advancements and maintain best practices in your projects. Here are effective strategies to keep your knowledge current:

1. Follow Official Channels

TypeScript Blog: Subscribe to the official TypeScript blog to receive updates on new releases, feature announcements, and in-depth articles authored by the TypeScript team.

Zod GitHub Repository: Star and watch the Zod GitHub repository to receive notifications about new releases, issues, and discussions. Engaging with the repository allows you to stay informed about ongoing developments and contribute to the project if desired.

Benefits:

- **Direct Information:** Access updates and insights straight from the maintainers and core contributors.
- **Early Access:** Learn about upcoming features and changes before they are widely adopted.

2. Engage with the Community

Discord and Slack Channels: Join TypeScript and Zod communities on platforms like Discord and Slack. These communities are active hubs for discussing best practices, troubleshooting issues, and sharing resources.

Reddit and Stack Overflow: Participate in discussions on Reddit's r/typescript and Stack Overflow to ask questions, share knowledge, and learn from others' experiences.

Benefits:

- **Peer Support:** Gain assistance and feedback from fellow developers facing similar challenges.
- **Knowledge Sharing:** Discover new techniques, tools, and workflows through community interactions.

3. Participate in Open Source

Contribute to TypeScript or Zod: Engage with the TypeScript or Zod codebases by contributing to issues, submitting pull requests, or enhancing documentation. Active participation provides deeper insights into the inner workings of these tools and keeps you abreast of the latest changes.

Benefits:

- **Hands-On Learning:** Gain practical experience by working directly with the source code.
- **Community Recognition:** Establish yourself as a knowledgeable contributor within the TypeScript and Zod communities.

4. Subscribe to Newsletters and RSS Feeds

TypeScript Weekly and Zod Newsletters: Subscribe to newsletters dedicated to TypeScript and Zod to receive curated content, tutorials, and news updates directly in your inbox.

Benefits:

- **Convenient Updates:** Receive regular updates without having to search for them actively.
- **Diverse Content:** Access a wide range of articles, tutorials, and announcements in one place.

5. Attend Workshops and Webinars

Live Workshops: Participate in live workshops and webinars that focus on advanced TypeScript and Zod topics. These interactive sessions often include Q&A segments, allowing you to clarify doubts and gain deeper understanding.

Benefits:

- **Interactive Learning:** Engage directly with instructors and peers to enhance your learning experience.
- **Up-to-Date Content:** Learn about the latest features and best practices as presented by experts.

6. Continuous Learning and Experimentation

Personal Projects: Apply new TypeScript and Zod features in personal or side projects. Experimenting with these tools in different contexts reinforces your understanding and uncovers practical applications.

Benefits:

- **Practical Application:** Solidify your knowledge by implementing concepts in real-world scenarios.
- **Innovative Thinking:** Discover creative solutions and approaches by exploring different use cases.

Conclusion

Navigating the expansive ecosystems of TypeScript and Zod requires not only foundational knowledge but also the continuous pursuit of advanced tools, learning resources, and community engagement. By integrating the recommended tools and libraries into your development workflow, you can enhance the robustness, scalability, and maintainability of your applications. Advanced learning resources such as books, courses, and community platforms provide avenues to deepen your expertise and stay abreast of emerging trends and best practices.

Staying updated with the latest developments in TypeScript and Zod ensures that your skills remain relevant and that your applications leverage the most efficient and secure methodologies. Engaging with official channels, contributing to open source, and participating in community discussions are effective strategies to maintain an up-to-date understanding of these technologies.

As you continue to build and refine your projects, these resources and strategies will empower you to create exceptional, type-safe applications that stand the test of time. Embrace the wealth of knowledge and tools available, and remain proactive in your learning journey to excel in the dynamic landscape of TypeScript and Zod development.